The Myth and Reality of No Child Left Behind

Public Education and High Stakes Assessment

A report issued on behalf of National-Louis University, 2008

Edited by
Todd Alan Price and Elizabeth Peterson

University Press of America,® Inc.
Lanham · Boulder · New York · Toronto · Plymouth, UK

University Press of America,® Inc.
4501 Forbes Boulevard
Suite 200
Lanham, Maryland 20706
UPA Acquisitions Department (301) 459-3366

Estover Road
Plymouth PL6 7PY
United Kingdom

Printed in the United States of America
British Library Cataloging in Publication Information Available

Library of Congress Control Number: 2008932750
ISBN-13: 978-0-7618-4314-6 (paperback : alk. paper)
ISBN-10: 0-7618-4314-0 (paperback : alk. paper)
eISBN-13: 978-0-7618-4315-3
eISBN-10: 0-7618-4315-9

™ The paper used in this publication meets the minimum requirements of American National Standard for Information Sciences—Permanence of Paper for Printed Library Materials, ANSI Z39.48—1984

Table of Contents

Preface

The purpose of this book is to explore the influence of high stakes testing, assessment, and evaluation over a range of critical educational issues.

We will examine the history of educational reform and the development of educational law in lieu of contemporary political struggles regarding accountability, testing, and students leaving the public school system. The chapters that follow comprise a series of reports, narratives, and case studies intended to shed light on the multifaceted manner in which *No Child Left Behind* has been perceived, adopted, implemented, questioned and sometimes resisted in a number of different locations.

No Child Left Behind as a policy for educational reform has serious implications for students, teachers, administrators and parents alike. As authors we hope to contribute to the debate concerning the costs and benefits, by putting forward an informed position through our research.

Special thanks to Elizabeth Peterson and Sondra Simpson for supporting efforts in the overall coordination and research, and for bringing together the second journal of the Gidwitz Center, *Common Concern,* a scholarly foundation upon which this book was launched.

Thanks to Tenena Soro for his valuable comments in the writing and editing of the chapter "English Language Learners in an Era of NCLB."

Thanks to Elizabeth O'Callaghan, who worked hard to compile and format these chapters.

This book is dedicated to those on the front lines, including our National-Louis University students and faculty.

I also want to personally acknowledge international colleagues and friends, educators like my wife, Xueqing Jiang, who strive to be honorable teachers in uncertain, yet hopeful times.

Introduction

The authors of this book view public education in the United States of America as the foundation upon which democracy resides and unfolds; a great social experiment to be certain. The process of educating people within a democracy, however, is a highly problematic one, stirring vigorous, even pointed debate.

The promise of public education has always been great: to ensure that a people are made knowledgeable and capable of prospering under a "republican democracy." Preserving that form of government for future generations is an explicit goal. Public education as such has moved from a lofty promise to a legitimate institution; yet the institution has changed over the lifespan of the republic, much as has the republic itself. Thus, it can be noted, the institution has undergone periods of profound contestation. That contestation is reflected in the fact that public education seems to be forever in a period of change and then stablization, of crises and then reform. This is due to swings in public opinion regarding the means and the ends, of this venerable construct, "school."

Contemporary educational reform focuses on themes of school accountability and student achievement, of local school district policy and state law, of federal school mandates and teacher preparation. The purpose of this book is to explore public education, focusing on the engine of contemporary educational reform and assessment: NCLB. Subsequently, we file this report.

We start by asserting that the purpose of education has shifted from the classic education objective of teachers teaching and students learning to one of aligning curriculum to standards and passing standardized tests. To provide a fodunation we look at the early educational pioneers and the history of testing.

We then detail contemporary political struggles regarding standards and standardized testing. We document the impact of the law on public education. High school students are dropping out of the system, or are rather systematically being pushed out. College students struggle to become highly qualified professionals. Teachers struggle to maintain their voice under the federally defined "highly qualified teacher" status imposed upon them. The authors file this report in a time when educational alternatives to public education are being advocated. We consider: what does schooling means today in an "ownership society"?

In the chapters that follow, the reader will find a thoughtful book which includes a series of reports, narratives, and case studies that shed light on the manner in which standardized assessment has been implemented in a number of different locations. We share the belief that NCLB as an educational reform has serious implications for all parties who care about education. As authors we hope to contribute to the debate, by putting forward an informed position through research.

Chapter(s) Preview

It is important to note that much is expected of public education. Since the birth of the nation, increasing demands have been placed on schools, parents, teachers and students. Educational administrators share a particularly heavy burden because of limited school resources. Our report takes these issues under consideration and provides a unique approach to the study of assessment past and present, as the different forms intersect in school policy.

In chapter one, "The Book of Testing" I start by describing how the development of compulsory education and moral standards evolved alongside the struggle of early pioneers to make public education available to all. Appreciating this story requires an understanding of the various mediating institutions that exist in the decentralized state system of the United States of America, including the role of religion, of professional associations, of state and local educational agencies, of teacher unions and of philanthropic institutions. In this first chapter, setting the context for the rest of the report, the author examines the idea of public education as building the "good society," and considers whether the No Child Left Behind federal mandate and the standards underpinning the law that are supposedly raising the bar for schools will truly include students left behind in the past.

Chapter two, "The Chicken Wins: The History of Assessment" has James Kusch asking the following questions: What are the types of assessment that are used and where did they come from? What are the alternatives, or in other words, what are ways to help schools to focus on achievement and to truly enact the principle of leaving no child behind?

In chapter three, "ETS and the American Dream" the authors ask the following questions: What is the testing industry? Where did the Educational Testing Service come from and how do they make the tests? What are the results for teacher education, for high school students, and for English language learners? This chapter was written by Alice Bicudo with contributions by Todd Alan Price and James Kusch.

In chapter four, "Fuzzy Math: Missing Tests, Missing Students, Missing the Mark" I consider: does NCLB and the testing it requires really boost the numbers, or perhaps are we unaware how it measures up?

Elizabeth Peterson determines the impact of the No Child Left Behind Act on the public school system in chapter five, "Drop Out or Pushed Out?" A high percentage of youth are leaving high school before completion. In the Chicago area, as elsewhere in the nation, the dropout rates among people of color (specifically African-Americans and Hispanics) limit their opportunity to achieve economic success. Recent data suggests that dropout numbers have increased at an alarming rate over the last several years since the No Child Left Behind Act went into effect.

Kristin Lems and Leah Miller write chapter six, "English Language Learners in an Era of NCLB." This chapter, as they describe, considers the implications of the key aspects of the law, as they relate to the teaching of English, foreign languages, and literacy in student's heritage language.

In chapter seven, "Who is Being Left Behind?" Martha Casazza and Laura Bauer examine the relationship between developmental education and adults, or students with articulation agreements who are pursuing two year degrees. They observe that adult students with sixth grade reading levels are coming to higher education unprepared, and they wonder, who is being left behind under the law?

In "Public Education and Privatization in the Ownership Society," chapter eight, Steven Thompson explores the meaning of education in an age of privatization. The political science of the law and the law's intentions; who are the interest groups at the forefront of the law, the policy aims an extension of what has been done in Chicago are described.

In chapter nine, "Hawaii, A Case Study of the Plantation Blues," Nancy Stone points out that prior to the onset of government funded and directed public education, Hawaiians, while under the authority of the missionaries were once considered the most literate people in the world. So what happened to push this state and these people into the tailspin that has sunk them to the bottom? This chapter will examine the structure, the history, the funding, the demographics, the policy practices and the politics that have driven this downward movement.

John W. Hunt writes chapter ten "The Modification of School Improvement and Staff Development Efforts in Response to the Failure to Make Adequate Yearly Progress." He points out that the law has forced schools to examine closely the scores of subgroups for the first time, while concluding that the high stakes testing impact has unintended consequences, some negative some positive. The positive consequences involve, for example, school improvement and staff development efforts.

Anne Grall Reichel documents the negative consequences like teacher frustration and concern over loss of voice in the decision-making process in public schools. In her chapter, "Unintended Consequences: The Teacher's Story" she points out that critical thinking and problem-solving have been sacrificed in the name of test preparation. Anne shares that our teachers are feeling betrayed by a system of testing that fails to see the whole child. Her premise is really quite simple; "we have failed to examine the unintended consequences of NCLB because we have failed to listen to the people who are doing the work."

Finally Virginia Jagla, in chapter twelve "A Ray of Hope: Service-Learning Insures Success for All" seeks to find some way in which innovation and creativity can be carved out of the law. She writes,

> who can argue with the premise of the No Child Left Behind law? Of course we want success for all students. Most teachers and administrators realized the one-size-fits-all approach originally adopted within the law would prove to be too challenging to fulfill. Now that the essential component of flexibility is being added to this federally mandated law, there may be a ray of hope.

Rather than ponder the myriad facets of this complex piece of legislation, this chapter considers one school's approach to addressing and meeting academic standards through the use of service-learning.

To conclude, history is important. The authors of this book are keenly aware of the story of public education's early advocates like Horace Mann, Catherine Beecher, and W.E.B. Dubois, who strove to transform the American school and the teaching profession, by determining the right size, shape, and furnishings of the buildings and classrooms, by establishing a common school fund, by improving teacher-training programs, and by arguing for a rich and inclusive curriculum. Champions of public education worked hard in the past to standardize, because standardization meant to improve and equalize the offerings of the public schools. In practice this meant to provide a core curriculum, to advance the distribution of quality textbooks, to train young women (and men) to become both professionals and cultural workers, to further develop subject matter, and to expand access to supplementary educational centers and social services. Progressive thinkers like John Dewey and Harold Rugg, to name but a few of the throng, challenged the institution to rethink pedagogy; in many cases they called upon the schools to change society rather than merely reflect it. Early educational pioneers fought mightily, as did the civil rights activists of what might be considered the first NCLB, the Elementary and Secondary Education Act of 1965 (ESEA), to make accessible to all social classes, to peoples of different creeds, color, gender and abilities, the opportunity to come through the door and be afforded at public expense an education of worth.

Public education started with the pilgrims, "the city on the hill," yet it hasn't been a uniform march to the promised land. Indeed the history of American education has long consisted of periods of standardization and back-to-basics, punctuated by brief periods of progressivism and creativity. The focus of this book is to understand the pendulum swing of educational reform, examining the most current attempt at educational reform in that light. NCLB, whose stated intention is to make certain that every student reaches the threshold of success, that we standardize competence and aim at 100% proficiency, by leaving, supposedly, no child behind, is something old, something new. Is NCLB a creative and/or progressive reform? Or is it a back-to-the-basics approach, a return to a supposed golden age of education that we have lost?

This much we know for certain. The NCLB Act, signed in 2002, follows more than two hundred years of advocacy, educational experimentation, crises and reform. Yet while the original ESEA was driven by public education advocates, NCLB appears largely driven by its most ardent detractors. Critics say we need to change the public education system *fundamentally* from the perspective that it is broken and its mission in need of revision. In this report we attempt to find out just what is broken, and whether NCLB is suited to provide a remedy.

Chapter 1
The Book of Testing

Todd Alan Price

America's faith in democracy once was evident in its support of public-schools. Locally controlled public education was the great equalizer to many an émigré, a bridge to economic opportunity and political enfranchisement in this, the great experiment in freedom and democracy.

Over time that faith survived challenges by private religious schools, of home schools, and the emergence of vouchers and charter schools.

The greatest challenge to the sustainability of public education had been levied first by Catholic schools and Father John Hughes in the 1840s. Catholic schools demanded a portion of the common school fund, but were denied on the grounds of separation of church and state. Thus Catholics went elsewhere, and their private schools grew in number.

Years later, a Supreme Court decision argued in 1925 that private schools could exist and flourish side by side with public schools.[1] The Republic thus maintained, funding of schools became a problem; property taxes would continue to rise causing some to bemoan paying their share of the public school tithe.

Throughout it all, more Americans than not continued to support public education.

Still, a new challenge to the viability of public education's future is not in the property tax, rather, it is with the federal government.

When the Department of Education mandates an evaluation system for each state, when each state in turn creates (or some would say adopts, from big business) standards that each school principal must adhere to, and when each teacher is directed to administer the high stakes, standardized tests that each student must take, then it becomes increasingly clear that local control is being subsumed by federal control through testing.

Beginning with the Carter administration, the Department of Education has grown, taking on more authority even in light of political challenges to its overall existence. Initially hostile to the idea of federal government involvement in public education, the Reagan Administration became directly involved in public education issues. The result is our commitment to public education has been shaken, first by the questioning of public education's "values" and second by the government demanding more "accountability."

From questioning the public schools secular values, the federal government moved toward sanctioning schools, replacing teachers and letting go principals if they failed to "prove" their worth, according to a statistic called the Annual Yearly Progress (AYP). Under the No Child Left Behind Act (NCLB) a school district could be shut down, taken over by the state and even restructured as a for-profit charter school system, if AYP is not met. On the other hand, private, religious schools are largely absolved from government interference because of the establishment clause which, again, calls for a separation of church and state.

An interesting point of departure for this story would be to consider that public schools developed from early religious roots. It is interesting to note, as some scholars do, the close relationship between religious faith and the development of faith in testing in the secular public school system. Where does faith in testing and/or lack of faith in public schools come from? What is the role of schools other than the public schools in a Republican democracy? Why is public education today, unlike the earliest days, of such heightened interest to the federal government? To provide answers we can look at the literature.

In the Beginning

Several scholars have written on the history of American public education, pointing often to the emergence of the Common School of the 19th century. This story usually begins with Horace Mann, riding a horse through the little towns, writing his twelve annual reports on improving education. This is followed by Catharine Beecher exhorting her young female teachers-in-training to relocate as fast as possible to fill positions in schools emerging on the Western frontier.

This is the secular story, but there is another story.

Several scholars place the "Genesis" of American public education back even further, to the middle of the 17th century. One particular story from this period tells of Pilgrims landing on Plymouth Rock, of the fabled "City upon a Hill"[2] of growing villages, peopled with hard working families, where children were to be seen and not heard. As these little communities struggled, adults worshipped and children were proctored to by a stern religious master, a theologian. With passage of the law, the *Old Deluder Act of 1647*[3] religious morality and corporeal punishment would be combined to, for the first time, mandate compulsory education, teach students to read the *King James Bible* and, subsequently, instill the proper amount of fear and respect in order to spread the Word.

While the "old" world was rapidly changing with advances in Enlightenment philosophy, in the New World of the Americas, early Colonists carried over the predispositions of their "old" world religious orders, accounting for the architecture, personal dwellings, social relations, and the school. During this pre-Revolutionary, Colonial period, (1620s to 1776) new churches were formed, members of the congregation flocked, a new revival was heard, and contentious denominational lines were drawn.

On the one hand, where the Episcopalians flourished there was resistance to the idea of paying for the education of other people's children. Schooling in such a case lay largely in the hands of private, church agencies and was supported by philanthropic funds or church tithes. The private management of the schools seemed to be located in the middle and southern Colonies where the Episcopalian and other similarly motivated denominations would predominate. Public management of the schools, on the other hand, was brought to life first by the New England communities and in the Puritanical settlements. The state of Massachusetts required that settlements with more than fifty residents provide an elementary school: "a precedent was thus set, with in almost every case, schools [being] paid for out of taxes" the early schools of Massachusetts were both publicly supported and publicly controlled.[4] Although religion advanced the idea of compulsory education in the early Colonial period, the idea of publicly supported education corresponded to a growing secularism, reflected in Enlightenment philosophy from Locke, Rousseau, Wollstonecraft, and Pestalozzi. What really transpired, despite the obvious European influence, was a movement toward everything new. While it was European liberal philosophy that influenced the ideas of curriculum and pedagogy, an American, Noah Webster pushed the idea of building a uniquely American language, casting out the old European texts, and ushering in the new American republic with the Blue Back Speller and the New-England Primer. Thus religiosity would morph with secularism over time, evolving into a uniquely configured citizenship education.

The diverse denominational styles of education, save for a strand of Protestantism, would be systematically replaced with a growing *Secularism* and *Liberal Humanism*. Liberal Humanists, many of whom were religiously educated, would advance the notion that education, though started by God-fearing peoples, should be directed toward meeting the needs of all, not just the fortunate (in the time of Calvin, preordained meant that before birth, each person was already slated for one fate or another). Given sufficient support, the ideals of citizenship and an American pragmatism would follow.

Philosophically speaking, the aims of public versus private styles, of ownership, funding and management were thus enshrined during the early Colonial pilgrimage. Public education grew out of the tension that separated publicly managed and privately managed schools. The tensions between the different philosophies are documented here:

> These differences were of the greatest importance. When the American people decided to establish public schools throughout the United States, they found that the job was easier where habits of public support and control were deep in the life of the people, as they were in Massachusetts, than it was where the private school had been the dominant educational institution, as in the middle and the southern states.[5]

This story, and other such stories are noted in the works of Lawrence Cremin and in a recurring, popular educational textbook called *The American School 1642-2004* by Joel Spring. Spring makes a powerful point regarding the history of public education. To some, school is experienced as a vehicle of social mobility here status is "conferred" yet to others it is more narrowly understood as a site of ideological control, where status is "confirmed."[6] Although history textbooks frequently speak of a collective, shared, American experience, different groups of people share different experiences in the pursuit of the American dream, and likewise have different experiences of "school." It all depends on one's personal and social experience while attending.

In sum, by telling a story about school, the student, parent and/or teacher should recognize that there are often many contradictory ways in which a story about school can be received, interpreted and understood. Stated another way, history has its share of winners and losers but over time, there are different versions of who won and lost and what winning and losing means. There is, for example, his story and her story, and there are stories of school that speak eloquently to the following: Colonization, accommodation, assimilation, marginalization, socialization, indoctrination, all of which speak to the phenomena of *Americanization.*

Rewind

Great contributions have been made to American public education by philosophers who have shared this value: an informed citizenry is the essence of American democracy. Adam Smith preached a moral philosophy *and* a new economics where a drop in the bucket (human capital) would ensure that all boats would rise; the good society (philanthropy) would moderate the excess of the burgeoning merchant class and business ethics would sustain the new economic system of capitalism.[7] John Locke envisioned the good society where the right to voice one's political belief would be honored (and not get one thrown into jail), where tolerance of divergent religious opinions is the norm, and where the role of education fosters these rights, and also, to boot, turns out a well-rounded man of business.[8] On the integration of education and nature, the need to acknowledge the natural rites of passage, and the belief that all humans go through developmental stages there is Jean-Jacques Rousseau.[9] Subsequent to and expanding on Rousseau, there is the dignity of the child, and a curriculum based on the science of teaching and learning here one finds the contributions of Johann Pestalozzi.[10] Furthermore where there is the idea of children's growth, there is Maria Montessori[11] expanding on ideas constructed by the creator of "gardens for children" or "kindergarten," Frederick Froebel.[12]

Several have written about the institution itself. For the interested student of education, the following list brushes upon only a few of those who are often cited in educational literature. Most significantly to the general enterprise of education for all, on the general diffusion of knowledge and the critical need for a uniquely secular, liberal and humanistic American public education, local elections for school boards, and a national system for ensuring the maintenance of a system of laws with checks and balances there is Thomas Jefferson .[13] Not to be outdone, there is a significant tribute to the rights of women as intellectual equals in a co-educational national system, by a radical feminist named Mary Wollstonecraft.[14]

Horace Mann, honored as the "father of public education" wrote 12 reports, detailing teacher wages, classroom size and accoutrements, and what teachers should know and how they should teach.[15] Catherine Beecher[16] more than any other defined the teacher as a woman, and invested great effort to advance the profession. Frederick Douglass[17] advocated for the rights of the America slaves to be emancipated and reap the benefits, as he had done, to an education of worth; Frederick Jackson Turner[18] gave traveling scholar lectures regarding the American frontier, and William Homes McGuffey created the most popular reader of his times, aptly named the McGuffey Readers.[19] Harold Rugg contributed to the creation of a popular Social Studies textbook series that challenged America to do better.[20]

There is a laundry list of scholars who have attempted to capture the essence of American public education, or to prescribe what should be the curriculum and instruction of most worth.[21] Ellwood Cubberley, for example, wrote a history of American public education that was based on school building construction and the role of the superintendent.[22]

To be certain, examinations have been used throughout the history of public education to determine what a student knows and how they know it. It is the issue of testing, evaluation and assessment that appear to be the most important determiner of curriculum decision making; the "big test"[23] reflects the standards that drive curricula today. Nicholas Lehman writes an excellent history concerning how standardized tests were advanced with the intention of serving a common good. Rising and declining scores of students, teachers, schools and school districts tell one story of how public education is doing. But another story needs to be examined. In this book, we the authors feel the story of how assessment was formed impacts strongly how the story of public education is told today, and has consequences for the stakeholders of public education, all of us.

Theory

- There are different forms of capital invested in society, not only the economic kind.[24] Social, cultural, symbolic and political forms of capital are, for example, invested in public schools. Students come out of the experience of school having accumulated different amounts of capital. A central question to ask is how are forms of capital transmitted and to whom?
- There are different types of values, norms, and mores circulating throughout culture[25] and subsequently, these values, norms, and mores circulate often uninterrupted in public schools. A central question to ask is whose values, norms and mores are honored in school?
- Finally, there are different ways in which history can be written. Given the subjective nature of historians as story tellers, the historiography[26] or the writing of history, is often about "great men" and "great wars," it is important to realize that any history, including that of the public education experience is subject to debate. The question to ask should be: whose voice is inscribed in the written history of school?

With these general caveats in mind we begin with a few suppositions:

Supposition one is this: American public education can be characterized as having passed through four distinct and classifying eras of educational stability and reform, as follows:

- *Compulsory Education in the Colonial Era.* This is reflected in the contributions of Puritanism, Colonialism, and Radicalism leading right up to the American revolution (1620-1776)
- *The Revolutionary Era.* The establishment of a republican form of government, citizenship education and Utilitarianism. (1776-1830)
- *The Common School Era.* Manifest Destiny, the Civil War, and the challenges of direct democracy in the form of immigration and Populism. (1830-1890)
- *The Progressive Education Era.* Political upheaval, Unionization, immigration, Progressivism; a period of scientific discovery and focus on curriculum and instruction. (1890-1957)

Sprinkled throughout are advances in student learning, professional development for teachers, unionization, curriculum experimentation, and political reformation.

Less distinct and less well defined are two recent eras in the story of public education:

- *The Back-to-the-Basics Era.* National insecurity with the launching of Sputnik, and a return to Conservatism; the Back-to-the-Basics movement. (1957-1980s)
- *The Globalization Era.* World Class Standards, Information Technology, High Stakes Testing. (1989-present)

These periods are characterized by an amalgamation of the others, but share features that have expanded in importance, namely, technology deployment used by administrators, teachers and students in the classroom, and the emergence of alternative (private) school systems.

Supposition two is this: while the history of public education is subject to interpretation there is, nonetheless, what appears to be stability: a common thread running through the American public education experience. That common thread is *democratic access*. School began with compulsory education; democratic access to education was conceived with the Northwest Territory Ordinance, and articulated in state constitutions during the Common School Era. The concept emerged and survived: *an equal opportunity afforded by a uniform, thorough and efficient public education system.*

Long before the modern language of learning disabilities, peer tutoring, advanced placement classes, attention deficit disorder, at-risk youth, teaming, block schedules, and site based management, a common language of the three R's, 'reading, 'riting and 'rithmetic took hold, and the kernel of an idea that compulsory education should be paid for by the citizens of a community through a local tax emerged, grew, and thrived. Even from the earliest days of the Puritanical colonies, there was support for the idea that an institution could be construed to provide for the benefit of all and to serve the common good. During the

Revolutionary Era, the idea of everyone being availed access to a democratic education in order to secure Citizenship gathered strength.

Years later, during the Common School Era, the Compulsory education idea was more clearly articulated and enshrined in the form of a system of highly-qualified teachers, uniform codes of conduct, blackboards, standardized text-books and rigorous tests.

Indeed, in our current Globalization Era, it is in the form of Common School Era generated tests that the idea of democracy is evaluated. In the Common School Era, tests were used, standards were applied, and immigrants were counted for political aims. During the Progressive Education Era, standardized tests were legitimated as a tool for civil rights, to ensure a meritocracy.

Something strange happened along the way to the 21 century. As America continues to diversify, the stakes are suddenly deemed to be higher, and, in other words, high stakes tests now determine curriculum under the rationale that to do otherwise (test en masse) is to deny some their opportunity. Thus in order that no child is left behind, every student in the 21st century is tested...but with instruments derived from the 1840s. To these phenomena we now turn.

Purpose of Evaluation

With greater waves of immigrants coming to the United States of America, during the 1840s, 1890s and 1920s, the government needed to exercise a form of social control. Manifest Destiny clearly meant that white Anglos were granted the right to annex land where they could exercise what to them must have seemed their proper role of governance. Not insignificantly, statistics became a way to keep tabs on people, especially the people added to the Republic from newly acquired territories. Statistics have been used as a sort of "state arithmetic"[27] to sort out different immigrants into groups, to determine what they will learn, where their life opportunities are, and how they will vote. In this story, evaluation is not neutral, but rather, it is a state strategy that occurs as a part of the production of ideas in a social field. The government of the Common School Era 1830-90, resembles the government today, if only that the government responds to immigration from within a complex social field, and that social field exercises ultimate power. In other words, government didn't create the "problem" of immigration, powerful actors within a social field did.

By state strategy, what is meant is that the government is responding to the social field, and attempting to exercise control (immigration "reform"). The government's power is revealed in the type of strategy used, for example, when it argues for the production of statistics and of one type of examination over another.

In one interesting case, the local government for the first time rolled out standardized tests to determine whether the children were learning or not. This transpired in Boston in 1845,[28] and Horace Mann, the evangelical public education advocate agreed to administer and collect the tests. The experiment was unique, it revealed that the students ranged widely in their skills and also that teachers' skills ranged widely too. Yet it would not be repeated again, until the 1920s when standardized testing was becoming akin to a science.

The idea that the federal government should naturally be able to sort people out using a test, to determine an evaluation in the first place, speaks to how public education has both changed and stayed the same over time. While the government frequently relies on polls to determine strategy, nowhere in the Constitution is there language that says that the federal government has the right to determine anything about the forms of evaluation in public schools. Despite Jefferson's best efforts at building a national curriculum, conservatives have often been wary of big federal government meddling in the affairs of local communities. Local school boards would determine the character of the curriculum, and state education agencies emerging from the Northwest Territory Ordinance (1789) determined that the individual states had the responsibility for ensuring a system of education for the denizens within. But the feds were expected to mind their own business.

Fast Forward

Indeed the first ESEA was formed as a matter of progressive policy-making that strove to force the public schools to become more equitable, diverse, just, and basically more public. Under the administration of President Lyndon Baines Johnson, the ESEA was signed in 1965, emerging out of the Civil Rights movement. Signed in front of his first grade teacher, Johnson put forth a carrot or a stick approach to recalcitrant Southern states.[29] In effect he said: either desegregate your schools or lose money allotted from the federal government. Knowing, as a fellow southerner, that the institutional racism of the South would never willfully submit to desegregation, Johnson offered a monetary incentive.[30] The result was a massive desegregation the likes of which the nation has never known then nor since.

The No Child Left Behind bill was signed into law by President George W. Bush before a teeming crowd of students and teachers in Hamilton City High School Ohio on January 8, 2002. NCLB, or the Education Bill HR 1, was slated to allocate $26.5 billion dollars to Public Education. With the September 11, 2001, New York City twin tower tragedy a recent memory, citizens rallied around the Commander-in-Chief; the President was riding a wave of popularity. The principal in Hamilton, Ohio glowed about how the nation could rest safely with the president's steady leadership and because of the good people he had surrounded himself with. The superintendent warned of children at risk, of the evils of illiteracy and, much like the fight against terrorism, this was a war desperately needing engagement. Public education was on the line. This story was put to good effect that day in the auditorium of the medium sized, folksy, urban school. Bush could claim to be fighting against terrorism on the one hand, and defeating the scourge of illiteracy and underachievement on the other.

President George W. Bush, a Republican, with bipartisan support of the Democratic party in the House and Senate, managed to project a vision of a day when all students would succeed, while speaking little at all about the consequences: dismantling traditional forms of governance of public schools in favor of "choice" in education, and subjecting teachers and students to the unsavory underside of standardized testing, narrowing the curriculum. Leaving no child behind, on that day in Hamilton, who could ask for more?

Yet the irony of this much celebrated day was that despite claims to the contrary by administration and supporters, NCLB would soon be attacked for being yet another unfunded mandate. Furthermore, the call for all schools, homogenous and diverse alike, to demonstrate Adequate Yearly Progress (AYP), would soon empower a profit driven regime of curriculum packaging (Reading First), of high stakes testing (ETS and Harcourt Assessment, Inc.) tutoring (Sylvan Educational Solutions and IGNITE) and enable lucrative and questionable assessment efforts ("Growth models," and "Safe Harbor" provisions). NCLB, by placing data before decision making would jeopardize the attainment of the very same principle the title of the law supposedly advocates for.

Consider for example, NCLB in effect claims to neglect no one by disaggregating specific subgroups from the whole group of students to get a better look at who is achieving and who is not. It strives to measure and categorize students by way of high stakes standardized test scores in order to prevent students from being left behind, and to ensure that they are given the instruction necessary to move ahead. Yet perverse incentives, as is the name of a title that criticizes the law, abounds. School districts may indeed feel discouraged in testing students with special needs, often the ones who are most in need of assessment, because those same students bring the test scores down for the entire school!

Questions for Research

We use a critical methodology for better understanding public education as an institution; we are claiming that because of the No Child Left Behind Act, a new educational institution is being constructed. We examine key indices and statistics that relate to the student population(s), to schools making Adequate Yearly Progress (AYP) and we use qualitative research to contextualize these findings. We start by asking:

- Where did the idea of high stakes testing come from?
- Where did No Child Left Behind come from and who owns its meaning?
- Who pays for it?
- Who manages its meaning and implementation?
- What does this say about who participates?
- Who stands most to gain or lose from the act...who ultimately benefits?

Notes

1. *Pierce v. Society of Sisters of the Holy Names of Jesus and Mary*, 268 U.S. 510 (1925).

2. Lawrence Cremin, *American Education; the Colonial Experience, 1607-1783* [1st ed.] (New York; Harper & Row, 1970).

3. Lawerence Cremin, 1970; (duly transcribed in *Records of the Governor and Company of the Massachusetts Bay in New England,* 1853).

4. Lawrence Arthur Cremin and Merle L. Borrowman, *Public schools in our democracy* (New York; Macmillan. 1956) p. 67

5. Lawrence Arthur Cremin and Merle L. Borrowman, *Public schools in our democrac,* (New York; Macmillan. 1956) p. 67

6. Joel. H. Spring, *The American School, 1642-2004.* 6th ed. (Boston: McGraw-Hill. 2005).

7. Fred R. Glahe, *Adam Smith and the Wealth of Nations: 1776-1976 Bicentennial Essays*. edited and with an introduction by Fred R. Glahe (Boulder: ColoradoAssociated University Press. 1978).

8. Peter Gay, *John Locke on Education.* Edited, with an introd. and notes, by Peter Gay. (New York; Bureau of Publications, Teachers College, Columbia University. 1978).

9. Jean Jacques Rousseau, *Emile* translated [from the French] by Barbara Foxley; introduction by P. D. Jimack (London: Dent; New York: Dutton, 1974). 444 p.

10. Johann Heinrich Pestalozzi, *How Gertrude Teaches her Children; An Attempt to Help Mothers to Teach their own Children and an Account of the Method, by Johann Heinrich Pestalozzi*; translated by Lucy E. Holland and Francis C. Turner, and edited with introduction and notes by Ebenezer Cooke (London, G. Allen & Unwin ltd.; Syracuse, N.Y., C. W. Bardeen. 1915).

11. Maria Montessori, *The Advanced Montessori Method.* Translated from the Italian. (Cambridge, Mass., R. Bentley, [c1917]. 1964).

12. Johannes Ronge, *A Practical Guide to the English Kinder-garten (Children's Garden) for the Use of Mothers, Governesses, and Infant Teachers: Being an Exposition of Froebel's System of Infant Training*. 4th ed. (London: A.N. Myers. 1871).

13. Charles Flinn Arrowood, *Thomas Jefferson and Education in a Republic;* edited by Charles Flinn Arrowood (New York, [etc.] McGraw-Hill book company. 1930).

14. Ulrich H. Hardt, *A Critical Edition of Mary Wollstonecraft's A Vindication of the Rights of Woman, with Strictures on Political and Moral Subjects* (Troy, N.Y.: Whitson Pub. Co. 1982).

15. Lawrence Cremin, "The Republic and the School. Horace Mann on the Education of Free Men." *Classics in Education. No 1* (Bureau of Publications, Teachers College, Columbia University, New York. 1957).

16. Catherine Beecher, *The Duty of American Women to their Country* (New York: Harper & Brothers. 1845).

17. William L. Andrews and William S. McFeely, *Narrative of the Life of Frederick Douglass: Authoritative Text, Contexts*. Criticism. 1st ed (New York: W.W. Norton & Co. 1996).

18. Frederick Jackson Turner, *The Frontier in American History, by Frederick Jackson Turner* (New York, H. Holt and company.1921).

19. Stanley W. Lindberg, *The Annotated McGuffey: Selections from the McGuffey Eclectic Readers 1836-1920* (New York: Van Nostrand Reinhold. 1976).

20. Rugg, Harold, *An Introduction to American Civilization; A Study of Economic Life in the United States, a Textbook in Geography and Civics with Historical Backgrounds, by Harold Rugg* (Boston, New York [etc.] Ginn and company. 1929).

21. Herbert Spencer, *Education; Intellectual, Moral, and Physical* (London: Williams and Norgate. 1902).

22. Ellwood Cubberley, *The History of Education: Educational Practice and Progress Considered as a Phase of the Development and Spread of Western Civilization* (Boston: Houghton Mifflin. 1920).

23. Nicholas Lehman, *The Big Test: The Secret History of the American Meritocracy* (New York: Farrar, Straus and Giroux. 2000).

24. Pierre Bourdieu, *Distinction: A Social Critique of the Judgment of Taste*; translated by Richard Nice (Cambridge, Mass. Harvard University Press. 1984).

25. Antonio Gramsci, *Prison Notebooks* (New York: Columbia University Press. 1992).

26. Fernand Braudel, *On History;* translated by Sarah Matthews (Chicago: University of Chicago Press. 1980).

27. Thomas Popkewitz, *Paradigm and Ideology in Educational Research: The Social Functions of the Intellectual* (London; New York: Falmer Press. 1984).

28. Otis W. Caldwell and Stuart A. Courtis, *Then and Now in Education 1845:1923 A Message of Encouragement from the Past to the Present* (Yonkers on Hudson, New York; World Book Company. 1924).

29. Stone Lantern Films, *School: The Story of American Public Education* foreword by Meryl Streep; introduction by David Tyack, with James D. Anderson [et al.]; narrative by Sheila Curran Bernard and Sarah Mondale; edited by Sarah Mondale and Sarah B. Patton (Boston: Beacon Press. 2001).

30. Anderson, 2001

References

Andrews, William L., and William S. McFeely. *Narrative of the Life of Frederick Douglass: Authoritative Text, Contexts, Criticism.* 1st ed. New York: W. W. Norton & Co., 1996.

Arrowood, Charles Flinn. *Thomas Jefferson and Education in a Republic.* Edited by Charles Flinn Arrowood. New York: McGraw-Hill book company, 1930

Beecher, Catherine. *The Duty of American Women to their Country.* New York: Harper & Brothers, 1845.

Bourdieu, Pierre. *Distinction: A Social Critique of the Judgment of Taste.* Translated by Richard Nice. Cambridge, Mass.: Harvard University Press, 1984.

Braudel, Fernand. *On History.* Translated by Sarah Matthews. Chicago: University of Chicago Press, 1980.

Caldwell, Otis W. and Stuart A. Courtis. *Then and Now in Education 1845:1923 A Message of Encouragement from the Past to the Present.* Yonkers on Hudson, New York; World Book Company, 1924.

Cremin, Lawrence. *American Education; the Colonial Experience, 1607-1783.* 1st ed. New York: Harper & Row, 1970.

Cremin, Lawrence, and Arthur and Merle L. Borrowman. *Public Schools in our Democracy.* New York: Macmillan, 1956.

Cremin, Lawrence. "The Republic and the School. Horace Mann on the Education of Free Men." In *Classics in Education, No 1.* Bureau of Publications, Teachers College, Columbia University, New York: 1957.

Cubberley, Ellwood. *The History of Education: Educational Practice and Progress Considered as a Phase of the Development and Spread of Western Civilization.* Boston: Houghton Mifflin, 1920.

Gay, Peter. *John Locke on Education.* Edited, with an introd. and notes, by Peter Gay. New York: Bureau of Publications, Teachers College, Columbia University, 1978.

Glahe, Fred R., ed. *Adam Smith and the Wealth of Nations: 1776-1976 Bicentennial Essays*. Boulder: Colorado Associated University Press, 1978.

Gramsci, Antonio. *Prison Notebooks.* New York: Columbia University Press, 1992.

Hardt, Ulrich H. *A Critical Edition of Mary Wollstonecraft's A Vindication of the Rightsof Woman, with Strictures on Political and Moral Subjects.* T roy, N.Y.: Whitston Pub. Co., 1982.

Lehman, Nicholas. *The Big Test: The Secret History of the American Meritocracy*. New York: Farrar, Straus and Giroux, 2000.

Lindberg, Stanley W. *The Annotated McGuffey: Selections from the McGuffey Eclectic Readers 1836-1920*. New York: Van Nostrand Reinhold, 1976.

Montessori, Maria. *The Advanced Montessori Method.* Translated from the Italian.Cambridge, Mass.: R. Bentley, [c1917], 1964.

Pestalozzi, Johann Heinrich. *How Gertrude Teaches her Children; An Attempt to Help-Mothers to Teach their own Children and an Account of the Method, by Johann*

Heinrich Pestalozzi. Translated by Lucy E. Holland and Francis C. Turner, and edited with introduction and notes by Ebenezer Cooke. London: G. Allen & Unwin ltd.; Syracuse, N.Y.: C. W. Bardeen, 1915.

Pierce v. Society of Sisters of the Holy Names of Jesus and Mary, 268 U.S. 510 (1925).

Popkewitz, Thomas.*.Paradigm and Ideology in Educational Research: The Social Functions of the Intellectual.* London; New York: Falmer Press, 1984.

Ronge, Johannes. *A Practical Guide to the English Kinder-garten (Children's Garden) for the Use of Mothers, Governesses, and Infant Teachers: Being an Exposition of Froebel's System of Infant Training.* 4th ed. London: A.N. Myers, 1871.

Rousseau, Jean-Jacques. *Discourse on Political Economy and the Social Contract: Jean-Jacques Rousseau; translated with introduction and notes by Christopher Betts.* Oxford; New York: Oxford University Press, 1994.

Rousseau, Jean Jacques. *Emile.* Translated [from the French] by Barbara Foxley; introduction by P. D. Jimack. London: Dent; New York: Dutton, 1974.

Rugg, Harold. *An Introduction to American Civilization; A Study of Economic Life in the United States, a Textbook in Geography and Civics with Historical Backgrounds, by Harold Rugg.* Boston, New York [etc.] Ginn and company, 1929.

Spencer, Herbert. *Education; Intellectual, Moral, and Physical.* London: Williams and Norgate, 1902.

Spring, Joel. H. *The American School, 1642-2004.* 6th ed. Boston: McGraw-Hill, 2005.

Stone Lantern Films *School: The Story of American Public Education*. Foreword by Meryl Streep; introduction by David Tyack, with James D. Anderson [et al.]; narrative by Sheila Curran Bernard and Sarah Mondale; edited by Sarah Mondale and Sarah B. Patton. Boston: Beacon Press, 2001.

Turner, Frederick Jackson. *The Frontier in American History, by Frederick Jackson* Turner. New York, H. Holt and Company, 1921.

Chapter 2 The Chicken Wins: The History of Assessment

James Kusch

The main purpose of this chapter is to provide a different perspective on the history of testing that spans the years 1843-2008; a view of how teachers learn to grade their pupils formally in methods courses and informally during the practicum experience; and some words on the production of knowledge as it relates to assessment.

In the following discussion I explore the broad relationships that exist between theoretically significant conceptions of assessment that appear in historical scholarly research and the actual practice of pupil assessment as it is transmitted to new teachers.

My argument is that teachers employ assessment to achieve classic pedagogical objectives such as developing sequences of lesson topics and strategies, judging lesson plans, and sanctioning pupil thought. But most particularly, I argue, teachers employ assessment to order pupil learning and to control classroom relations. Assessment then becomes an element of social control to the extent that it defines and orders classroom knowledge and values.

There are backlash affects of testing on learning and teaching that are complex and that are rarely discussed. The history of the testing movement provides an operational view that affects what is to be learned about what students learn and teachers teach when we privilege teaching to the test.

Charles Murray and Historiometry

Saturday, October 24, 2004, a new book on an old idea was reviewed by the New York Times. Charles Murray, a previous co-author with Richard J. Herrnstein of a controversial book, *The Bell Curve,* comes out with another, his latest (funded by the Bradley Foundation, the same sponsor of the school voucher movement's canon[1]) entitled *Human Accomplishment: The Pursuit of Excellence in the Arts and Sciences 800 B.C. to 1950.*[2]

Why, you may ask, consider Murray's book in a discussion of tests and measurement?

One reason is that Herrnstein and Murray with *The Bell Curve* reinvigorated what was thought to be a dead issue, arguing that intelligence is not only innate, but can largely be attributable to race. With *Human Accomplishment*, Murray continues this line of thinking, contributing a significant part of a much broader picture of the history of ideas, and in this case the history of assessment...or at least a particular idea of assessment that is much favored and richly funded by neo-conservative think tanks like the Bradley Foundation and the American Enterprise Institute.

What then does Murray actually say and how does he contribute to the history of assessment and the literature on tests and measurement?

Murray's main contention and *Human Accomplishments'* main idea is this: human achievement can be reduced to a number and tabulated by a computer!

Murray takes an almost exclusively quantitative approach, relying on a relatively obscure statistical method known as historiometry. Murray tells of Sir Francis Galton, an English scientist and eugenicist who brought the method into scholarly vogue. The book ranks the giants of the World Literature, or the Western World Literature...all men...on an ordinal scale from the top, Shakespeare, to the bottom, Ibsen, by virtue of numerical rank. Murray inventories Western accomplishments in astronomy, biology, chemistry, earth sciences, physics, math, medicine and technology to prove dominance of European and North American men. According to his statistics Murray claims 72% of "significant figures" of arts and sciences came from Britain, France, Germany, and Italy.[3]

Murray further claims that the reason for a Northern European's success is Christianity. Human intelligence is a "gift from God". It is argued that human excellence can be traced to Christian belief; even Jewish literary scholars owe their success to Christian culture, or so Murray argues in his final analysis!

Let's turn to tests and measurements and explore antecedents of Charles Murray.

The Early Views on Testing

My discussion of testing here is genealogical by design and is based upon certain assumptions. Namely, current views of testing and measurement are not new at all; they are firmly anchored in 19th century thinking. The purposes, practices, and uses of testing and assessment have changed very little since the mid-19th century. Where a system or scheme of thought is so firmly set in time will it not benefit similar groups today as it did then and exclude others as it did when it was formulated?

Think of possible implications for what and how we teach when our thinking of assessment is based upon 19th century ideas. Why is it that we seemingly have not moved beyond that style of thought? If our current curriculum and style of teaching reflects issues that are important in 2008 why employ older means of reckoning what we do?

That is the problem I pose and these are the questions for you: what are the ways we can assess learning which reflect the times in which we live? What are alternative histories of assessment and testing?

Standard Morality

J.S. Mill wrote that, in a utilitarian sense, social behavior could be judged by reference to moral principles. Mill thought we could measure morality and social behavior on an ordinal scale. For example, a moral quality such as happiness could be ascertained by "competent judges" by reference to what is most desirable. Think about how you would count or quantify a quality like "paying attention." In 1843 Mill wrote:

> There must be some standard by which to determine their goodness or badness absolute or comparative of ends or objects or desires. Whatever that standard is, there can be but one: for if there were several ultimate principles of conduct, the same conduct might be approved by one of these principles of conduct, the same conduct might be approved by one of these principles and condemned by another and there will be needed some more general principle as umpire between them.[4]

Consider that today there is much interest in assessing dispositions for teacher candidates. Are these ideas new, or merely a throwback to Mill and 1843?

I would propose that we can link mid-19th century thought on testing and assessment with English thought on evolution and scientific method after Mill and Darwin. The manner in which we obtain and retain knowledge proceeds in an orderly manner so that gaining knowledge is both a predictable and a measurable process. Testing is an act by which we measure a gain in knowledge, but there is a limitation on this type of thinking; consider, for example, do any of us know of classrooms and students that are entirely predictable and measurable?

Hereditary Genius

Francis Galton developed a series of psychometric surveys which helped establish a psychology of individual differences and a new inferential calculus for codifying empirical associations of those differences. At least two works of Galton illuminate thinking on tests and measures.

First, his 1869 study *Hereditary Genius* "hit" upon the idea of using obituaries and entries in a biographical dictionary to show a correlation between reputation, intelligence and heredity.[5]

Second, was his work with fingerprints...arguably Galton is the father of fingerprint techniques. He posited that true difference among all humans could be located in their fingerprints.[6]

With a classification of knowledge and life opportunities in the social sciences, we can further understand the drive by social scientists and educational psychologists to establish classificatory schemes and sets of standards in public education.

While control of standards is a central and typically under-analyzed feature of economic life, classifications such as those created by Murray et al. may or may not be standardized. If they are then there is no need to test for improvement or achievement because intelligence, like morality in Calvinist times is innate, preordained. If they are not...then they are limited to a local community or special interest group of limited duration.

The Early Testing Movement

In the late 19th century, there was an information explosion...the development of myriad systems of classification and standardization of modern industrial and scientific institutions. It was vogue to classify, measure and standardize just about everything. The categories so produced lived in industry, science education and government. They ranged from measurement of machine tools to measurement of people's forearms and foreheads. The standards were sometimes physically tiny measures: how big should the standard second of time be, an eyeglass screw, or an electric pulse rate? Government agencies, industrial consortia, and scientific committees created the standards and category systems. Most of these activities became silently embodied in the built environment and in common sense notions of good practice.

The work of Galton appeared in America through the work of James M. Cattell who coined the term "mental test"[7] and Edward Thorndike who used the term mental test in his construction of "achievement tests".[8] Cattell claimed that his work with mental testing enabled him to measure individual differences among students using paper and pencil tests and using methods free of introspection. Cattell thus supplied experimental psychology with a utilitarian framework. Since Thorndike defined mind as the sum total of connections between one's environment and one's responses, he provided a behaviorist rationale for standardized testing. Standardized tests gave teachers the opportunity to observe statistically representative subsets of a predetermined sort. As such the test was an indicator of present performance and a predictor for future performance.

But critical questions lingered (and still do): what are the differences between information and knowledge? Questions such as this one would be trumped by the desire for scientific time management and the emergence of a "cult of efficiency."[9]

Testing and Social Efficiency

On a mass scale standardized testing provided a means of coping with a large and growing population of students in the schools. Between 1890 and 1910 the general population of the U.S. grew by 68% while the number of high school students grew by an astounding 711%.[10] The United States of America had fast become a younger nation.

During that 20 year period the established curriculum in schools came under attack from groups in and out of education. These groups wanted the curriculum to respond to social efficiency movements that were then ascendant in industrial life. In that context we can understand why the CEEB (or College Board) was founded. The College Board provided a way of screening and sorting student's applications to colleges and universities. The CEEB created standardized examinations for those purposes. For the first time the idea of individualization emerged as a key concept and age grade statistics were collected to measure qualities of school systems and to give evidence of who individuals were and where they fit academically and socially.

During this, what has largely been described as "the Progressive Education Era"[11], two major purposes emerged for conducting assessments. These are summarized in the following: 1) testing was seen as a means by which schools and universities could collect and measure information about pupils on a mass scale and 2) testing gave a means to judge teacher's competence.

This would have great impact on education, throughout the twentieth century.

In the latter part of the 20th century other related purposes emerged:

> 3) examinations were seen as a way to reflect degrees of learning rather than simple attendance;
> 4) examinations were used to evaluate the "quality" of a teacher or a school;
> 5) examinations established preferential treatment in the allocation of money for salaries, buildings, equipment and the like;
> 6) examinations were seen as a way to motivate teaching and learning by specifying the detail of the systems' expectation for learning;
> 7) examinations led to undue concentration on material to be examined (teaching to the test);
> 8) examinations served as a way to legitimize knowledge and signaled an acceptance of new school subjects;
> 9) examinations allocated opportunity for students in life, rank ordering students, sorting them out as academic winners and/or losers.

In reviewing this history one should ask, do distinctions between these purposes for assessment provide a model for our 21st century theory of assessment?

Testing and Educational Psychology

Early pioneers like William James, Stanley Hall, James C. Cattell, Henry Goddard, Carl Bingham, and Edward Thorndike, used psychology to resolve thorny questions about schooling such as: 1) how do we obtain and retain valid knowledge; 2) why are some pupils bright and others dull; and 3) how might educators base promotion of pupils?

Stanley Hall was a student of the psychologist and philosopher William James at Harvard University where he developed theories in his writing that would make his philosophy practical only if its method were scientific. Soon Hall was appointed to the faculty at John Hopkins University, where he hoped to establish a chair in physiological psychology. His complaint was of the pitiful state of philosophy; he claimed that philosophy in the United States of America did not exist. What was taught was physiology...what one could lay hands on, see, and measure. Hall had returned to John Hopkins from study in Germany where he had studied the precursors of Sigmund Freud and others in what was called philosophical psychology. Hall eventually merged the American notions of philosophy with physiology into a "new" subject, "psychology".

Hall was at a time in his career where he explored different pathways including medicine, he extended his studies to psychopathology but, sensing the groundswell of interest in the United States for educational reform he reasoned that the most promising line of work would be to study the application of psychology to education. He lectured educators on the need to apply psychological science principles to their classroom pursuits. When Hall received a permanent post at Hopkins it was as a professor of psychology and pedagogy. He was able thus to persuade others of the links between child psychology, abnormal psychology and philosophy. Linkages between mind, physical attributes and their abnormalities...all could be measured.

In the 1890s at the University of Pennsylvania, James Cattell was applying capacity psychology to mental measurement of students. There in collaboration with the anthropologist Franz Boas he constructed a series of tests correlating anthropometric measurements to physical and mental development. Famous experiments conducted there were with empty skulls that test experts would fill with dry lentils to demonstrate skull size and mental capacity. The more the lentils a skull could hold the more the intelligence! Cattell wrote:

> We do not at present wish to draw any definite conclusions from the results of the tests so far made. It is of some scientific interest to know that students entering college have heads on the average 19.3 cm long...that they have an average reaction-time of 0.174 seconds, that they can remember seven numerals heard once, and so on with other records and measurements. These are mere facts, but they are quantitative facts and the basis of science. Our own future work and that of others must proceed in two directions...to what extent are the several traits of body, of the senses and of mind interdependent? What can we learn from the tests of elementary traits regarding the higher intellectual and emotional life? On the other hand we must use our measurements to study the development of the individual and of the race, to disentangle the complex factors of heredity and environment.[12]

In 1912, a psychologist named Henry Goddard used the *Binet* test, originally from Alfred Binet of France, to "prove" Jewish and Italian immigrants were intellectually inferior. Carl Bingham, a Princeton psychologist who helped develop educational testing, used data from World War I Army intelligence tests on East and Southern European draftees to provide the intellectual justification for the 1924 Immigration Act that halted immigration of these groups. He argued, incorrectly, that these groups' entry into the US had lowered the general intelligence level here. In point of fact, the tests measured acquired skills, not intelligence. Naturally as non-native speakers, they could not compete with native speakers on a test that measured language competence. The tests showed absolutely nothing about the immigrant's ability to learn.[13]

To the point, early IQ tests rely on late 19th century physical anthropologist's assumptions about genetic superiority and inferiority. They believed that by measuring skull sizes, they could determine which "races" had superior intelligence. These experiments (anthropometric tests) sought to prove Northern European's racial superiority by showing they had larger skulls than Africans.

Several years later, in the late 1970s, Stephen Jay Gould re-analyzed their data and found that these so-called racial differences were non-existent; brain sizes overlapped between different races. Franz Boas himself demonstrated that genetic traits like skull size can go through sharp changes from one generation to the next: they are not necessarily retained across generations.[14] What these results mean is that *in sum there is absolutely no scientific basis to the idea that intelligence is genetically transmitted.*

The Chicken Roosts

Despite the rejection of intelligence testing on a philosophical level by most educators, standardized testing continues to grow. On another note, much of educational assessment has drawn from the assumptions and theories of the early testing pioneers.

Edward Thorndike was a graduate student of William James at Harvard who lived in an apartment in James's basement. He studied and measured the behavior of chickens in mazes and in their feeding habits. Thorndike watched for the positive and negative responses of chickens in his experiments. He postulated that human subjects would respond similarly. Thorndike envisioned a mind that was machine-like in which there were thousands, millions, of connections. Despite all of these connections, the basic modus operandi was that humans would respond to positive and negative reinforcement no different than the chickens in the maze.

Out of his experiments Thorndike developed achievement tests that questioned the value of school subjects. He administered the same intelligence test to 8564 high school students between 1922 and 1923; he then divided that group according to subjects studied. Once he corrected for factors such as initial ability and special training, the value of these courses of study in raising intelligence could be computed. We would then know how much better Latin or Math was in raising general intelligence than, say for example, science. His conclusion: we find notable differences gained in the ability to think as measured by these tests, but they do not seem to be due to what one studies.[15] In other words, those who have the most to begin with, gain the most during the year. Again, the chicken's theory wins.

Testing and Social Meliorism

A final interesting irony in the history of assessment is that several testing pioneers believed that standardized testing would build a "meritocracy."[16] From the earliest days of Thomas Jefferson who believed that public funding was needed to "rake a few geniuses from the rubbish" to Henry Chauncey, founder of the Educational Testing Service[17] who was motivated to level the playing field for admission to the Ivy League colleges…testing to some was seen as the great equalizer.

An extensive documentation of the development of the testing industry has been completed in *The Big Test,* by Nicholas Lehmann. Lehmann notes with dry wit, that these very same icons of our present day…the Chauncey's of the world, stewarding the drive for worldwide standards…have created the testing oligopoly we are all saddled with. In public education, with a mish mash of charts, numbers, frequencies, and tabulations, in this author's view, little remains of Dewey's love of, and realization of excellent teaching and authentic learning.

Classroom Assessment

How then do we address the problems and trouble that NCLB legislation produces for an already aggravated condition, the testing mess? This book is a start as it begins to sort through constituencies that benefit from and are diminished by the goals and efforts of NCLB.

I see NCLB as an alert to consider anew the aims and purposes of schooling in the United States. In many respects NCLB is based upon taken-for-granted assumptions about educators and students alike. It provides a normalizing view of assessment as if there exists a consensus that all agree upon. To address the problems and troubles of NCLB requires that we not only take stock of the history of assessment generally but also conduct in depth study of how those who are charged with the responsibility for assessing our children learn about classroom assessment in teacher preparation coursework. Arguably there has been little if any research done that tracks the way in which teachers learn to grade their students.

Assessment in the classroom consists of information gathering by teachers that concerns the learning of pupils, the efficacy of teaching, and the integration of lesson planning into curriculum. Once assessment is defined in this manner, however, it becomes necessary to identify the pedagogical methods and consequences of such information gathering. In short, the very effort to define classroom assessment suggests that it is important to link the means that are used with the ends that are served when teachers assess their pupils.

Recent research on classroom assessment contends that there are formal and informal procedures for pupil assessment that combine elements of instructional feedback and social control. In the pursuit of instructional feedback, teachers gather information about the capabilities, understanding, and learning of their pupils[18] additionally, in the interest of classroom control, teachers regulate access to knowledge and thereby control the behavior of their pupils.[19]

Most research has treated these issues in the context of regular classroom instruction by experienced teachers.[20] There is, however, very little published research on the goals and consequences of classroom assessment in the context of pre-service teacher education—the very place at which assessment first enters into the professional life of the teacher. This fact suggests that practitioners and teacher educators would benefit from information about the approaches and implications of instruction in classroom assessment during pre-service teacher education.

At least three potential benefits should derive from the careful analysis of instruction in assessment during the time that student teachers are in the practicum classroom:

- Classroom teachers may choose to reevaluate their assessment practices when they reconsider the ways that they originally developed their approaches to assessment.
- Cooperating teachers—those who provide initial pre-service mentoring—may recognize more clearly the long-term consequences of preferences and models that they present to student teachers who work in their classrooms during the period of their practicum.
- Instructors in teacher education programs may wish to present alternative methods to student teachers in the hope that a broad repertoire of methods might permit individual teachers to match their teaching with the learning styles, resources, and environments of their pupils.[21]

Research Questions and Methods

Core Questions

This chapter grows from questions that were framed by theoretical concerns about the origins of intellectual and social control in teaching--questions that have been brought into focus by practical experience gained over the 26-year period during which I have served either as a public school teacher or a teacher education instructor. Three pressing questions are suggested by this chapter.

First, what dimensions of assessment are most salient in the practice of student teachers? At issue here is the possibility that there are distinctive aspects of assessment that are stressed more than others in the practicum classroom. The effort to answer this question is partly taxonomic and partly descriptive. On the one hand, it is useful to differentiate between the aspects of assessment that can reasonably be expected in the practice of teaching. On the other hand, it is also useful to learn whether observations of student teachers suggest patterns in the particular dimensions of assessment that they emphasize.

Second, how does assessment actually enter into the practice of student teachers? In this regard, it is useful to trace some of the ways that the influence of a methods course instructor compares with the influence of a cooperating teacher in the practicum classroom. If it is possible to distinguish some of the precepts that are taught in a methods course from those that are advanced by a cooperating teacher, it may be possible to delineate the interplay of methods instruction and practice on the part of student teachers.

Third, what are the likely consequences of stressing certain dimensions of assessment during the practicum experience? In short, once the interplay of assessment instruction and practice has been clarified, it is appropriate to consider the broader issues that arise when student teachers learn to assess pupils in the practicum classroom.

So given the relatively new assessment paradigm, the wall to wall federal sanctions on schools from the No Child Left Behind Act should they not assess correctly where then does knowledge reside?

Places of Knowledge

The term "No Child Left Behind" rests uncomfortably on a point of ideological division, although the lines of demarcation and debate are less clear. Places of knowledge…where do they come from and how do the words "Highly Qualified Teachers," "Supplemental Educational Services," "Choice" and "No Child Left Behind" mirror or mask truth(s)? The proposition of No Child Left Behind is one that continues to bedevil academics and educators alike. The purpose of the authors in writing this book is to attempt to understand the various meanings and intentions that motivate the web of beliefs that comprise this proposition. To begin, as one of the authors, I try to argue that there are at least three types of meaning in the web of beliefs of No Child Left Behind:

- Linguistic
- Semantic
- Hermeneutic

Understanding meaning as such requires that we unravel other overlapping beliefs concerning the language games that make understanding possible.

Let's take for starters linguistics. The linguistic meaning of No Child Left Behind is a matter of stringing together dictionary definitions of each of the four words. There is an emotional response to the idea of a left behind child. No one, certainly not teachers, wants to leave a child behind, thus the appeal of the slogan No Child Left Behind is apparent and real.

The semantic meaning concerns the relationship of the proposition to reality, where some scholars analyze semantic meaning as a nomenclature. For example, there may be a one-to-one correspondence between the concepts and the reality that they represent: children stuck and unnoticed in classrooms, as a social reality could be an example. Does No Child Left Behind rescue such children? Is that what it means? So the meaning of the concept is a thing, a quality, a relation, such that the presence of this thing in reality makes it correct to predicate the concept of reality, left behind children.

Questions of hermeneutics are different from questions of semantics in as much as they concern the meanings of utterances, not the truth conditions of abstractions. With hermeneutic meanings we might inquire: what do authors mean when they propose No Child Left Behind as a solution? Or if they say No Child Left Behind is unfunded? Or if they say No C hild Left Behind is a "slogan?" All are apparently reasonable and intelligible things to say about these phenomena.

Conclusion

A quote from William T. Harris former president of the National Education Commission, the president of the National Association of School Superintendents, and the United States commissioner of education sums up our testing dilemma today.

> Our schools are, in a sense, factories in which the raw material (children) are to be shaped and fashioned in order to meet the various demands of life. The specifications for manufacturing come from the demands of the twentieth century civilization, and it is the business of the school to build its pupils according to the specifications laid down.[22]

I wonder about how the teacher views life based on this outlook and how the teacher sees and reacts to the shift in the paradigm we are now engaged in as we move into national (international, too) standards for education. I have come to the following conclusions, that

> 1) it is not easy to recognize emerging forms of power because the social technologies, including educational testing, are enacted before the exercise of power is recognized as such;
> 2) it is useful to understand what is taken-for-granted as unchangeable in any system of thought;
> 3) several questions remain regarding NCLB which concern me and should be taken up in future discussions:
>
> A. What is the organizing schema? (called the system of reasoning or principle of coherence)
> B. How is the subject constituted? (especially test-takers in relation to the object of the testing and to the bigger social motivation)
> C. What is the role of the critical intellectual?

In the schema of NCLB the general principle is privileged over individuals; general principles, in other words are held to be more valid and more important. NCLB is a technology that ignores deliberative dimensions of curricular analysis. It affords curriculum a low status and is evidence of the fact that one cannot understand the history of education in the United States during the 20th Century unless one realizes that Edward Thorndike, observing chickens won, and John Dewey curriculum planning lost.

Questions for further review

- What do contemporary writers such as Charles Murray contribute to the literature on tests and measurement?
- Why is it that we seemingly have not moved beyond a 19th century style of thinking about tests and assessments?
- What are the alternative histories of assessment and testing?
- What are ways we can assess learning which reflect the times in which we live?
- Are classrooms and students you know predictable and measurable?
- What are the differences between information and knowledge?
- Do distinctions between purposes for assessment provide a model for 21st century theory of assessment?
- Are current assessments under the No Child Left Behind Act designed to reinforce the existing socioeconomic order or does the prevailing socioeconomic order use the assessments to justify their standing and way of life?

Notes

1. John E. Chubb and Terry M. Moe, *Politics, Markets, and America's Schools* (Washington, D.C.: Brookings Institution, 1990).

2. Murray, Charles, *Human Accomplishment: The Pursuit of Excellence in the Arts and Sciences, 800 B.C. to 1950* (1st ed. New York: Harper Collins, 2003).

3. Murray, 2003.

4. Alan Ryan Harmondsworth, *Utilitarianism and other Essays.* J.S. Mill and Jeremy Bentham; edited Middlesex, England (New York: Penguin Books, 1987).

5. Sir Francis Galton, *Hereditary Genius: An Inquiry into its Laws and Consequences* (London; New York: Macmillan, 1982).

6. Galton, 1892.

7. J.M. Cattell & L. Farrand, "Physical and mental measurements of the students of Columbia University." *The Psychological Review, volume 3*, no. 6(1896): 618-648.

8. Edward L. Thorndike [and others], *The Measurement of Intelligence* (New York, Bureau of Publications, Teacher's College, Columbia University, 1927).

9. Kliebard, Herbert, *The struggle for the American curriculum, 1893-1958.* 2nd ed. New York: Routledge, 1995; and Raymond E. Callahan. *Education and t he cult of efficiency; a study of the social forces that have shaped the administration of the public schools* (Chicago; University of Chicago Press 1962).

10. David B. Tyack, *The one best system: a history of American urban education* (Cambridge: Harvard University Press, 1974).

11. See Kliebard, 1995.

12. Cattell, 1896.

13. J. Feagin and C.B. Feagin, *Race and Ethnic Relations* (Englewood Cliffs, NJ: Prentice-Hall, 1993).

14. S. Gregory, and R. Sanjek, *Race* (New Brunswick: Rutgers University Press, 1994).

15. Thorndike, 1927.

16. Nicholas Lehman, *The Big Test: The Secret History of the American Meritocracy.* 1st rev. pbk. ed. (New York: Farrar, Straus and Giroux, 2000). 406 p.

17. Henry Chauncey and John E. Dobbin, *Testing: its Place in Education Today.* [1st ed.] (New York: Harper & Row, 1963).

18. Linda M. McNeil, *Contradictions of Control: School Structure and School Knowledge* (London; New York: Routledge, 1986).

19. Michael W. Apple, *Ideology and curriculum* (London; Boston: Routledge, 1979).

20. John Franklin Bobbitt, *Curriculum-making in Los Angeles* (Chicago, Ill., University of Chicago. Supplementary education monographs, pub. In conjunction with the School review and the Elementary school journal, no. 20, June, 1922).

21. James Kusch, *Teaching in a surveillance mode: a case study of how methods course syllabi and practicum classrooms construct assessment a sclassroom control.* (Dissertation, UW-Madison Theses, Memorial Library, 1995.) x, 290 leaves.

22. William T. Harris, "The National Educational Association: its organization and functions." *(A paper read before the Department of Superintendence of the National Educational Association, at Philadelphia, February 24th, 1891).*

References

Apple, Michael W. *Ideology and Curriculum.* London; Boston: Routledge, 1979.

Bobbitt, John Franklin. *Curriculum-making in Los Angeles.* Chicago, Ill., University of Chicago. Supplementary education monographs, pub. in conjunction with the School review and the Elementary school journal, no. 20, June, 1922.

Burns, Edward. *The Development, Use, and Abuse of Educational Tests.* Charles C. Thomas: Springfield, Illinois, 1979.

Black, Hillel. *They Shall Not Pass.* William Morrow and Company: New York, 1963.

Callahan, Raymond E. *Education and the Cult of Efficiency; A Study of the Social Forces that have Shaped the Administration of the Public Schools.* Chicago; University of Chicago Press, 1962.

Cattell, J. M., & L. Farrand. "Physical and Mental Measurements of the Students of Columbia University." *The Psychological Review,* volume 3, no. 6 (1896), pp. 618-648.

Charters, W.W. *Curriculum Construction.* New York. The Macmillan Company, 1923.

Chauncey, Henry, and John E. Dobbin. *Testing: its Place in Education Today.* 1st ed. New York: Harper & Row, 1963.

Chubb, John E., and Terry M. Moe. *Politics, Markets, and America's Schools.* Washington, D.C.: Brookings Institution, 1990.

Feagin, J., and C.B. Feagin. *Race and Ethnic Relations.* Fourth edition Englewood Cliffs, New Jersey: Prentice-Hall, 1993.

Galton, Francis, Sir. *Hereditary Genius: An Inquiry into its Laws and Consequences.* 2d ed. London; New York: Macmillan, 1892.

Gregory, S. and R. Sanjek. *Race.* New Brunswick: Rutgers University Press, 1994.

Harmondsworth, Alan Ryan. *Utilitarianism and other Essays.* J.S. Mill and Jeremy Bentham; edited Middlesex, England; New York: Penguin Books, 1987.

Harris, William T. "The National Educational Association: its Organization and Functions." (A paper read before the Department of Superintendence of the National Educational Association, at Philadelphia, February 24th, 1891).

Herrnstein, Richard J., and C. Murray. *The Bell Curve: Intelligence and ClassStructure in American Life.* 1st Free Press pbk. ed. New York: Simon & Schuster, 1996.

Hoffmann, Banesh. *The Tyranny of Testing.* Foreword by Jacques Barzun. New York: Crowell-Collier Press, 1962.

Kirst, Michael W. *Who Controls our Schools? American Values in Conflict* Stanford: Stanford Alumni Association, 1984.

Kliebard, Herbert M. *The Struggle for the American Curriculum, 1893-1958.* New York: Routledge, 1986.

Kusch, James. *Teaching in a Surveillance Mode: A Case Study of How Methods Course Syllabi and Practicum Classrooms Construct Assessment as Classroom Control.* (Dissertation, UW-Madison Theses, Memorial Library, 1995).

Lehman, Nicholas. *The Big Test: The Secret History of the American Meritocracy.* 1st rev. pbk. ed. New York: Farrar, Straus and Giroux, 2000.

McNeil, Linda M. *Contradictions of Control: School Structure and School Knowledge* London; New York: Routledge & K. Paul, 1986.

Murray, Charles. *Human Accomplishment: The Pursuit of Excellence in the Arts and Sciences, 800 B.C. to 1950.* 1st ed. New York: Harper Collins, 2003.

Thorndike, Edward L., and others. *The Measurement of Intelligence.* New York: Bureau of Publications, Teacher's College, Columbia University, 1927.

Tyack, David B. *The One Best System: A History of American Urban Education.* Cambridge: Harvard University Press, 1974.

Tyler, Ralph W. *Basic Principles of Curriculum and Instruction.* Chicago: University of Chicago Press, 1949.

Chapter 3
ETS and the American Dream

Alice Bicudo

In the previous chapter, the evolution of a way of thinking that equates knowledge with scoring well on standardized tests was described. Also noted was how a standardized testing "paradigm" mushroomed, or stated another way, how the values and behaviors associated with the measurement of intelligence developed, leading to what is quite literally a "testing mess."

Indeed, in this two part chapter, *The Testing Mess,* it's worth noting just how bad things have become; how sorry and deplorable the state of standardized testing is, not only in the United States, but in the world today for both aspiring teachers and struggling students. The following chapter(s) relies not on statistics, but narratives from those on the frontline(s), namely, teachers-in-training and teachers in the classroom. Given the testimony, it seems appropriate to say testing in the age of No Child Left Behind leaves everyone behind, not only students, but often their teachers.

To be a teacher

Peering in from outside of, or beyond the classroom walls, much of the discussion about education fails to acknowledge what is generally accepted with little resistance: that is, that in essence, progressive educators like John Dewey lost and modernists like Edward R. Thorndike have won.[1]

Whether it is the formation of curriculum, the development of subject matter, the fostering of creative teaching strategies, and/or the evaluation of systems of inquiry and learning, would-be 'progressive' educators talk a good game. However, a progressive theory which represented a thoughtful, reflective and meaningful interpretation of the wonderful possibilities for teaching and learning,[2] was discarded, years ago, for a modernist theory which, absurdly, likens and reduces human learning merely to an analysis of behavior. This analysis of behavior differs little from the theory developed by Thorndike while observing chickens pecking away to get food.[3]

Whenever educators examine curriculum, instruction, and assessment, it often appears as if we have fallen asleep, forgetting everything we have learned...our progressive education lessons. It seems in this the 21st century that progressive educators often discard what they know to be better, and instead settle on the old behaviorist model of the 1900's.

As far as evaluation goes, the Bell Curve,[4] Social Darwinism, and/or Behaviorism is outstanding in most classrooms; in every corner of the world for that matter; *standardized testing reigns supreme*. A veritable testing industry has emerged to produce the high stakes standardized tests used, it seems, by everyone, effectively trumping every other form of teacher or faculty produced assessment.

Testing, Inc.

At the forefront of that testing industry stands the Educational Testing Service (ETS) which determines not only assessment by producing multitudes of testing tools, but also, and disturbingly so, the professional lives of most teachers-in-training.

Several powerful testimonies to the dreadful results of standardized testing are readily available but they might as well not be well known. It's almost as if a deeply held secret has been revealed over and over again, and yet, no one has the courage to stand up and say that the emperor wears no clothes. We know that standardized tests and standardized assessments are hopelessly flawed, and yet we keep using them. A few excellent early exposes on the 'testing mess' include: Hoffmann, Banesh (1962) *The Tyranny of Testing;* Black, Hillel. (1963) *They Shall Not Pass;* and Burns, Edward. (1979) *The Development, Use, and Abuse of Educational Tests.*

Yet perhaps the most comprehensive, damaging, and perhaps least well known is a dissertation, *The Reign of ETS,* by Allan Nairn, (1980).[5] Allan Nairn (not the journalist) a graduate student at the time makes the case that ETS is the ultimate gatekeeper for measuring one's worth as a teacher...and that is where our story begins.

The testing industry where companies like ETS, Harcourt Brace Assessment Inc., McGraw Hill, and others reside, dominates assessment to such an extent that most impartial observers would get over their impartiality and become very concerned about this testing oligopoly's role as gatekeeper and teacher-maker.

For many years, standardized tests have been used to determine who gets what in society, which groups prosper and which groups stay in place. Tests classify and categorize different immigrant groups, exercising social control while using state arithmetic. Yet tests fail to measure human potential, and many times the test evaluators simply get the arithmetic wrong.

At a time when there is continuing talk of a wall going up on the U.S./Mexican border to keep out 'illegal immigrants,' the authors ask in response, who needs a wall when we continue to rely on companies like ETS to protect the supposed national interest. . . through standardized testing?

The Resistance

Many educators have fought against high stakes testing and the testing industry. Initially, several concerned educators, including a substitute teacher working to procure certification in Spanish teaching, gathered at the National Coalition of Education Activists (NCEA)[6] conference in July of 2002. Alice, a second year teacher-in-training, attended NCEA to voice her own specific concern that numerous teachers like herself across Ohio were struggling with the Praxis II test, a gatekeeper for foreign language teaching in the public schools. Upon hearing her story and those of the other teachers at the conference, it seemed apparent that the problems caused by standardized testing were widespread, not only among K-12 students, but also amongst graduate students/teachers-in-training in teacher education programs.

During the conference, a presentation by two organizations concerned with the misuse of standardized tests drew much attention. The first organization was *FAIRTEST*[7] and the second was *SUBSTANCE*[8] a Chicago newspaper. The stories were amazing and upon hearing the problems in this session, it was clear that the crises in public education had been ellipse by a pandemic of high stakes tests.

Monty Neil, the *FAIRTEST* director, painted a widespread epidemic of mistakes made with the distribution, implementation, and the scoring of standardized tests. George N. Schmidt, editor of the *SUBSTANCE* newspaper then spoke of how the testing industry guarded with great secrecy the test question items. The testing industry, in one example, went to litigation against the *SUBSTANCE* newspaper and Schmidt, when the newspaper released examples of the test questions which the paper argued were culturally biased and racist. While poor test scores are to be dreaded, one question that arose almost immediately concerned the inflation of test scores; wouldn't administrators be inclined to "make their scores higher, especially if they were being evaluated on having done so? If not discrepancies in the logging of statistics at a local school, other deeper problems emerge, such as, what do statistics used in standardized tests do and what do they really mean?

If anything, the conference provided a workshop on the problems, now the issue was how to fight back?

The Coalition to Stop ETS

Alice chose to build a coalition. Several teachers-in-training joined Alice and formed *the Coalition to Stop Educational Testing Service*. They started to gather stories from other teachers around the state of Ohio, who had equally compelling narratives of studying for the test, taking the test, waiting for the test scores to come back, failing the test, and having to scramble to re-apply for the next testing date. . . all the while spending hundreds, if not thousands of dollars. Alice and her fellow student Ana tried to get their Youngstown teacher education program, the Ohio Department of Education (ODE), and even their elected

Ohio representatives to address their grievance with this standardized testing process and with the ETS Company itself. Yet theirs was no easy journey, nor was there an easy road to take. They were consistently told that 'our hands are tied' and their efforts to seek relief were to no avail.

At an initial meeting on August 31st, 2002, a small gathering of concerned educators spoke to the problems they encountered with ETS. The authors were made aware of the 'trials and travails' of students like their selves in teacher education programs. As a faculty at a popular teacher education university, I became interested in hearing the stories of individuals who had been greatly challenged by the faulty ETS testing practices, especially those associated with one particular test, the Praxis II.

The purpose was clear. The authors had been invited by the small informal network, to help construct a discussion and to see what if anything could be done via action research and through the support of my university. The following key questions/concerns came out of that meeting:

- Where is the test being graded and does the location of grading effect the correct answers?
- Who is grading the test? Other teachers or hired graders and/or free lancers from other lines of work?
- How were the poor testing taking conditions, e.g., excessive noise, malfunctioning recorders, etc., rectified?
- What was being done about little or no turnaround time to retake the next offering of the exam?
- What was being done about non-existent to poor information and feedback to takers of the exam?
- What is the content covered and how can universities properly prepare their students to take the exam?
- What are the pass rates, cut scores, and who determines the content of the exams?

Alice, Ana and another student from Canton, Julie, had developed lengthy narratives of their trials and travails with the test; they spearheaded an effort to contact others with similar experiences. In sum, they wondered why the Praxis II test was used as the gatekeeper to entering the profession when each were acknowledged by their contemporary professors as being well-qualified to teach in the classroom.

An effort was made to enlist other interested individuals to attend the "Taking the Test" workshop. The workshop was the ideal place to launch a campaign to stop ETS by collecting the stories of those who have struggled with the test. The Coalition's intention was to organize in order to bring pressure on, not only the industry, but also the proxies of the industry who continue to use this test at the expense of future teachers as well as students. The findings were distributed to colleagues across Ohio. During a workshop at Kent State, in the intervening weeks between August 31st and the September 14th the Coalition started to gel.

The group continued meeting via the Internet and through telephone conferences. In order to investigate this particular "testing mess" situation, a steady correspondence between Alice, Ana, Julie and others was maintained.

Meanwhile my own research assistant dug up preliminary information on the ETS...

> Educational testing service is the world's largest private educational testing and measurement organization and a leader in educational research. ETS develops and administers more than 12 million tests worldwide.
>
> ETS's primary purpose has been the development of tests and other assessment tools to provide information (including test scores and interpretative data) to test takers, educational institutions, and others who require this information.
>
> ETS currently employs approximately 2,300 regular employees, including more than 1,100 professional staff members with training and expertise in education, psychology, statistics, and psychometrics.
> Additional areas of staff expertise include computer sciences, sociology, and humanities, Nearly 600 staff members have advanced degrees, including 240 who have doctorates.
>
> LOCATONS: Hato Rey, Puerto Rico- Oakland, CA- Tampa, Fl- Washington, D.C. Netherlands.
> REVENUES: ETS currently generates annual revenues of more than $600 million, and looks forward to aggressive growth in the future.[9]

and their *for profit* subsidiaries:

> "The Chauncey Group International truly has a global reach. For example, our Test of English for International Communication® (TOEIC®), which assesses English language proficiency for non-native English speakers, was delivered last year to more than two million people in 60 countries around the world. ETS created The Chauncey Group in 1996 to specialize in professional assessments, licensure and certification."[10]

We were struck by how much the testing industry resembled a petro-chemical company, pursuing ever greater market share. The Coalition's learning curve grew, and we became further convinced that this industry was the wrong one to be administering tests and evaluating teacher proficiency, let alone determining who does or does not teach in the state of Ohio or anywhere else. But who were we to say?

The Big Test

It was at this point that the teachers in training went through a workshop to prepare for the exam. The following information provides a glimpse of what is an otherwise secretive and guarded process. Each section is a breakdown and brief description of the Praxis II test given in 2002.

> Each question is worth 13 1/3%...ETS supposedly is looking for a "teacher-speaker," not a "native speaker."
>
> Do ALL suggestions that are in the questions/statements given to you on the exam . . . don't leave anything out. Use ALL the time they give you.
>
> SPEAKING: 6 questions
> 1. Picture description
> -when describing, go top to bottom or foreground to background
> -stay cohesive and flowing/correct mistakes when you make them
> -assessors looking for patterned errors
> -people cannot see what you are explaining-need to be able to imagine what you describe
> -use present, past, future, conditional-practice key verbs
> -use the whole 2 minutes
> -invent a "story" for the picture
> -can't mix dialectical speech
>
> 2. Role play
> -use transitions, connectors, key words, phrases (good advice for all questions in the PLS)
> -requesting something in order to solve a problem
> -take brief notes/speak freely and resourcefully
>
> 3. Instructions/Picture Narration
> -use circumlocution (always) if you don't know the word
> -more than likely, will use formal commands (unless instructed otherwise in the prompt: "tell your friend . . .")
>
> 4. Describing abstract concept/opinion
> -one minute
> -outline your speech
> -think very carefully and provide examples
> -transition, connectors, etc.
>
> 5. Brief talk
> -no slang or informality
> -speak slowly and carefully with a minimum of hesitation
> -outline with key info
>
> 6. Oral Paraphrase
> -hear passage 2 times
> -demonstrate facility with language and accuracy of the vocabulary
>
> WRITTEN: 3 Questions
> 1. Picture Narration
> -choose appropriate verb tense as signaled by intro sentence
> -can change tenses when appropriate

-connectors, keep it flowing, "circumlocate"

2. Formal letter
   -know your salutations and closings
   -formal tone and vocabulary
   -follow verbs given in prompts

3. Writing questions
   -have to cover the subject matter
   -grammar/spelling/sentence construction all count HEAVILY because the test only requires a small bit of info from you (not like the letter or narration)

SCORING

-Comprehensibility
*How much of an effort does scorer have to make to understand you? They are not sympathetic listeners.

-Accuracy of content
*Does the response accurately and appropriately address each task presented?

-Grammatical control
*Do you demonstrate control over high frequency structures?

-Fluency
*Can you use complex sentences, connectors, transition words, subordinate constructions, etc.?

Following the workshop, where the test overview and preparation was done, inquiries were made by the group into the process and the procedure of ETS. Findings were summarized as follows:

- ETS is not only involved in testing, but they are involved in licensure or certification stipulations set forth by each individual state (we will continue to follow this lead).
- Not only students who aspire to teach K -12, but even professors of higher education in Spanish have had significant problems with the PLS. One Spanish professor, we learned from the professor who "taught" the workshop, had failed the exam seven times!
- During the Kent State workshop to help students pass the test, we learned that the professor who was administering the workshop had never taken the test. Of course it was asked how that would ultimately benefit the students. This professor when asked how she obtained the information that she was sharing with the participants replied that this information came from students and professors who had taken the tests and not from ETS.
- This professor also explained that different dialects were worth more; student with a native dialect might be graded on a different scale and actually expected to perform higher due to the fluidity of their conversational skills. Of course this led to another question: why should it matter for the purpose of teaching high school students the basics of Spanish whether or

> not we are native speakers or near native speakers of Spanish? It seems as if a scale which changes depending on where someone is from lends itself to the possibility of discriminatory practices. This calls into question whether the test is administered in a fair and equitable manner.

To add a sense of urgency to our political and research struggle ahead, at about this time a New York Times article came out decrying some of the implications of this major so-called "non-profit" company, a company that, it was reported, had proceeds over 600 million dollars annually.[11] Tamar Lewin[12] cited ETS salaries that exceeded all but two college presidents in the entire U.S. Add to this million dollar bonuses, it certainly called into question the alleged non-profit status of ETS and more importantly appeared to question their social mission. Alice shared her concerns:

> "One could reasonably draw the conclusion that if testing were a necessary enterprise that the company that holds a large share of the market that bills itself as a non-profit company with a social mission would not conduct itself in such an outrageous manner. It has also engaged in an obvious conflict of interest by setting up a for-profit subsidiary designed to prepare students for the exams of its non-profit entity. "

The authors asked the teachers (including their selves) to use personal narratives to get at the heart of the matter; to compile and present evidence to the Ohio Department of Education in order to eliminate the test as the certification requirement.

The narratives of Alice, Anna and Celeste follow. These narratives a re compelling for their authenticity and supported by other stories that started to break in the news.

> *Narrative 1 Alice:* My own study stems from my own personal experience, and began January 19, 2001 when I traveled to Muskingum College to take the Praxis II exams in Spanish...the Productive Language Skills and Spanish Content Knowledge exams. Both exams were created and scored by the Educational Testing Service (ETS). These tests are two of a battery of three that one must pass in order to meet the requirements set forth by the state of Ohio in order to become a certified teacher in Spanish. I am happy to have passed the Spanish Content Knowledge exam the first time I took it with 12 points above the minimum standard. However, I have not yet met the standards set up by the State Department of education in Ohio with regards to the Spanish Productive Language Skills test. This event has led me to a struggle to find out why I have not passed this particular exam. I should also mention that Ohio requires a prospective teacher to take a test called the "Principles of Learning and Teaching." I took it on November of 2001, and was able to pass it with 7 points more than the required minimum standard.
>
> Along the way I have met with other students who are in the same type of predicament as I am, and who wonder why they can't teach in the state they grew up in. In addition, another student and I have met with state officials and communicated with the Ohio Department of Education in hopes of getting some

support for our future. They have offered us no hope. After graduation, I began working independently as an interpreter/translator for local businesses in my area. Some of the interpreting assignments that I have done include being a simultaneous interpreter for the Ohio Industrial Commission during court sessions. The Test the Spanish Productive Language Skills test consists of nine questions, six oral and three written essays. The oral part consists of a description of events that occur within a different set of scenarios (grocery store, post office etc). Generally, one is given about one minute to think about the answer and 30 seconds to one minute to answer each question orally into a tape recorder. ETS provides students with a guidebook to help prepare for the test. However, this guidebook contains serious grammatical mistakes that the test makers made.

Once I realized that I hadn't passed the test the first time, I immediately asked for a recount and paid the additional $50.00 that was required. Along with my check, I sent a brief note describing some of the technical problems that had occurred during the test session; in particular, some of the tape recorders didn't record. I was appalled to find that according to the stipulations set forth by ETS, it would take another six weeks to receive my recount decision. Approximately, a week after sending my check and note to ETS, I received a phone call from one of the people in charge of solving problems related to the exams at ETS who simply asked me to further explain my note and concerns, and told me that my test would be sent to California to be re-scored. Surprisingly, one day after the phone call, I received a letter stating that my exam had been rescored, and that my score of 165 was to remain the same. Once I realized that my test could not have been sent to California and scored in less than 24 hours, I began to question ETS's testing practices.

In terms of service, ETS has found clever ways to make additional money. The actual test costs $80.00, and one has to wait approximately six weeks to receive the results. If one wants to hear the results in less than six weeks time, it is possible to hear one's own scores over the phone, by paying an additional $20.00 after four weeks of having taken the test. The phone score disclosure has become a must, since, in case you didn't pass the exam, you would have to pay an additional $25.00 late fee to register for the next available exam date. Another interesting aspect, deals with the other possible charges related to the test. For instance, if you cannot register online, which happens frequently, and it happens to be too late to register via mail, than you must pay an additional $45.00 dollars to register over the phone, in addition to the $25.00 late fee. In my last attempt, I was late in registering and had to pay $167.00 total just to take the test. Since that time, I have taken the test three more times and have received the scores of 161, 166, and 161 respectively, which is not enough to obtain the Certification requirement of 167 set by the State of Ohio.

In October of 2001, Mr. Gary Reel, my campus supervisor during student teaching, went beyond his call of duty to help me. He was able to get in touch with several people including Tom O'Brien who works directly with the Praxis exams, and with Jennifer Wassum who works for ETS and for the State Department of Education in Ohio. As a result, I received what appeared to be a detailed letter regarding my performance during my first three exams. As it turns out, the letter did not address any mistakes that I may have made, and went on to basically repeat the same information given by ETS in the preparation book for this exam. During this month, my cooperating teacher, Mrs. Little, a Spanish teacher at Niles McKinley High School in Niles Ohio, wrote to ETS asking for some explanations regarding my situation. A month later, she received a letter that stated that ETS doesn't discuss their policies or exams with anyone other than the person who takes their exams.

In November of 2001, I spoke with Dr. Morelli, the Supervisor for all student teachers at Y.S.U, and she told me to contact Pamela Greene at the State Department of Education. I wrote Ms. Greene an email which explained, somewhat briefly, what my situation was about. Four weeks later, after sending a second email, I received her answer, which stated that the office she worked for (educator preparation), didn't have any interaction with ETS. She went on to state that a meeting was going to be held in January of 2002 by the Ohio Teacher Education Certification Advisory Committee (OTECAC) to review not only the exam in question, but also all exams in other subjects. In January of 2002, I along with my colleague, another student who has excelled in Spanish, went to speak with our then assistant Dean, Dr. Phillip Ginnetti, in the College of Education at Youngstown State University. During the meeting, we were told that he had "his hands tied" by whom, we didn't find out, and that this problem with the Praxis exams (all subjects) was one that all Deans had brought to the attention of the Ohio Department of Education. Nothing more was said on the subject. In February of 2002, we went to speak with Ohio State Senator Tim Ryan who politely promised to help solve the problem. He said that it was inconceivable to him that such good students were having this type of trouble. He also said that he believed he could fix the problem, and that we could relax about it. In March of 2002, after several calls made to the Senator, we were able to speak to Seth, an office assistant. He informed us that Senator Ryan had written a letter to ETS to inquire about our situation, and that ETS had told him that the exams were confidential and any details associated with the exams were not open for discussion. In addition, Seth told us that Senator Ryan had spoken with Senator Gardner who sits on the education committee, and Gardner explained that no one could touch ETS, because Ohio had entered a contractual agreement with them. On April 26, 2002 we met with Tony Atwater, University Provost at Y.S.U who told us to email him a brief description of what our problem was. Upon the receipt of this email he would then make sure that our Dean at the college of Education would "untie his hands." We are still waiting for an answer, and we still don't know who has their hands tied up.

In May 2002, I spoke with Dean Edwards, the former head of the college of education, and with Dr. Angle, a special education professor at Y.S.U. Our casual conversation took place at an art festival in our area. Dr. Angle, amazed to hear about my situation, offered to call John Nicholson, the head of the certification department at the state department of education. Two weeks later I met with Dr. Angle and she told me that Mr. Nicholson had informed her that the problems associated with the Praxis Foreign Language Exams were being investigated, and that it would take at least a year, if not more, to get any type of resolution. Mr. Nicholson went on to say that, since, I had come so close to the required score, that the next time I took the exam I would pass it. In June 2002, I took the exam for the 4th time, and contrary to Mr. Nicholson's predictions I did not pass the test.

During the months listed above, I researched all available information about ETS in our library, and came across an advertisement for essay scoring titled "US-NJ-Work from Anywhere-Online Essay Scoring" which asked for anyone who was a teacher, active or retired, student teachers, graduate students and anyone non-credentialed holding a bachelor degree to apply. The assignment involved the scoring of essays in the CAHSEE (California High School Exit Examination). I wondered whether the same qualifications are required for those who score the Praxis II exams. At this time, I have yet to be able to find out who is responsible for scoring the exams. This has been a continuous struggle with very little hope in sight. Along with many other students, an organization is forming to fight this issue. Many other students who have aspired to become teachers have given up this exam anxiety and are now actively seeking other types of employment. Many have gone to states that have different requirements or states that don't subscribe to ETS's testing practices. Massachusetts and New York are some of the examples. Meanwhile, my investigation is continuing to grow.

Narrative 2 Ana: Before I moved into my new house, I had an entire folder filled with everything I owned in regards to the Praxis. This folder included old test results, notes on my meetings with certain people (mentioned below), and correspondence with ETS. I have been searching for this folder for the past 2 days, and I cannot find it anywhere. Also, my mom paid for the tests with a credit card, and no longer has the statements. Therefore, my chronology is going to be quite sketchy. I only remember 4 dates for certain (I plan to ask ETS for the other date). TEST DATES: November 2001, June 2002, September 2002, January 2003 COST: The Spanish Productive Language Skills test costs $70, registration fee $35, to register by phone $25. I was reimbursed $95 because of poor testing conditions once, and I paid $50 once to receive an early score report. Therefore, this one exam has cost me approximately $605. This total does not include other tests that I have taken with ETS (PLT & Spanish Content Knowledge), nor the phone bills that I have paid for calling them to register since their 1-800 number never works. Also, although I have not received my score on the Jan. 03 test, I am expected to register for the March 03 test in case I have failed. I must do so by Thursday, otherwise I will pay a $35 late fee. However, if I did pass, and I register on time, they will not reimburse my $35 registration fee. Either way I am out another $35. The people whom I've spoken with follow. PEOPLE: Senator Tim Ryan (now Congressman for Ohio), Dr. Phillip Ginnetti (now Dean of Education at YSU), Provost Tony Atwater (YSU). I do not remember the dates that I met with these people since my folder is currently lost. However, Alice has copies of this information since we met with these people together. I hope this works for you. Once again, sorry for all of the missing information. I plan to keep searching for my folder so that I may be able to give you more specific information.

Narrative 3 Celeste: I am a student in one of Dr. DeBlois Introduction to Education classes. She has recommended that I contact you regarding the fact that no one has passed the Spanish Praxis exam in the state of OH. I wish to be a Spanish teacher, yet I am told that I cannot even become a student teacher without passing this impassable exam. I am a second generation American. My four grandparents immigrated to the US in the 20's. My father is a retired Spanish and German teacher and he along with my mother reared their children in a home where both Spanish and English were required to be spoken. I have

> a love and a great enthusiasm for the Spanish language. I understand that you are spearheading a cause to rectify this assault on new teachers of the Spanish tongue. I would like to join forces with you on this and I have asked my father if he is interested. He is a very respected educator in Canton, OH. What can be done about this? Am I just to throw in the towel regarding my dream of becoming a Spanish school teacher? Please reply to me as your help and advice would be greatly appreciated. My name is Celeste Perez-Hazlett. I am very disheartened at this juncture in my journey into education. Thanks!

The narratives point to the same nagging questions and concerns listed earlier in the chapter and highlight an uncaring, unfeeling testing bureaucracy, as well as an impotent government, that adds no value to the students these teachers would serve, if indeed they were ever to get in front of students.

Further research yielded results which explain that ETS continues to push an expansionist agenda.

Delores Santos,[13] a Columbian faculty member, was introduced to our group by Dr. Kusch. Santos described in detail how ETS had taken its business world-wide with little transparency into its products. Other than world domination in the testing industry observers, like our group were then and still are left wondering: what social mission is this multi-national testing conglomerate serving, besides increasing its bottom line?

The Ohio Department of Education Blinks

After these narratives, the collaborative research, and the constant testing mess stories that came the author's way, a question arose over how to get this message out to a wider audience. Although we were just learning the scope of ETS, we were still committed to bringing these collective stories to light. Alice and Anna pursued going public with their own story(s) to a television news program. The authors solicited getting conference presentations together, finding supportive colleagues in the academic profession, and writing this book you are now reading.

As time passed one participant asked a key question of their schools. What was ETS' role in teacher education? Specifically:

- Who selected these examinations? The state? The Universities? ETS?
- What are the passing rates broken down by University?
- How many education professors have taken the examination? How many passed?
- How valid and reliable are the exams and where is that data?

One professor wrote back to state that the universities had nothing to do with the examinations and believed that the Ohio Department of Education mandated them. He stated the passing rate for his university and believed those professors who did take the exam did well on them. No response was made to validity or reliability of the exams.

But then the unexpected happened to challenge the rationale of continuing to use a test that was so clearly alienating teachers. In April of 2003, the test and the company were examined. Subsequently, and without warning, the Ohio Department of Education dropped the Praxis as a test requirement to teach in that state.

The Aftermath

Only through a number of disjointed efforts could the Coalition to Stop ETS start to piece together what had actually happened. Anecdotal stories began to make their way into the press. Mark Fisher of the Dayton Journal wrote of one such story, an individual who quit his job to pursue his dream of becoming a teacher . . . only to be stymied several times by the testing bureaucracy wall that had been set up.[14] Unfortunately for this individual, ETS had made some mistakes and he had actually passed the exam. It's unsure whether this delay in getting the right score cost him a teaching job but it certainly didn't help. Of course this individual has no recourse to regain the time or effort the errors cost him. It's just another cost of administering these kinds of examinations and that cost is almost always borne by the individual and not the testing bureaucracy.

The testing mess is clear. While it is important to note that the contractual relationship between ETS (Praxis II) and the Ohio Department of Education was severed; many more undocumented cases of errors have been uncovered. In but one of many dreadful examples, 4,100 teachers-in-training . . . wrongly scored and failed...are only the tip of the iceberg. The New York Times reported that ETS settled a class action lawsuit with wrongly failed test takers awarded $11.1 million dollars for being denied the opportunity to even interview for teacher job.[15] Yet apparently nothing much has changed as high stakes standardized testing continues...to miss the mark.

K-12 students are impacted even more seriously by failed tests; "real" failures' or often as our findings show 'imagined' ones.[16] No one is immune from being caught in this trap of high stakes testing and the consequences are significant and in some cases final.

Notes

1. Kliebard, Herbert M. *The Struggle for the American Curriculum, 1893-1958.* (New York: Routledge, 1986); Cremin, Lawrence Arthur. *The Transformation of the School; Progressivism in American Education, 1876-1957.* (New York, Knopf, 1961).

2. Dewey, John. *Democracy and Education; An Introduction to the Philosophy of Education, by John Dewey.* (New York, Macmillan, 1916).

3. Thorndike, Edward L.; and others. *The Measurement of Intelligence.* (New York, Bureau of Publications, Teacher's College, Columbia University, 1927).

4. Herrnstein, Richard J.; and Murray, Charles. *The Bell Curve: Intelligence and Class Structure in American Life.* 1st Free Press pbk. ed. (New York: Simon & Schuster, 1996).

5. Nairn, Allan and associates. *The Reign of ETS: The Corporation that Makes Up Minds*. Publisher: (Center for the Study of Responsive Law. 1980).

6. National Coalition of Educational Activists

7. *FAIRTEST,* The National Center for Fair & Open Testing, Cambridge, Massachusetts. <http://www.fairtest.org/index.htm>

8. *SUBSTANCE*, Chicago, Illinois. <http://www.substancenews.com/>

9. Educational Testing Service. <http://www.ets.org/>

10. Chauncey International, <http://www.prometric.com/Chauncey/default.htm>

11. Lewin, Tamar. "Corporate Culture and Big Pay Come to Nonprofit Testing Service," (*The New York Times*. 2002).

12. Lewin, 2002.

13. Santos, Doris. *'Expand, Expand, Expand'...Testing as Big Business*. 2004.

14. Fisher, Mark. (Dayton Journal News Story. 2004).

15. Arenson, Karen. "Case Involving Errors in Teacher Test Is Settled," (*New York Times,* March 15, 2006).

References

Arenson, Karen. "Case Involving Errors in Teacher Test Is Settled," *New York Times,* March 15, 2006.

Chauncey International. http://www.prometric.com/Chauncey/default.htm

Cremin, Lawrence Arthur. *The Transformation of the School; Progressivism in American Education, 1876-1957*. New York, Knopf., 1961.

Dewey, John. *Democracy and Education; an Introduction to the Philosophy of Education, by John Dewey*. New York, Macmillan, 1916.

Educational Testing Service. http://www.ets.org/ *FAIRTEST.* The National Center for Fair & Open Testing, Cambridge, Massachusetts.

Fisher, Mark. Dayton Journal News Story, 2004.

Herrnstein, Richard J. and Charles Murray. *The Bell Curve: Intelligence and Class Structure in American Life.* 1st Free Press New York: Simon & Schuster, 1996.

Hoffmann, Banesh. *The Tyranny of Testing.* Foreword by Jacques Barzun. New York: Crowell-Collier Press, 1962.

Kliebard, Herbert M. *The Struggle for the American Curriculum, 1893-1958.* New York: Routledge, 1986.

Lewin, Tamar. *Corporate Culture and Big Pay Come to Nonprofit Testing Service.* New York Times, 2002.

Nairn, Allan. *The Reign of ETS: The Corporation that Makes Up Minds*. Publisher: Center for the Study of Responsive Law, 1980.

Santos, Doris. *'Expand, Expand, Expand'...Testing as Big Business*. 2004.

SUBSTANCE. Chicago, Illinois. http://www.substancenews.com/

Thorndike, Edward L. [and others] *The Measurement of Intelligence.* New York: Bureau of Publications, Teacher's College, Columbia University, 1927.

Chapter 4
Fuzzy Math: Missing Tests, Missing Students and Missing the Mark

Todd Alan Price

Introduction

The authors contend that the No Child Left Behind Act has set up a series of negative incentives that seek to reward the exclusion of the most vulnerable student population in order to boost the school's overall scores. Unfortunately, these schools believe they have little choice but to manipulate the testing population so they do not lose already precarious funding. In addition, the use of standardized tests as a sole measure of student performance is misleading and has directly led to problems of underreporting as well as an increase in test preparation work which most observers believe detracts from what should be happening in classrooms.

The Nelsonville-York school district in Appalachia is a case in point. This small school district has severe challenges…equal to those of Chicago and much larger urban neighbors in the North. Sixty percent of the Nelsonville-York student body is on free and reduced lunch yet NCLB punishes districts such as theirs for having too many special needs students.

One member of the assessment team summarized the problem eloquently: "even with accommodations they (special education students) cannot meet the same standard. . .[the] very lowest functioning can take the alternative testing, but only 1%! Every student over that 1% fail it, even if they pass!"[1] By the same fuzzy math, a student could be counted several times given race, need, and socio-economic status: "our special education children are not passing the test…they also fall into the category of poverty. One child [can be] impacting us in three categories"[2]

The bottom line is that the law pits the test *against* not only the student, but teacher, the administrator and the school district. The stakes are high. In Ohio, 1 in 6 students are in poverty, coming to school already disadvantaged. As one of the Nelsonville-York teachers argues, by using alternative testing for a number of students larger than the allowable 1%, "we do what's best for the [special needs] children and take the hit on the failure marks of the test."[3]

Chicago's Missing Tests and Missing Students

While the testing mess was playing out in Ohio, a series of articles emerged from Chicago which questioned the testing required by the NCLB law, wondering how the badly needed supplementary services were to be provided. Toward that end, the authors spoke on the phone with one of the reporters from the Chicago Tribune who reported on these testing problems surfacing with the 'new' mandates of NCLB being deployed.

These Tribune reporters, Darnell Little, Jodi Cohen, Diane Rado and Stephanie Banchero, had culled reams of public education test data information from the Chicago Public School System (CPS). That information demonstrated how thousands of scores are tossed out every year because the tests are invalidated, don't conform to the standardized testing rules set by the state, a state like others driven by the quest to make adequate yearly progress (AYP) under NCLB. Little pointed out how the testing validity was becoming a real challenge because so many tests were thrown out, scores were thus exaggerated, inflated, and generally speaking a testing crisis existed.[4] Coupled with the work that the authors had done previously, hearing, compiling and documenting the stories of teachers-in-training, we were nonetheless surprised.

Rampant problems in administering these high-stakes exams were continuing to be identified by Cohen, Rado, and Little. In a late 2004 Chicago Tribune article stated:

> 72,000 reading and math tests were tossed out because the state disregards the results for students who enrolled too late in the academic year, or those who skipped major portions of the test. The exemption for those enrolled after Sept. 30-meant to avoid penalizing a school for children educated elsewhere-disproportionately applies to minority and low-income students, those most likely to move during a school year. The exemption for incomplete and invalid tests-intended to weed out administrative errors and tampering-ends up applying most often to disabled children. Minority students were systematically excluded by sub-groups because they failed to reach the 40 student threshold that Illinois requires for sub-group reporting.

In addition, students' tests were also disqualified for late enrollment, incompleteness or other problems which eliminated 10.7 percent of black students' tests and 9.3 percent of special education students' tests, while disregarding just

3.7 percent of white students' tests. It would appear that NCLB "reforms" and the problems associated with caused suspect behaviors on behalf of schools.

My colleague, Elizabeth Peterson compiled and examined statistics to expound upon another relevant problem: that of dropouts, or students often pushed out by the bureaucracy being fed by the testing frenzy. She noted:

> One in five 16-24 year olds drop out of high school. As high as the overall number might be, the numbers are even higher for the individual minority groups, minority groups that are considered "subgroups" under "No Child Left Behind." According to the 2000 census, 1 in 3 Hispanic youths and 1 in 5 African Americans youths drop out of school before achieving a high school diploma. Schools that have higher minority populations, pressed to bring each child up to testing standards, actually benefit from students dropping out, especially if the students who drop out are the same ones that might not reach the standard. There is no way to tell for certain if students are dropping out on their own accord or if they are actually being pushed out of schools in an attempt to boost scores. Most reports provide the numbers, but not the reasons students drop out; clearly the reform measures have not been successful in reducing drop out numbers and maybe responsible for increasing them. Since 1996, dropout rates in Chicago have remained consistent for Whites and Hispanics but have soared from African Americans. From 2001-2002 the number of Hispanic male drop outs increased 15% while the increase among African American males soared to over 27%.[5]

Clearly, better reporting of scores does nothing to address what is happening to those who continue to be left behind, who drop out or are pushed out. Indeed, given the negative incentives, one surefire way for a school district to improve is to let students leave who would otherwise bring the average down, and to report less special needs students in general.

Harcourt Assessment, Inc.: Missing the Mark

Another example from Illinois involves the administration by Harcourt Assessment of Texas of the Illinois State Achievement Test (ISAT) to the state's students. In 2005 the teacher's manuals and test books were delivered late, were incomplete and some of the tests were illegible.[6] In late 2006, the Chicago Tribune reported that a "series of computer glitches, printing mistakes, labeling blunders and human error by school and testing officials have conspired to seriously delay the state's 2006 school report cards"[7] Cheryl Corley from NPR also notes these severe problems with schools in southern Illinois failing to receive the test materials, and rightly suggests that given the increase in testing under the NCLB (from grades 3rd to 8th), test companies are scrambling to meet the increased demand.[8] Lost tests have also been shown to negatively impact schools in that tests that cannot be found and can cause a school that has been passing to fail for lack of enough passing tests in a specific grade level.[9]

Conclusion?

The smoking gun of the testing mess is in the testing industry, the politicians, the principals, teachers, or the schools of education. Ultimately, though, the problems of the testing mess reside in the logic of a centuries old assessment system which by its nature is doomed to be imperfect and flawed. As Kusch described in the previous chapter the Testing Movement, these 'mistakes' are built into a system which is intended to try to stop and measure a moving target, that is, with high stakes standardized tests we are trying to capture the essence of what is knowledge, much like using a huge, porous net to capture a butterfly…yet the testing mess and madness goes on with a vengeance, partially due to the enactment of new NCLB requirements to 'prove' the adequacy of 'highly qualified teachers' and to develop teacher and student proficiency through test scores only. The community of educational administrators and educators themselves appear to be mute on this continuous battle of a testing hierarchy.

As Arenson concludes "As long as standardized testing companies continue to make errors in what are regarded as high-stakes tests, you can expect to continue to see cases filed."[10] Denied the ability to register work or get promoted, the aggrieved individuals try to get a second chance but no one appears ready to stop the insanity.

Questions

- Who selects the examinations? The state? The Universities? ETS?
- What are the passing rates broken down by school? By University?
- How many have taken the examination? How many pass?
- How valid and reliable are the exams and where is the data?

Notes

1. Price, Todd Alan, Geoff Berne, and Karen Rybold Chin, *No Child Left Behind report. Public education in the crosshairs.* On the Earth Productions, educational series. [Oconomowoc, WI]: Northwest Ordinance Productions, Inc. 2005.

2. Price, 2005.

3. Price, 2005.

4. Cohen, Jodi S., Diane Rado and Darnell Little, "Test Scores don't Count the Neediest: Many Minorities, Late Enrollees Left Out of State Tallies" *Chicago Tribune,* December 16, 2004.

5. Peterson, Elizabeth and Todd Alan Price. "A Response to "Test Scores don't Count the Neediest: Many Minorities, Late Enrollees Left Out of State Tallies" *Chicago Tribune,* December 16, 2004.

6. Clements, Kate. "Testing Problems prompt questions from House Republicans." *The News-Gazette.* March 25, 2006.

7. Banchero, Stephanie. "School Test Data Tardier Than Ever," *Chicago Tribune,*November 23, 2006.

8. Corley, Cheryl. "A Struggle to Handle 'No Child' Testing Madness," *National Public Radio,* 2006, http://www.npr.org/templates/story/story.php?storyId=5361238

9. Rado, Diane, "Missing tests stir fight: State vowing to label school as failing due to exams it can't find" *Chicago Tribune,* Published November 5, 2006.

10. Arenson, Karen. "Case Involving Errors in Teacher Test Is Settled," *New York Times,* March 15, 2006.

References

Arenson, Karen. "Case Involving Errors in Teacher Test Is Settled," *New York Times,* March 15, 2006.

Banchero, Stephanie. "School Test Data Tardier Than Ever," *Chicago Tribune,* November 23, 2006.

Black, Hillel. *They Shall Not Pass.* William Morrow and Company. New York: 1963.

Burns, Edward. *The Development, Use, and Abuse of Educational Tests.* Charles C. Thomas, Publisher Springfield, Ill. 1979.

Clements, Kate. "Testing Problems prompt questions from House Republicans." *The News-Gazette.* 2006.

Cohen, Jodi S., Diane Rado and Darnell Little, "Test Scores don't Count the Neediest: Many Minorities, Late Enrollees Left Out of State Tallies" *Chicago Tribune,* December 16, 2004.

Corley, Cheryl. "A Struggle to Handle 'No Child' Testing Madness." *National Public Radio.* 2006. http://www.npr.org/templates/story/story.php?storyId=5361238

Peterson, Elizabeth and Todd Alan Price. "A Response to "Test Scores don't Count the Neediest: Many Minorities, Late Enrollees Left Out of State Tallies." (Unpublished letter to editor of the *Chicago Tribune,* December 16, 2004).

Price, Todd Alan, Geoff Berne, and Karen Rybold Chin. *No Child Left Behind report. Public education in the Crosshairs.* On the Earth Productions, educational series. Oconomowoc, WI: Northwest Ordinance Productions, Inc. 2005.

Rado, Diane, "Missing tests stir fight: State vowing to label school as failing due to exams it can't find" *Chicago Tribune,* Published November 5, 2006.

Chapter 5 Drop Out or Pushed Out? Who's Counted Out in High Stakes Testing

Elizabeth Peterson

An increasing number of youth are leaving high school before completion. At the same time the labor market for teens and young adults is deteriorating. Gone are days when those without a high school diploma could look forward to getting a job good enough to support themselves and a family. These "disconnected" young people lack the credentials needed to become fully employed, self-sufficient young men and women in today's increasingly knowledge and skills based society. In 2005 the National Governors Association on State High School Graduation Data released a report that indicates about a third of all high school students do not graduate from high school. The report goes on to say, "outcomes for minority students are significantly worse. About three-fourths of white students graduate from high school, but only about half of African American and Hispanic students do."[1]

The purpose of this chapter is to explore the impact, if any, that federal policy, namely No Child Left Behind, has had in reversing the drop out crises in Chicago area schools; and what, if anything, is being done in the schools to help them comply with the legislation while at the same time reaching out to provide opportunities to young people who have already fallen through the cracks. Great care was taken to look beyond the statistics; numbers only tell us part of the story. In this chapter we talk to administrators and teachers, and hear firsthand how current policy has affected how they have responded to the needs of the young people that they serve.

Who is a dropout?

In Chicago, as elsewhere in the nation, dropout rates particularly among people of color have increased. For African Americans and Hispanics, the lack of a high school diploma drastically limits their opportunity to achieve economic self-sufficiency and has in many ways contributed to the economic decline in predominantly African American and Latino communities. Once out on the streets these high school dropouts drain public resources. High school dropouts are 15% less likely to be employed and earn 30% less than those who have either completed high school or have a GED. Because they cannot obtain gainful employment they are more likely to end up on public assistance or to join the ranks of the prison population. The only way we can even begin to tackle this problem is to first determine how many young people have dropped out, who they are and why they dropped out. Then we must find ways to reengage young people in the schools so those who are at risk of dropping out find opportunities for success in schools, while at the same time reaching out to those who have dropped out but want to come back.

It is hard to determine how many dropouts there are because there is no one system for calculating dropout rates. According to the National Governors Task Force, "The quality of state data on graduation and dropout rates is such that many states cannot account for the status of their students as they progress through high school or beyond. Further, states calculate and report this information in such different ways that comparisons are nearly impossible."[2]

In a report prepared for the National Center for Education Statistics (NCES) dropouts were defined as individuals who were enrolled in school at some time during the previous school year, but were not enrolled at the beginning of the current school year. Dropouts are individuals who have not graduated from high school or completed a state or district approved education program. The following exclusionary conditions would also prohibit an individual from being classified as a dropout: transfer to another public school district, private school, or state or district approved program, temporarily absent due to suspension, involvement in an approved school program, or death.[3]

Even within these established parameters there is some inconsistency in how it is determined that a student has dropped out. In 2005 the National Governor's Task Force recommended that states immediately adopt a standard four-year adjusted cohort graduation rate to begin to address this problem. Using a complex formula, the Graduation Rate equals the number of on-time graduates in the year divided by the number of first time entering ninth graders in the year minus four plus the number of students transferred in minus the number of students transferred out. In this definition graduates are those earning high school diplomas. Students earning modified diplomas, for example a special education diploma would only count if the modified diploma is the standard that the state and school system have set for the student in an individualized education plan (IEP). Students who earn a GED do not count as graduates.[4]

Despite the inconsistency in determining who exactly makes up the dropout population, the fact remains that a high percentage of students drop out of high school each year.[5] Over the last decade between 334,700 and 544,000 tenth through twelfth grade students left school *each year* without successfully completing a high school program. The cumulative effect is that millions of young people are out of high school, but lack a high school credential. In that same year (2004-2005) it was shown that fewer than one out of three teenage high school dropouts were working. Research conducted by The Center for Labor

Market Studies at Northeastern University in Boston indicates that there is a connection between education and a young person's ability to find employment. The employment rate for people between 16 and 24 years of age has declined in recent years to just over 50%. The only group whose employment rate rose in the last four years are those with a bachelor's degree or higher.[6]

So, who is the high school dropout? Although high school dropouts can be found in all racial and socioeconomic groups, high school dropouts are more likely to be either African American or Hispanic youths from economically disadvantaged families. For whatever reason these young people have found the challenges they face in our nation's schools to be more than they can handle. The problem is that life outside of school is equally if not more challenging and these young people are not equipped to handle the challenges most adults face.

When asked, dropouts give many reasons for leaving school. Most often the reasons given are a combination of personal problems and school related problems that culminate in the decision to leave school. According to Schwartz, "dropouts often have a long string of failures that stretch back to the earliest grades."[7] Schwartz goes on to say that often students who eventually drop out of school begin to experience difficulty in elementary school and have been held back a grade or two. They are more likely to have been placed in low ability groups or remedial classes or even being diagnosed as being a special needs student.

Youngsters who drop out tend to be habitually tardy, and they cut classes or skip school entirely. And when they do show up, they're often suspended or expelled for breaking school rules.[8]

All Students	46,588,307	68.0%
By Gender:		
Male Students		64.1%
Female Students		72.0%
By Race/Ethnicity:		
American Indian		51.1%
Asian		76.8%
Hispanic		53.2%
Black		50.2%
White		74.9%

Figure 1. National Graduation Rate Profile[9]

Aside from the problems that these young people face in schools, they often have serious personal problems as well. Pregnancy is often cited as the reason given by teen-aged girls who drop out. Boys and girls who have familial responsibilities find it difficult to keep up in school while holding down a job. The lives of kids who drop out are often unstable and fraught with problems. The conditions that they find in their homes and their community do not provide a foundation for academic success. When I asked one young man why he dropped out of high school he said that he was scared every day that he was in school. The gangs in his community were very strong and he feared that if he remained in school, he would be forced to join a gang. Gang problems, addiction to drugs and/or alcohol, trouble at home with parents, trouble with the law, have all been cited as reasons behind the decision to leave school.

It is one thing if a child gives up on school; it is another thing when the school or school system gives up on the child. Now with the pressure schools and school systems face since accountability is tied to high stakes testing a new worry comes. Kids may find that the decision to leave school is not theirs to make; schools that feel there is too much at stake to keep low performing children in school will find a way to push them out. A 2002 study of New York City public schools found that an alarming number of high schools students were not voluntarily dropping out of school but were being 'discharged' by the school system.[10] According to this study, " . . . these discharges may be forced 'push outs' by school administrators of students, who have a legal right to remain in public schools. Both students and parents complained that there was no process for the discharge, they were never informed of their rights to stay in school until the age of 21, and were not offered support services to improve academic performance or attendance."[11] The study found that in 2001 discharge rates exceeded drop out rates with 55,015 discharges reported compared to 14,549 reported drop outs for the same group of schools.

No Child Left Behind and High Stakes Accountability

Since the passage of NCLB in 2002, high school graduation rates have been more closely scrutinized than they were in the past. The many opponents of the law have been quick to focus on the many flaws in the legislation, but even the harshest critics admit that certain aspects of the law look good on paper. Such is the case with graduation rates. Under NCLB for the first time high schools and school systems are held accountable for graduating students. Although much attention has been paid to the high stakes testing that is required under the law, testing is only one measure of success for an individual high school. The other is the number of children who actually complete their education over a four-year period.

A study released in April 2004 indicates that high stakes exit exams have not significantly affected high school graduation rates.[12] In this study, a regression model was used to evaluate whether adopting a high school exit exam affects graduation rate. Graduation rates were calculated for 18 states from the class of 1991 to the class of 2001. The researchers could not conclude from their analysis "that high school exit exams had an effect on graduation rates, positive or negative and if any effect exists, it could not be distinguished from ordinary fluctuations in graduation rates."[13]

Other researchers have a different view and feel that however well intentioned the law is on paper, the reality is that The No Child Left Behind graduation rate accountability provisions have fallen short of their potential in trying to improve school success for those who are most disadvantaged. Orfield, Losen and Wald (2004) found that, "the racial disparities in graduation rates that exist at the federal, state, district, and school levels are pervasive and deep."[14] While graduation rates for whites remain stable at around 75%, graduation rates for historically disadvantaged racial and ethnic groups remains just over 50%.[15] According to Swanson (2005), "The situation appears to be even more dire for students in our nation's largest high poverty urban districts, where as few as one-third of *all* students graduate.[16] In these places, completion rates among certain disadvantaged groups of students are often lower still."[17] Chicago as the nation's third largest city is one such urban center.

Dropout or Push out? A Chicago Case Study

The Chicago public schools initiated high stakes testing long before NCLB mandated testing nationwide. Beginning in the 1995-96 school year, all eighth graders were required to meet minimum scores on the Iowa Test of Basic Skills before they were promoted to high school.[18] Eighth graders who failed the test either repeated the grade or if they were too old to remain in elementary school they were moved into "transition centers" that were designed to ready these students for high school. By ending social promotion the hope was that over time high school drop out rates would decrease because only those students who were high achievers would enter high school. There was some concern that by implementing such a policy drop out rates would in fact increase. Students who are held back could be more likely to drop out.[19] Allensworth's study found that initially following the implementation of the eighth grade promotion gate policy retention rates increased. More eighth graders were held back from entering high school in the first year after the policy was enacted. But by year four, retention rates tapered off and began to decline. This occurred, according to this report, "because student achievement increased substantially and because more students were promoted despite not meeting the cutoff or were moved into special education and excluded from test reporting."[20]

According to "official" reports, the dropout rate in Chicago has decreased over the past few years (Figure Two: CPS 5-year Cohort Dropout Rates). However, experts who have suggested that the numbers are deceptive for the reasons cited earlier have refuted these reports. Even with fewer low performing kids moving into the ninth grades the numbers have not significantly improved. Allensworth (2004) found that retention at the eight grade promotion gate actually increased the likelihood of dropping out by age 17 by about 8 percentage points and increased the likelihood of dropping out by age 19 by 13 percentage points.[21]

A report released by The Urban Institute (2005) indicates that Chicago's Public high schools, with a racial/ethnic makeup that is 90% minority, graduates less than half of the 435,261 students enrolled.[22] While most White and Asian students can expect to graduate on time (65.3% and 80.6% respectively); for African American students only 42% graduate on time and only 50% of Hispanic students can expect to complete their studies within four years (see Figure Three: Chicago's High School Graduation Rate Profile; also, see Figure Four: CPS Freshmen On Track Rates).

CPS Citywide Report		2004 Dropout Rate	2005 Dropout Rate	2006 Dropout Rate	2007 Dropout Rate
CITYWIDE	OVERALL	46.9%	44.7%	44%	41.6%
GENDER	Male	55.1%	52.3%	51.6%	49.8%
	Female	37.8%	36.6%	35.8%	33.2%
RACE/ ETHNICITY	Asian	24.3%	24.6%	24.6%	21.3%
	Black	51%	49%	48.1%	45.4%
	Hispanic	43.8%	41.4%	41.1%	39.6%
	Native Am	46.4%	42.9%	41.3%	47.1%
	White	41.6%	39.8%	37.8%	35.8%

Figure Two: CPS 5-year Cohort Dropout Rates[23]

All Students:	**435,261**	**48.8%**
By Race/Ethnicity:		
American Indian		**–**
Asian		**80.6%**
Hispanic		**50.8%**
Black		**42.1%**
White		**65.3%**

Figure Three: Chicago's High School Graduation Rate Profile[24]

	2004			2005		
	On track Rate	# On Track	Total # of Students	On track Rate	# On Track	Total # of Students
OVERALL	57%	15,874	27,983	59%	16,359	27,709
MALE	49%	6,807	13,820	51%	7,070	13,751
FEMALE	64%	9,067	14,163	67%	9,289	13,958
	2006			2007		
OVERALL	58%	16,394	2,2698	57%	15,728	27,550
MALE	50%	6,997	13,956	50%	6,840	13,635
FEMALE	66%	9,397	14,313	64%	8,888	13,915

Figure Four: CPS Freshmen On Track Rates[25]

Although research does suggest that the higher poverty levels among African Americans and Hispanics (coupled with the fact that often the schools that these students attend are in segregated and low income communities increases the likelihood of high school drop out) some community leaders fault the local school districts and feel that their communities and the people within their communities have been written off (see Figure Five: Figure Five: CPS/IL Comparative Statistics). In September 2003 the Chicago Tribune reported that dropout successes depend on who counts citing that school officials had been accused of publicizing rates that made them look better. According to the school system 70% of its students were graduating. Later it was found through a longitudinal approach that compared 9th grade enrollments and 12th grade enrollments that over half of the 9th graders had been lost in the four-year period. The Tribune also reported that a number of dropouts reported that they did not leave voluntarily, but were pushed out of the public high schools.

Sixteen year-olds who are not expected to graduate by their 21st birthday can be 'disenrolled' according to state law and that is what happened to these students when they fell behind. In both cases cited, the students returned to class only to be told that they were no longer on the roster. Both students enrolled in alternative high schools to complete their degrees. The response to the possibility that the schools are giving up on low performing kids was swift. Community leaders quickly organized and meetings were held to draw attention to what one community leader said was akin to "flushing them [the kids] down the toilet." The failure of the schools to serve one predominantly Hispanic neighborhood has prompted one community leader to say that the schools are guilty of educational "genocide" and that at least three generations have been lost.[26] Oddly enough including graduation rates as one of the accountability measures mandated by NCLB was supposed to prevent school systems from pushing out lower performing students. Under NCLB academic assessments are the primary indicator of performance, but to provide balance the high school graduation rates were to provide a secondary academic indicator.[27] "This provision is intended to serve as a safeguard to discourage schools from raising their achievement levels by pushing out lower-performing students. A 'gaming' strategy of that kind would result in higher achievement scores on average and would help schools to avoid sanctions. But these apparent gains would be attained at the expense of producing more dropouts and fewer graduates, thereby undermining the intent of the law."[28]

So if pushing children out of the system defies NCLB mandates, how are schools able to get away with it? Simply put there is a loophole that does not include students who leave school, but reenroll in one of the 27 special and alternative schools in the state report card. This in turn makes the dropout rate look much better than it actually is. Orfield, Losen, and Wald refer to push out as "the dark side" of high stakes testing.[29] Narratives taken from students from New York to Alabama speak of this new trend. As was the case in Chicago, students were shocked to learn that they were not going to be allowed to return to school or that they were denied graduation due to poor test performance. Once out of school there are few options for these young people. There are not

Reporting Groups	2004	Dropout Rate	# of Dropouts	n
CPS		46.9%	14,272	30,431
IL		5.3%	32,445	610,317
CPS % of IL Dropouts			44%	
CPS % of IL n				5%

Figure Five: CPS/IL Comparative Statistics[30]

enough alternative high school slots for all of the students who need them. Some go on to get a GED, but many never finish their formal schooling. In an article that appeared in the *New York Times,* it was reported that nearly 100,000 people between the ages of 16 and 24 are out of school and out of work in Chicago. "Many of them are leading the kinds of haunted lives that recall the Great Depression. They hustle, doing what they can-much of it illegal-to get along."[31]

In Their Own Words: CPS Teachers and Administrators Talk about the Dropout Crisis and NCLB

Since the No Child Left Behind legislation was passed in 2002 Chicago area school districts have worked to comply with the law and know firsthand how challenging it is to improve the school experience for all children. No one knows more about how policy changes affect schools than the men and women who must enforce the policy. As one administrator said, "all educators are in this to do the right thing." All school district personnel: administrators, teachers, counselors and support staff believe that all children have a right to a high quality education. More often than not, however, the voices of those who work daily in support of schools and children are lost in the numbers and statistics that are released to the public. Thirteen Chicago area school district and school administrators were invited to talk about their impressions of NCLB and the dropout crisis as it exists in Chicago area schools. Several topics emerged that seemed to cut across all of the districts and programs that these individuals represented.

Topic 1: NCLB is a Very Complex Law

In almost every case each administrator began the discussion by saying that on the surface no one would dare argue with the intent behind the No Child Left Behind Act. The intent of the law they feel is sound and they believe in the goals of NCLB according to the Chicago Public Schools are 1) strong accountability; 2) raising the bar continuously to move forward and 3) utilizing a strong combination of administration, school, and parent involvement in improving the school experience for students. The problems come in enforcing legislation that is very complex and the bureaucracy that often comes with federal mandates.

According to one administrator, "the quibbles are around the over bureaucratization of the rules and regulations that tie our hands and impede our ability to do things that make sense." One administrator from a suburban school district said that she felt that administrators have been effectively silenced when it comes to discussions of NCLB because any dissension was seen as whining and "it's hard to whine about kids and their education."

> There needs to be a larger awareness. More of the dialogue must come from a number of voices as the research gap is ridiculous. It is hurting us as we try to tackle these issues. We need to underscore that people at the school level have a great deal of knowledge about this law and its limitations. We need to be unified.

Most of those interviewed agreed that although there are a few exceptions, most of the schools are making progress. They recognize that they have a long way to go, especially in a city as diverse as Chicago, but they see NCLB as an "all or nothing" law that doesn't recognize small gains.

> The good intentions of supporting all students and all subgroups has the potential to be lost if the program is not fine-tuned. Strict NCLB compliance doesn't distinguish between dismal schools that are real problems and those that are good schools that show improvement. Both types of schools are labeled the same. There is clearly a problem with an accountability system that uses a baseball bat.

Although graduation rates are taken into account there is a sense that test scores are still what matter most. The two suburban high schools selected for this case study have a diverse student population and boast high graduation rates for all students. Yet one of these schools was cited because test scores were low for some subgroups. According to an administrator, "The current NCLB accountability system might be a more effective system if it was weighted instead of all or nothing against one criterion. If we look at graduation rates we are performing at a far higher rate than state rates with an 80-90% African American and Hispanic graduation rate."

NCLB has forced schools to focus on the test and in the minds of some this has had a negative impact on the high school experience. NCLB has forced schools to place more emphasis on testing math and reading. "It is particularly problematic that social studies, writing, and not to mention the fine arts are being eliminated. These are subjects that need to be a part of a comprehensive high school experience." Although no one would admit that the focus has shifted "to teaching to the test," the concern is that teachers are spending more time learning how to integrate what is needed into their curriculum. "It is interesting how teachers have come along in this process. This is not how they were trained. They were trained to help educate kids, but they were not trained in data driven test construction. However, awareness has increased that we don't just need programs created, but this [data driven testing] must be moved into the classroom.

Topic 2: Dropouts, Academic Achievement and NCLB

Three of the administrators interviewed work directly with students who have dropped out. They all agreed that changes in state policy and NCLB have had a significant impact on their work.

> Over the last seven years emphasis has shifted from attendance to academic achievement. The Illinois state policy is that after 20 school day absences, a student can be dropped due to attendance. There was a change in legislation last year (2003) that moved the compulsory age to 17. This is being implemented now. This legislation states that kids can't drop themselves out of school. Thus new applications will decrease and schools will be required to re-enroll those students that want to come back. However, there are no programs or incentives or funding provided with this law. It is simply a mandate and the schools are left to figure it out. This is difficult.

The lack of funding and/or incentives is seen as a major problem with most recent legislation that focuses on schools. Lack of proper funding and support encourages schools to look for any loopholes that they can in order to showcase themselves in a more positive light. Anecdotally these administrators agree that just before testing time they experience an increase in the number of students that call to get on the waiting list for slots at the alternative high schools. "Although it is not measured, I believe this happening is related to schools purging rosters to shed those [students] that are not doing well."

Many of those who try to enter the alternative school system are very far behind. "What do you do with a student that has been out for a year and is severely behind in credits? They may have a whole year or more to make up. What do you do with the kid?" Some of these kids are only reading at the 4th or 5th grade level. High stakes testing does little to address the issues that many kids that drop out face.

> Generally kids that drop out don't go back for their GED or go back to school. And often if they are black males, they aren't working either. We have pockets with historical poverty. But in 30 years there has been no structural change. The penalty is on the wrong place. There should be no penalty on the schools. This is a systemic issue. Everyone needs to ante up and be able to say, "We can't graduate students without basic skills." In the alternative high schools we only have a 2-3 year window to focus on those essentials and this is not enough.

Some of the schools have tried to deal with the gap in academic achievement by providing additional academic support to those students that need it. As stated earlier the Chicago Public Schools closed the promotion gate from 8th grade to high school in 1998 and according to one administrator this alone has led to some decrease in the high school dropout rate because if students are going to drop out, they are more likely to do so before they enter high school. Most leaders acknowledge that drop out is a problem that starts long before a child reaches high school. Since ending social promotion in 1998 schools have struggled to find ways to assist those students who are struggling before they get to the point of dropping out. Under NCLB Supplemental Educational Services (SES) are to be offered by all schools that do not meet AYP (annual yearly progress). In Chicago SES is designed to "provide good quality options for after school programs." The primary function of the program is to prevent school drop out. It provides something very different from what after school programs traditionally offered which were enrichment and recreational types of activities. Reading and math tutoring are the specific focus of SES.

Time will tell whether SES will have any real impact on achievement levels (and hence graduation rates). "With so few hours per week, it will be difficult to correlate the hour of reading so many weeks with raising scores to the national norms. Here we are dealing with target that is of the lowest income, [students] that are nationally among the lowest performers and with the most obstacles to learning."

One of the suburban school districts has a different approach to working with kids who come with academic challenges. The administrators in this school district pride themselves with, "holding on to kids, especially those who aren't contributing to high test scores." The district created a special "safe" school within the high school for those students that are not academically ready. This school focuses primarily on freshmen and sophomores who aren't really making it, but have the potential to do so. The program is designed to work with these students and get them caught up before they give up and drop out of school. School leaders feel this has been a powerful intervention that has enabled them to hold on to kids who might have otherwise dropped out.

In addition to the special school, other programs have been put into place in this district to assist students who need extra academic support. Incoming eight graders who need extra help go to summer school before they even enter high school. For the weakest readers, a Humanities enriched program is offered and tutors are available for any student who wants one through a tutoring center. Students can access tutors during their free periods or after school. Up until now this district has not implemented SES but next year 20% of their budget will go to SES to meet state requirements.

Topic 3: Changes in the Dropout Population in Chicago

When slots are available, students who drop can opt to reenroll in one of the 27 alternative high schools in the city. The administrators of these schools attest that the demand for slots increased since NCLB.

> Most of the students at [school] find their way to this school after dropping out of the traditional school programs. Some are not necessarily dropouts but wanted to leave their old school environment and come to a smaller school. For some, they became disinterested in the work of traditional schools, the sub-

ject matter in the traditional program was not relevant to their existence or their lives. So they stop going . . . the type of kids coming in are for different reasons. The criterion for the population that we serve is that the students must be dropped from their old school.

In 2003 the Chicago Public Schools passed a policy designed to make it more difficult for children to opt out of the school system. The policy requires parents to come in with their kids to sign drop forms. But, according to one administrator, this policy has not decreased the flow of students into the alternative school system because kids are now entering the system through referral.

> A referral means that a student is not being dropped from the CPS system but is being transferred. By law the students are not able to transfer [into alternative schools]. The concept of referral defeats the purpose and the criteria of the alternative schools-that the student must be willing to come to the school. We prefer that the students come on their own versus being referred. The referred students are less interested. There is a difference in their enthusiasm. Our school has a very open environment that supports and respects individual students and their right to explore and express themselves. This openness has been a critical incentive for some students. We've noticed a change since NCLB has been in effect. This change is the fact that the students coming in are lower in skill level. The skills are getting lower and the students are getting older with fewer credits. The student's skills are especially lower in math, reading, comprehension, and critical thinking. Some of the kids come with no credit hours whatsoever.

Transition centers were developed for students who are struggling with basic skills. Eighth graders who were not ready for high school were supposed to go into the transition center in order to boost their basic skills competency and then matriculate into the high school. But more than one administrator pointed to the transition center as being like a funnel; kids enter and then disappear.

Topic 4: NCLB's Impact on Teachers

One of the ironies of this legislation is that it is creating a drain on the teaching staff. Through the SES (supplemental services) provision, private entities are being brought in to provide remediation for those students who are considered at risk within the system. However, the individuals who are hired by the private providers are in fact public school teachers. "It is a misnomer that a private provider has their own teachers. The CPS teachers are doing all of this. Of the private providers, 80-90% of the after school instructors are CPS teachers. The private providers don't have their own staff."

Teachers have an excellent opportunity to boost their income through working for a private provider. But many think that the money would be better spent if it could supplement the activities that take place during the actual school day. Most private providers don't want to work with high schools. When CPS asked only 5 or 6 of the 28 providers chose to serve high schools as well as the elementary grades.

> "They don't want to tackle this population. The curriculum [of the providers] is very targeted. They are also paid by enrollment and it is harder to keep the high school students in. The younger ones have a higher attendance rate and more money is spent."

NCLB also mandates that schools have 100% certified highly qualified teachers. This mandate is especially challenging for the smaller alternative high schools that serve the dropout population. "Trying to get 100% highly qualified teachers means that we must be competitive in terms of salaries. However, we simply don't have those kinds of resources." Even when good teachers are hired, the population that they serve has very different needs.

> "Our faculty is working much harder than many other education professionals because of the caliber of student being dealt with. The amount of time and energy invested to deal with these students' mental, emotional and motivational issues as well as the academic issues is tremendous. These students have social and human services barriers to overcome to keep coming to school. These can be as difficult as dealing with criminal justice, substance abuse, sexual promiscuity, and child rearing issues that they may be experiencing. [The school] has a small group, large group concept where we counsel individual students and deal with their academic issues. Thus, our educators require more skill than others. NCLB has been devastating to [school] in terms of teachers. We had a strong group of college degreed teachers that were passionately committed to and effective with this particular student base. However, they were required to take the teaching certification tests as part of the 'qualified teacher' program in NCLB. Some refused to in order to make a political statement. There were others who have had trouble passing the tests that are biased and unfair. They do not speak to the cognitive background of African American, some women and minority working professionals."

In the end, the school had to let a large number of their experienced teaching staff go to stay in compliance with the requirements of NCLB. "These were people who understood our students, came from a similar background and had a passion for helping them."

In Conclusion: The Fate of Public Schools

What does the future look like with accountability and testing? According to public opinion the outlook is not very optimistic. Much of what one hears in the press reflects the view that as it is now, public school education in many cases is failing, particularly for those that are failing at each stage. These administrators did not feel this way. They felt that a lot of what we hear reflects misinformation and misunderstanding. They cite the fact that so many improvements have already been made in the schools that doesn't get reflected in the press. They feel there is a general sense out there that there is some kind of 'magic bullet' that can solve all the problems right now, some sort of 'one size fits all' way that will reach all children. But as in all things, it is much more complicated than that. As one administrator said, "If it were that easy don't you think someone in public education would have done it already?"

So, what questions should the public be asking in order to better understand the impact of NCLB? When asked, nearly all of the administrators agreed that the first question people need to ask is, "What is a failing school?" The public doesn't understand how schools are judged to be failing.

> Everybody gets labeled in certain ways in NCLB and you can miss the fine grain details, like is this school actually making strides or is it a school that is stagnant? The most important thing that gets lost in NCLB is that schools do not either work or don't work for kids in some sort of universal way. There are certain things about a particular school that make it an appealing choice for one parent and not as appealing for another. Thus, a child might be doing really well in an environment even though most kids aren't making standards. After the label is in place, then as a 'consumer' parents have to look at the particular situation in the particular school and determine if the school is working for their child, regardless of what the charts say.

These educators agree that there may come a time when all of the Chicago schools end up on the 'failed' list. When this happens, does it mean that the public school system has failed all children? Absolutely not, they say. All of the administrators asked said that the only way they feel the public perception will change is if [a specific affluent suburban school] suddenly ended up on the failed school list.

The public needs to ask, "What do we really want our kids to be and to do? What are the essential skills?" There needs to be a dialogue about whether skills that are being tested are the only skills that are being taught. And if this is the case, where are kids supposed to learn all of the other things that we know they'll need in order to be productive citizens? We all know that schools can't teach all kids all things, but the public schools do have the tremendous responsibility for preparing children for their future roles. Who will pick up the slack if schools are charged with only providing the basics? NCLB has pushed the blame onto schools and teachers for a systemic problem.

Parents who are struggling with children who face academic challenges need to know that help is available. Parents and students who have been pushed out or disenrolled need to know their options. Parents must be more vocal and stand up for their child's right to remain in school. By law students have the right to remain in school until age 21, but more often than not when students are disenrolled no one comes forward to speak on their behalf. Under No Child Left Behind schools are required to offer supplemental support to any student who is in need of academic assistance, but parents need to know how and when to seek support for their children.

The public also needs to question why there is such a lack of funding for such an extremely ambitious goal. None of the administrators asked had a problem with the goal, they all believe that all children deserve a high quality education, but they feel that the goal warrants proper support. In Chicago approximately 200 thousand children are eligible for SES support, but only 80 thousand can be served with current funds. Our state funding is flawed, yet the school district is seen as 'washing away money' when we are just trying to keep up with the law and do the right thing. This is a story that isn't being told.

Questions for the Public

1) What is a failing school? Does this mean that all children in these schools receive a poor education?
2) What skills are essential for our children? What must they learn to be well-rounded adults?
3) What are my child's rights? What are the options for children who are having difficulty making it in school?
4) Where is the support? Where will the money come from if 100% school success is to be a reality?

Notes

1. National Governor's Association. "National Governors Association Task Force on State High School Graduation Data," (Washington D.C., 2005), p. 9

2. National Governor's Association. "National Governors Association Task Force on State High School Graduation Data," (Washington D.C., 2005), p. 3

3. Kaufman, Alt, and Chapman. "Dropout Rates in the United States."(*National Center on Educational Statistics,* 2000).

4. National Governors Task Force, 2005, p. 7

5. Alexander, K., Entwisle, D., and Kabbani, N., "The Dropout Process in Life Course Perspective: Part I, Profiling Risk Factors at Home and School," (Baltimore, MD: Johns Hopkins University, 2000).

6. Sum, A., "Lost in the Wilderness: The Deteriorating Labor Market for Teens and Young Adults in Illinois 2000-2004," (2005)

7. Schwartz, Wendy. "School Dropout: New Information About an Old Problem."(National Center For Education Statistics. 1995). <http://eric-web.tc.columbia.edu/digests/dig109.html>

8) Schwartz, Wendy. "School Dropout: New Information About an Old Problem."(National Center For Education Statistics. 1995). <http://eric-web.tc.columbia.edu/digests/dig109.html>

9. *Source: Provided by The Urban Institute/Education Policy Center, 2005

10. Gotbaum, B., "Pushing Out At Risk Students: An Analysis of High School Discharge Figures." (*The Public Advocate for the City of New York and Advocates for Children,* 2002).

11. Gotbaum, B., "Pushing Out At Risk Students: An Analysis of High School Discharge Figures." (*The Public Advocate for the City of New York and Advocates for Children,* 2002), p. 2.

12. Greene, J. and Winters, M., *Public School Graduation Rates in the United States.* (Center for Civic Innovation/The Manhattan Institute, 2002).

13. Greene, J. and Winters, M., *Public School Graduation Rates in the United States.* (Center for Civic Innovation/The Manhattan Institute, 2002), p.5

14. Orfield, G., Losen, D., and Wald, J., "Losing our Future: How Minority Youth

are Being Left Behind by the graduation Rate Crisis." (*The Civil Rights Project at Harvard University,* 2004), p. 2

15. Orfield, G., Losen, D., and Wald, J., "Losing our Future: How Minority Youth are Being Left Behind by the graduation Rate Crisis." (*The Civil Rights Project at Harvard University,* 2004).

16. Swanson, C., "Who Graduates? Who Doesn't A Statistical Portrait of Public High School Graduation, Class of 2001." (Urban Policy Institute/ Education Policy Center, 2005).

17. Swanson, C., "Who Graduates? Who Doesn't A Statistical Portrait of Public High School Graduation, Class of 2001." (Urban Policy Institute/ Education Policy Center, 2005), p. 1

18. Allensworth, E., "Ending Social Promotion: Dropout Rates in Chicago After Implementation of the Eighth-Grade Promotion Gate." (*Consortium of Chicago School Research,* 2004).

19. Allensworth, E., "Ending Social Promotion: Dropout Rates in Chicago After Implementation of the Eighth-Grade Promotion Gate." (*Consortium of Chicago School Research,* 2004), p. 1

20. Allensworth, E., "Ending Social Promotion: Dropout Rates in Chicago After Implementation of the Eighth-Grade Promotion Gate." (*Consortium of Chicago School Research,* 2004), p. 10

21. Allensworth, E., "Ending Social Promotion: Dropout Rates in Chicago After Implementation of the Eighth-Grade Promotion Gate." (*Consortium of Chicago School Research,* 2004), p. 15

22. *Source: Provided by the Urban Institute/Education Policy Center 2005

23. Chicago Public Schools. *Dropout and Graduation Rates, 1999-2007/Cohort Dropout and Graduation Rates.* Retrieved February 10, 2008, from Chicago Public Schools: Office of Research, Evaluation, and Accountability.<http ://research.cps.k 12.il.us/ cps/accountweb/Reports/citywide.html>

24. *Source: Provided by the Urban Institute/Education Policy Center 2005

25. Chicago Public Schools. *On Track Rates, 2004-2007 High School Freshmen On Track.* Retrieved February 10, 2008, from Chicago Public Schools: Office of Research, valuation, and Accountability.<http ://research. cps.k12.il.us /cps / accountweb/ Reports/citywide.html>

26. Medina, 2004

27. Swanson, C., "Ten Questions (and Answers) About Graduates, Dropouts and NCLB Accountability." Urban Policy Institute/Education Policy Center. 2003.

28. Swanson, 2003, p. 1

29. Orfield, Losen, and Wald, 2004. p. 3

30. Chapman, C., & Hoffman, L. *Event dropout rates for public school studentsin grades 9-12: 2002-03 and 2003-4* (NCES 2007-026). US Department of Education, National Center for Education Statistics. Washington, DC. Retrieved from <http ://www pathwaystocollege.net/PCNLibrary/ViewBiblio.aspx?aid=2247>

31. Herbert, B., "Locked Out at a Young Age." *The New York Times*, October 20, 2003.

References

Alexander, K., Entwisle, D., and Kabbani, N., "The Dropout Process in Life Course Perspective: Part I, Profiling Risk Factors at Home and School," Baltimore, MD: Johns Hopkins University, 2000.

Allensworth, E., "Ending Social Promotion: Dropout Rates in Chicago After Implementation of the Eighth-Grade Promotion Gate." *Consortium of Chicago School Research,* 2004.

Alternative School Network. "Reconnecting Youth," 2003.

Black, S. "Out of the Picture." *The American School Board Journal,* 1998.

Black, S. "Unfinished Business." *The American School Board Journal.* 2004.

Chapman, C., & Hoffman, L. *Event dropout rates for public school studentsin grades 9-12: 2002-03 and 2003-4* (NCES 2007-026). US Department of Education,National Center for Education Statistics. Washington, DC. http://www.pathwaystocollege.net/PCNLibrary/ViewBiblio.aspx?aid=2247.

Chicago Public Schools. *Dropout and Graduation Rates, 1999-2007/Cohort Dropout and Graduation Rates.* Retrieved February 10, 2008, from Chicago Public Schools: Office of Research, Evaluation, and Accountability.http: // research.cps.k12.il.u s/cps /account web/Reports/citywide.html.

Chicago Public Schools. *On Track Rates, 2004-2007 High School Freshmen On Track.* Retrieved February 10, 2008, from Chicago Public Schools: Office of Research, Evaluation, and Accountability. http :// research .cps .k12 .il.us /cps /accountweb /Reports/citywide.html.

Gotbaum, B., "Pushing Out At Risk Students: An Analysis of High School Discharge Figures." *The Public Advocate for the City of New York and Advocates for Children,*2002.

Graduation Counts. A Report of the National Governors Association Task Force on State High School Graduation Data, 2005.

Greene, J. and Winters, M., *Public School Graduation Rates in the United States.* Center for Civic Innovation/The Manhattan Institute, 2002.

Herbert, B., "Locked Out at a Young Age." *The New York Times*, October 20, 2003.

Kaufman, Alt, and Chapman. "Dropout Rates in the United States." *National Center on Educational Statistics,* 2000

"National Governors Association Task Force on State High School Graduation Data," Washington D.C. National Governor's Association, 2005.

Orfield, G., Losen, D., and Wald, J., "Losing our Future: How Minority Youth are Being Left Behind by the graduation Rate Crisis." *The Civil Rights Project at Harvard University,* 2004.

Schwartz, Wendy. "School Dropout: New Information About an Old Problem." National Center For Education Statistics. 1995.http: // ericweb tc. columbia. Edu /digests/ di g109.html

Sum, A., "Lost in the Wilderness: The Deteriorating Labor Market for Teens and Young Adults in Illinois 2000-2004," (2005)

Swanson, C., "Who Graduates? Who Doesn't A Statistical Portrait of Public High School Graduation, Class of 2001." Urban Policy Institute/ Education Policy Center, 2005.

Swanson, C., "The Real Truth About Low Graduation Rates: An Evidence Based Commentary." Urban Policy Institute/Education Policy Center, 2005.

Swanson, C., "Ten Questions (and Answers) About Graduates, Dropouts and NCLB Accountability." Urban Policy Institute/Education Policy Center. 2003.

Swanson, C., and Chaplin, D., "Counting High School Graduation When Graduates Count: Measuring Graduation Rates Under the High Stakes of NCLB." Urban Policy Institute/Education Policy Center. 2003.

Chapter 6
English Language Learners in an Era of NCLB

Kristin Lems and Leah D. Miller

The No Child Left Behind (NCLB) Act of 2002 has ushered in a raft of sweeping and stressful changes in schools across America. With high stakes tests bearing high stakes consequences, each school and each school district in the country must now track its subgroups to see that they make ever-increasing percentages of adequate yearly progress (AYP). If one or more of the subgroups does not make the amount of yearly progress established by that state's board of education, the school is put on an academic watch list, then on probation, and can eventually be subject to restructuring.

English Language Learners (ELLs) comprise one of the subgroups, and because of that, ELLs have gone from the sidelines to the crosshairs in record time. NCLB requires all states to "assist all limited English proficient children, including immigrant children and youth, to achieve at high levels in the core academic subjects so that those children can meet the same challenging state academic content and student academic achievement standards as all children are expected to meet."[1] Because ELL test scores are now part of the public record of each school and school district, ELLs are receiving new attention, and the programs that teach them English are receiving new scrutiny. The ways in which NCLB has altered the landscape for the teaching of English language learners is complex and multidimensional. It has affected professional preparation and development, program models, classroom instruction, and assessment. Moreover, it has changed the dialog about the teaching of ELLs. This chapter will provide an interpretive overview of NCLB as it pertains to the teaching of English as a new language.

Policies toward English Teaching in the U.S.

The question of just how immigrants to the United States and language minorities within the United States ought to learn English has a long and colorful history, reflecting changing political tides. The U.S. Constitution does not specify an official language, and the United States has thus far not established one. In fact, until World War I., the decentralized U.S. educational system allowed for immigrant groups to set up and maintain schools offering their home language as the language of instruction.[2]

In 1968, the Bilingual Education Act, or Title VII of the Elementary and Secondary Education Act (ESEA) was passed as part of the wave of social reforms that flowed from the Civil Rights Act of 1964. The Act authorized money to be spent on teaching both oral and academic English to children from language minority backgrounds. The ambiguous language of the Act, however, provided no road map for English language instruction, stating only that language minority students had a right to specialized instruction to meet their needs. This was enshrined in the Supreme Court decision *Lau v. Nichols*, decided in 1970. Justice Douglas wrote this preface to his opinion:

> No specific remedy is urged upon us. Teaching English to the students of Chinese ancestry who do not speak the language is one choice. Giving instruction to this group in Chinese is another. There may be others. Petitions ask only that the Board of Education be directed to apply expertise to the problem and rectify the situation.[3]

In some ways, this stance foreshadowed the current language of NCLB, which does not point to any teaching method or approach, but clearly specifies English language proficiency as the desired outcome.

No Child Left Behind and English Language Learners

Title III of the No Child Left Behind Act, entitled "Language Instruction for Limited English Proficient and Immigrant Students," consists of 304 sections and is 45 pages long. Its first section

> 1) calls for state education agencies to adopt programs for ELLs that are scientifically proven to be the most effective;[4]
> 2) requires an accurate census of immigrant children as a determinant in assigning funding;
> 3) calls for ELLs to reach state academic achievement levels comparable to those of native speakers;
> 4) and provides guidelines for how grant money should be allocated.

It also requires ESL teachers to be fluent in English, stipulates that students ultimately be transitioned into programs "that are not tailored to limited English proficient children," calls for an annual increase in the percentage of students making progress, and requires schools which do not reach these levels to submit an improvement plan. Title III also states, "Nothing in this part shall be construed to require a state or local educational agency...to establish, continue, or eliminate any particular type of instructional program for limited English proficient students." The Act also carefully states that the use of Native American languages should not be restricted.[5]

The second major section, called "Improving Language Instruction Educational Programs," lists a number of mandatory features that should be found in programs for ELLs, including valid and reliable tests, systematic data gathering, and trained teachers. Conspicuously absent is any mention of maintenance or development of the home or heritage language.

Other sections discuss professional development, how grant funds shall be distributed, and conditions under which grants will be renewed. At the end is a glossary of terms, and there, one finds the sole nod to bilingual or dual language instructional models:

> Language instruction educational program means an instructional course...that may make instructional use of both English and a child's native language to enable the child to develop and attain English proficiency, and may include the participation of English proficient children if such course is designed to enable all participating children to become proficient in English and a second language.[6]

The parental notification section requires parents be given information about the programs offered at their children's school, but does not require providing a rationale about the programs offered, and offers an option to refuse ESL or bilingual services. The end of the document announces that the former Office of Bilingual Education and Minority Languages Affairs is henceforth renamed the Office of English Language Acquisition, Language Enhancement, and Academic Achievement for Language Minority Students. Except for appearing in the renaming, the word "bilingual" is completely absent from the document.

Consequences of NCLB for English Language Teaching and Learning

In some ways, the Act is ecumenical in its treatment of English language programs, as was the original Bilingual Education Act. It does not promote or criticize any instructional method or program model. On the other hand, the removal of the word "bilingual" signals that bilingual education is not considered a national educational goal.[7] In fact, a blue ribbon committee was empanelled to review research assessing the effectiveness of various models of instruction for ELLs. When the National Literacy Panel for Language Minority Children and Youth concluded, after three years of study, that students consistently performed better when some instruction is conducted in their native language, the Department of Education decided not to publish the report. This left many asking if results that contradicted an "English only" policy position had been suppressed.[8] *Developing Literacy in Second-language Learners: Report of the National Literacy Panel for Language Minority Children and Youth,* the full report, has recently been published by Lawrence Erlbaum Associates, rather than by the government.[9]

The most positive byproduct of NCLB is that schools can no longer overlook the need to provide high quality services for ELLs (Crandall, 2005). This is important for states without strong programs for ELLs, but even in states like Illinois, for example, where there was already a strong degree of accountability in meeting the needs of ELLs, the interest level has heightened even more.

Marilyn Poole, a retired teacher who developed the first ESL program at an Illinois high school some years ago, put it succinctly:

> During my career, I fought for program changes in my school that would enhance the learning opportunities for ELL students. I heard comments from the administration about "those students" or "your student." Very rarely did I hear "our students." NCLB changed all that. Now the administration is all too consumed with the progress of these students because it is these students as well as another subgroup who are causing my (ex) building's failure to meet expectations.[10]

Another positive aspect of NCLB is the professionalization of the teachers of English language learners. Since NCLB requires all teachers to be highly qualified, teachers who want to work with English language learners anywhere in the country are now required to complete formal training to develop expertise in teaching English language learners. ESL professionals overwhelmingly support maintaining and upgrading our professional qualifications. A teacher recently sighed, "If I hear anyone else say 'all you need to be an ESL teacher is being able to speak English' again, I'll scream!" When professional credentials become more demanding, the field offers more opportunities and rewards. The ESL and bilingual education fields are no exception.

All public school students are affected by NCLB, including ELLs. Like all the other students affected, ELLs must show adequate yearly progress in key content areas; in addition, they are also responsible for showing adequate yearly progress in English language proficiency. The real problem with NCLB for ELLs lies in the first of these two. If states do not have an instrument in place to form an alternative to the standardized tests taken by native speakers, the ELLs end up having to take the same tests – with all the resulting failure. They are being asked to compete with native speakers while lacking native speaker language proficiency. W. Wilson puts it succinctly: "Common sense dictates that if you administer a test to students in a language they don't understand, they probably won't do well on it."[11]

To strengthen the rigor of programs that would allow ELLs to meet the language requirement, a number of states got together to form the WIDA Consortium, which created the WIDA English Language Proficiency Standards (WIDA Standards). The very detailed WIDA standards have four distinct but interrelated dimensions.

1) *Domains* The WIDA standards describe the language used in the domains of listening, speaking, reading and writing.
2) *Content Areas* There are five different sets of standards which cover the academic language required to learn content in the language arts, math, science, and social studies, as well as in the more holistic domain of social and instructional language.
3) *Grade clusters* The standards are broken into age appropriate grade level clusters for grades pre-K through 12.
4) *Proficiency levels* Each one of these accommodates different levels of language proficiency within the standards, from the total beginner to the transitioning student.

That means that, for example, a tenth grade high school social studies teacher doing a unit on the Civil War could ask more proficient ESL students to write a letter from the point of view of a soldier, and ask less proficient students to write sentences describing a picture of a soldier. This prevents the practice of putting less proficient students off in a corner with nothing to do and thereby "fall through the cracks." By looking at the standards in order to design learning tasks and the language that goes with them, teachers can address the full range of language proficiency levels found within their classrooms. Having different ways of looking at the WIDA standards gives teachers guidance in preparing differentiated instruction for their ELLs, whether in a dedicated ESL setting or within a mixed classroom of native speakers and ELLs.

The WIDA standards are in use in the 15 member states of the WIDA Consortium, and they are freely downloadable at the WIDA website (The WIDA Consortium, 2004). Even teachers in states that are not in the consortium can make full use of the standards in their own teaching. This, we think, is a tremendous leap forward in the teaching of English language learners.

New Assessments

The WIDA Consortium also created the ACCESS test, an annual, secure test that separately measures each ELL student's language proficiency gains in listening, speaking, reading and writing. States that are members of the Consortium pay to make use of the test in their districts. The test was introduced on a large scale in the winter of 2006. The ACCESS test closely reflects the WIDA standards, and ACCESS allows for future changes in standards; Jim Bauman, one of the primary developers, said, "As standards change, items that map to those standards will change."[12] However, not every state has the benefit of clearly defined standards, and not all have developed valid and reliable assessments of either content areas or language proficiency. While the ACCESS test is a positive development for its 15 member states, the nation still has a patchwork quilt of assessments designed for ELLs and ELL accommodations to content tests for native speakers. Because the assessments differ so widely from state to state, it is hard for teachers to gauge the language proficiency of children moving into their states because the scales differ so much.

Diversity Dangerous to School Success

There are other negatives that accompany grouping ELLs into a subgroup of their own. Schools with populations that are linguistically, racially, and economically diverse, in addition to the presence of special ed. students, have a greater possibility of failure under NCLB since the scores of only one subgroup can put a school at risk. As a consequence, schools that do the "heavy lifting" of public education, those with a lot of diversity, may have the hardest time complying with NCLB because they have the most subgroups.[13]

ELLs may also be the only measurable subgroup in a more homogenous district, and in some cases, their scores may threaten a school's ability to meet NCLB requirements. Educators are aware of this, and concerned. "I don't want to see English language learners become scapegoats," declared former Illinois State Board of Education president Randy Dunn.[14] Seen against that backdrop, NCLB can be fairly accused of making children more vulnerable. It has created a system in which an entire school district can be penalized because of one subgroup.

Finally, there are profound negative consequences to high stakes testing in its own right. These consequences come not only from the possibility that schools may close or be taken over if children's scores do not improve at a fast enough rate. It is also because of the way such testing can compromise the curriculum. Teachers feel exasperated by the amount of time stolen from their teaching to prepare for and administer the tests and the effect all the testing has on many children. They also question the value of the tests themselves. This creates a moral dilemma for many teachers. In Illinois, for example, ACCESS testing can take up to a week to administer. On top of that, ELLs have to take the native language content tests over a period of two or more days, with all of the test preparation that entails. Depending upon the resources of the school or district, teachers may be called upon to organize the testing procedures. This further reduces their ability to offer quality instruction.

It has not been possible in this brief chapter to fully explore the twin issues of American educational policy and national immigration policy, but they will surely impact if, and how, NCLB is reauthorized. In the meantime, we can hope NCLB, if reauthorized, will not only mandate, but also fund, positive initiatives to better all children. At least for now ELLs are "on the radar."

Notes

1. U.S. Department of Education, 2002, 276. <http://www.ed.gov/index.jhtml>

2. C. Ovando, "Political issues in bilingual/bicultural education." In W.I. Israel (Ed.), *Political issues in education* (Washington, D.C.: The Council of State School Officers, 1978), p. 101-15.

3. Lau v. Nichols, Supreme Court, 1974, in Crawford, 2004, pp. 113, 393.

4. U.S. Dept of Education, 2002, Section 267.

5. see Sections 267-281.

6. p. 307

7. S. R. Katz, "Does NCLB leave the U.S. behind in bilingual teacher education?" *English Education, 35*, 2 (2004): 141-152. W. Wright, "A Catch 22 for language learners." (*Educational Leadership 64*(3), 2006): 22-27.

8. James Crawford. "Federal 'Practice Guides' on ELLs Omit Native Languages." (2007) Institute for language and academic policy, Retrieved February 15, 2008 from <http://www.elladvocates.org/>

9. D. August and T. Shanahan, Eds. *Developing literacy in second-language learners: Report of the National Literacy Panel for Language- minority Children and Youth.* Mahwah, N.J.: Lawrence Erlbaum Associates, 2006.

10. M. Poole, *Email Interview.* Recorded January 4, 2006.; U.S. Department of Education, 2002; and *No Child Left Behind Act of 2001.* Pub. L No. 107-110, 115 Stat, 1425. Retrieved June 7, 2007 from: <http://www.ed.gov/policy/elsec/leg/esea02/index.html>

11. Wilson, 2006.

12. J. Bauman, "WIDA and ACCESS for ELLs ™." Workshop for universities and colleges of education and regional offices of education. Naperville, IL, Jan. 27, 2006.

13. The Associated Press, 2003.

14. Randy Dunn, January, 2006.

References

August, D., and Shanahan, T., Eds. *Developing literacy in second-language learners: Report of the National Literacy Panel for Language- minority Children and Youth.* Mahwah, N.J.: Lawrence Erlbaum Associates, 2006.

Bauman, J. *WIDA and ACCESS for ELLs* ™. (Workshop for universities and colleges of education and regional offices of education). Naperville, IL, Jan. 27, 2006.

Chicago Tribune, "Study: US unfair to diverse schools" Nation Section. 2003.

Crandall, J. *No teacher or teacher educator left behind: Collaborating to survive in a sea of standards and accountability.* (Paper presented at the meeting of the Illinois Teachers of English to Speakers of other Languages/Bilingual Education Convention), Chicago, IL, March, 2005.

Crawford, James. "Federal 'Practice Guides' on ELLs Omit Native Languages." Institute for language and academic policy, 2007. Retrieved February 15, 2008 from http://www.elladvocates.org/

Crawford, James. *Educating English Language learners.* Los Angeles: Bilingual Educational Services, 2004.

Dunn, R. (Speech presented at the Annual Conference of the Illinois Association of Multicultural Multilingual Education), Oakbrook, Illinois, January 2006.

Katz, S. R. "Does NCLB leave the U.S. behind in bilingual teacher education?" *English Education, 35*, 2 (2004): 141-152.

Ovando, C. Political issues in bilingual/bicultural education. In W.I. Israel (Ed.), *Political issues in education (pp. 101-15).* Washington, D.C.: The Council of State School Officers, 1978.

Ovando, C.J., M.C. Combs, and V.P. Collier. *Bilingual and ESL Classrooms: Teaching in Multicultural Contexts. Fourth Edition.* New York: McGraw-Hill, 2006

Poole, M. *Email Interview.* Recorded January 4, 2006.

U.S. Department of Education, *No Child Left Behind Act of 2001.* (Pub. L No. 107-110, 115 Stat, 1425, 2002). Retrieved June 7, 2007 from: http://www.ed.gov/policy/elsec/leg/esea02/index.html

The WIDA Consortium, 2004. Retrieved February 15, 2008 from: http://www.wida.us/

Wright, W. "A Catch 22 for language learners." *Educational Leadership 64*(3), 2006: 22-27.

Zehr, M.A., "'No child' effect on English-Learners mulled." *Education Week 25*, 25, 2006: 14-15.

Chapter 7
Who is Being Left Behind?

Martha Casazza and Laura Bauer

Introduction

> My parents couldn't afford college, and my dad once told me that he couldn't go to school because he didn't have money. I understood his decision, but I refused to accept that as my fate. So I took the initiative to search for scholarships and worked various jobs, and with hard work, dedication and discipline I was able to put myself through school. And today a promise is being fulfilled and a goal has been achieved. This is my story of how my journey began. (Alejandro Maldonado, 2005 graduation speech)

With funding for *No Child Left Behind* (NCLB) being focused disproportionately on educational programs for children, what is happening to academic support programs designed to retain high school students at risk for dropping out? What is happening to financial assistance programs for those who cannot afford to go to college? What has happened to academic assistance programs for those students who do make it through the doors of higher education but who are underprepared or misprepared?

The United States has a long history of providing access to colleges and universities for students who need different types of support systems. Federal legislation has driven much of this support through programs such as the Servicemen's Readjustment Act (the GI Bill), which has enabled millions of returning veterans to pay for college, and the various federal *TRIO programs* which focus on comprehensive assistance for low income students who aspire to college. Over the last century, our system of higher education has expanded to accommodate an increasingly diverse set of learners who seek an education beyond high school. More high school graduates than ever before view higher education as a necessity to obtain employment that is self-fulfilling and increases their chance for upward mobility. Our economy depends on highly educated individuals who are prepared to work in fields where communication skills and the ability to understand diversity are imperative.

Access to higher education is a social imperative and no longer an option simply for a select few. For many, however, there must be resources available for access to be meaningful. With the refocusing of already limited federal and state resources solely on early education, many adolescents and young adults are being ignored; their pathways to college are becoming longer and more complicated. They have difficult personal and educational choices to make often as a result of financial constraints and often must base decisions on pressing family issues and tuition rates rather than professional goals. In some cases, these choices lead them to drop out of high school or perhaps take a less rigorous curriculum in high school in order to find extra time to work. This impacts both the level of preparation and the level of diversity across four-year colleges and universities as well as the work force.

Limiting educational support for adolescents and young adults also indirectly cycles back to the NCLB legislation. By narrowing educational opportunities for parents and older siblings, young children will lack the mentors and role models that are significant factors in their educational achievement, and the parents themselves will have a difficult time finding meaningful employment to support their children's future educational aspirations. It perpetuates an endless cycle.

To address these concerns, this chapter will explore:

- Today's Students
- Historical Overview of Federal Involvement
- The High School Connection
- How High Schools and Colleges Can Make a Difference

Today's Students

> I did have several students who have made a significant impact on my career as a developmental educator. Two that come to mind are Sonia and Francisco. They were both students in the College Assistance Migrant Program at the University of Texas-Pan American. They both came from humble beginnings, struggling financially but determined to get an education. They both accepted the challenges before them and did excellent work. It was not easy for them, but they stuck it out and made it. What impressed me the most about them was their persistence and determination to make something of themselves. [1]

As the American population becomes more diverse and as high school students increasingly set their sights on a college education, high schools and colleges must continue to evolve in order to meet ever-changing demands. The need for a college degree will continue to increase. Between 1960 and 2001, college enrollments went from 4.1 million to 14.8 million. 90% of high school seniors expect to attend college while only 47% of high school graduates have completed college preparatory curricula. As a reporter, Stephanie Banchero noted in The Chicago Tribune on August 17, 2005, recent ACT scores across the

United States show that 20% of 1.2 million test takers met all the bench marks in science, math, reading and English. [2] Approximately 40% of all high school graduates took the ACT, and the pool is becoming larger and more diverse each year. Minority students taking the ACT have increased 24% since 2001 with the number of Hispanic students growing by 40% and African Americans by twenty three percent during the same time period. [3]

40% of students in four-year postsecondary institutions take remedial courses while the overall percentage for all institutions is 53%. Enrollment across colleges and universities is expected to grow and by 2015, one to two million additional young adults will seek access to a higher education, many of whom will come from low income and minority families. [4] A great number of these students will also be the first in their families to attend college and will, therefore, need guidance through the educational process...from setting realistic expectations, to enrolling in a college-preparatory curriculum in high school, to applying for financial assistance and identifying the right college for them.

In addition to increasing enrollments, more students today are taking out loans to pay for their education. According to the College Board, tuition and student fees rose 10.5% in the 2004 academic term at four-year public universities and 6% at four-year private universities. [5] When adjusted for inflation, students paid 51% more in 2004 than they did in 1994. [6] The annual *number* of student loans for college tuition has grown from 4.8 million in 1992/1993 to 10.8 million in 2003/2004. [7] The total *amount* of the loans has increased from $19.8 billion to $50.5 billion for the same time periods. [8] With 41% of African Americans and 33% of Hispanics living in households with incomes that fall below the "minimum but adequate" level set by the U.S. Department of Labor, [9] the rising costs of college tuition hit especially hard. Even 48% of students from families making $100,000 and more who received a bachelor's degree took out federal loans. [10]

While college is becoming more expensive, it is also becoming a requirement if one wants career choices. Employers are looking for individuals who can process information and possess good communication skills. There are few unskilled jobs left today. As early as 1997, 96% of manufacturing firms indicated that they provided some education and training for their hourly employees. At least two-thirds of them also indicated that they provided remedial instruction in reading, writing, math and problem solving. [11] From 1998 to 2008, 14.1 million new jobs will require a bachelor's degree or at least some postsecondary education, more than double those requiring high school or below. [12]

Clearly it is imperative to increase access to colleges and universities, but these efforts must begin in high school. Currently the dropout rate of Hispanic students is double the rate of white teenagers. Hispanic students drop out of high schools at the rate of 15% and as noted by Fry "...the need to work is clearly one major reason Latinos dropout." [13] Also according to the Public Agenda report, "With Diploma in Hand" there is data that suggest Hispanic students are often "...derailed on the road to higher education by low expectations from teachers, poor understanding of the admissions processes, and little adult support." [14]

According to Carnevale, "If we were successful in giving minorities access to their share of seats in college, there would already be another 185,000 minorities with bachelor's degrees in America." [15] He contends that minority enrollment in colleges should reflect their percentages in the general population. Based on that formula, there should be an additional 200,000 African Americans and 430,000 Hispanics in college today. He also stresses that while African Americans and Hispanics each account for approximately 12% of the nation's population, each minority represents less than 6% of students at the most selective colleges and universities. [16]

Access, when effectively implemented, increases diversity while enhancing the quality of education. Chang maintains that the opportunity for interaction with a racial group other than one's own enhances a "student's academic development, satisfaction with college, level of awareness, and commitment to promoting racial understanding..." [17] This diversity, according to Chang, can affect the "institutional climate" – and contribute to "student retention, overall college satisfaction, college GPA, intellectual self-confidence and social self-confidence." [18] Shriver and Weissberg, in a recent quantitative study, found that "social and emotional learning programs significantly improve students' academic performance." [19]

Historical Overview of Federal Involvement

Beginning in 1862, the federal government became directly involved in education at all levels. This had a substantial impact on who would attend college, and it opened the doors to wider participation. One of the federal initiatives was the first Morrill Act signed by President Lincoln in 1862. This act guaranteed to each state thirty thousand acres of land per congressman to support colleges dedicated to teaching agriculture and the mechanic arts. The second Morrill Act, in 1890, further broadened the mission of universities by prohibiting federal funding to states that practiced discrimination in higher education.

These two Acts were significant in their combined effect on the evolving purpose of higher education. States began to establish A&M (agricultural and mechanical) universities and increase funding to public universities in order to provide more technical training. This funding was highly debated. The private institutions in the Northeast viewed government intervention as inequitable and quite threatening; they were concerned about whom it might bring into the halls of higher education. In addition to governmental calls for a change, business leaders also began demanding change; they wanted a curriculum that prepared students more directly for the job market. One Chicago businessman, Richard T. Crane, argued that "a college education, because of its classical and literary emphasis, was a worthless undertaking for any young man who wished to succeed in the business world." [20]

In 1907, more than half of the admitted students to Harvard, Yale, Princeton and Columbia did not meet the standard entrance requirements. [21] These schools then added developmental courses to their curricula. The most common of these were remedial reading and study skills courses. By 1909, over 350 colleges were offering "How to Study" courses for under prepared students, and by 1920, 100 study habit books had been published.[22]

By 1917, seventy-six junior colleges had been created across the country which continued the trend of opening the doors to higher education to more students. The President's Commission on Higher Education stated, "virtually 50 percent of the population has the ability to complete fourteen years of schooling, that is, through junior college and that nearly one-third has the ability to complete a college course in liberal arts or professional training."[23] Within the next 13 years, the number of college students doubled. This trend, of course, was hotly debated by educators who felt there were already too many students enrolled who were below the more traditional standards. Nevertheless, higher education became more of an expectation for a high school graduate. In 1900, 1.6% of the college-aged population enrolled in college, and by 1960 that had increased to 22.2%.[24]

It is clear that students were being accepted to colleges and universities who had not had the opportunity for appropriate preparation in their high schools. Consequently, academic support systems began to grow. In 1929, a survey was sent to all state universities requesting information about their offerings in remedial reading. Almost 25% of those responding indicated that they tried to identify poor readers upon admission and slightly fewer actually provided some type of remediation.[25] Some of the respondents had begun to implement mandatory remediation. At Ohio State University, probationary students were required to take remedial reading. One dean returned the survey with the comment, "I am sorry that we have nothing to report as done, but I am heartily delighted that you are beginning to work along this line. I don't know anything more timely."[26]

Added to this increasing recognition that academic support systems were important was the unpredicted outcome of the Servicemen's Readjustment Act of 1944, more commonly referred to as the GI Bill. Originally written to reward military service following World War II and also to head off the potential economic chaos of so many G.I.s returning home from the war, this legislation had far-reaching effects. Under its education provisions, 2.2 million veterans were enabled to attend two and four-year colleges and universities. Another 3.5 million enrolled in vocational schools. By 1947, veterans made up 49% of college enrollments.[27] Many of these returning veterans were married with children and were often the first generation in their families to consider attending college. With this government funding, colleges developed guidance centers, reading and study skills programs, and tutoring services primarily to serve the new students.[28] Along with the veterans came increasing numbers of women, students with special needs, and students from impoverished backgrounds. Academic support systems grew and became more comprehensive to meet increasingly diverse needs.

The availability of student financial assistance continued with the Higher Education Act of 1965 which was followed by two reauthorizations in 1972 and 1992. One of the most significant outcomes of this legislation was the Pell Grant, the largest federal grant program for college students. This award is based on financial need with no academic criteria attached to it. The amount of the award depends on the level of funding that Congress allots each year. In fiscal year 2005, the maximum grant was frozen at $4050 for the third year in a row. This was despite the fact that the cost of living and college tuitions continue to rise. The number of Pell Grant recipients has gone from 176,000 in 1973/74 to over five million in 2004/05. [29] About one third of all college students receive some type of aid under this program, and the vast majority come from families with an annual income of less than $35,000. [30] Despite its success in increasing access for low income students, a change in eligibility was announced in 2004 that cut out approximately 90,000 students and reduced the amount of grants available for over one million students. In addition the overall number of low income students receiving Pell Grants has decreased 17% over the last decade at the most selective schools. [31] This is occurring at the same time that the number of bachelor degrees achieved by individuals from low income families has remained level for the last decade and "improved only slightly since 1970." [32]

Another means of federal assistance comes in the form of loans. The Perkins loan is a low-interest loan for students who demonstrate financial need. The educational institution itself is the lender and uses government funds to help subsidize an eligible student. Since fiscal year 2003, the amount of available monies appropriated for the Perkins loans has decreased from $166,411,000 to $66,132,000 in fiscal year 2005. [33] While the number of students aspiring to go to college and the tuition rates are increasing exponentially, the federal appropriation for this loan program is being decreased.

In 1965, as part of the Economic Opportunity Act, several additional programs were created in response to the federal government's "War on Poverty." Two of these programs, described as *TRIO programs*, *Talent Search* and *Upward Bound* currently serve 900,000 students. Their focus is to work with high school students from low income families who will be the first generation in their families to attend college. They provide both academic and personal assistance to students to enable them to attend college and succeed. *Talent Search* provides grant funding to colleges and universities in order for them to establish programs that identify high school youth with potential and encourage them to complete high school and continue on for a postsecondary education. Both of these programs were slated to be eliminated for the 2006/2007 school year in the early stages of the federal budget process, but funding for *TRIO* was maintained at the fiscal year 2005 level of $836,500,000 for 2006.

Programs as described above for college bound students are constantly being threatened with elimination and are being maintained simply at previous levels of funding which do not keep up with the cost of living. This makes it difficult for low income students to receive the assistance they need for tuition without working, and it also makes it difficult for schools to pay for programs like *Talent Search* and *Upward Bound* that have provided educational access for over forty years. At the same time, funding for programs under the *No Child Left Behind* legislation have seen a forty percent increase in the past five years. In fiscal year 2001, they were funded at $17,400,000,000 and by fiscal year 2005, the appropriated funding was $24,400,000,000. [34]

The High School Connection

> When I was in 8th grade, I was living in a cycle. This cycle was repetitive, dramatic and included violence and drugs. I felt trapped and it appeared to me that there was no way out. I soon realized that this cycle that surrounded me would eventually lead me to a disordered life. I started wondering, 'What am I going to do after I graduate?' College was never in my mind as a freshman and, financially, college seemed impossible. (Alejandro Maldonado, 2005 graduation speech)

Increasing minority and low-income student access to higher education in the United States is not optional, nor will it cause the decline of standards of excellence and quality across our educational system. A large body of research supports the notion that first generation college students and minority students share multiple risk factors and are less likely to persist than those from other family backgrounds. [35] These students lack what Bills defines as "cultural capital" or that which defines one's social status. [36] They then have little familiarity with the academic cultural norms for that situation and will frequently not know how to participate in experiences that could lead to higher levels of achievement. Programs with both social and emotional elements have been designed to provide experience with such opportunities and they have been shown to significantly improve student performance. [37]

The NCLB Act seems to further marginalize these students. Loukes and Cameron maintain that while the NCLB Act asserts that "school choice" must be provided as an option for families whose children attend Title I schools that fail to make Adequate Yearly Progress (AYP), high performing high school districts are not mandated to accept these students. [38] Loukes and Cameron also point out that there may not be any high performing high schools nearby, so transportation also becomes a problem and an expensive one. [39] Often parents must take time off from work to accompany their children to distant schools. Those children who do travel alone must pay transportation costs that they cannot easily afford. An example of how these factors impacted a program designed to provide a preparatory college program for high school students occurred in 2004 at National-Louis University in Chicago. Students were recruited from the Chicago Public Schools, and they eagerly registered for the weekend program. When it came to actually getting to the university to participate, however, the majority of students did not come because they reported that the bus and train fare was too costly and their parents were too anxious to let them cross particular streets in the city due to safety concerns.

The concept of AYP itself is troubling; it is based on a "single test, a snapshot of the student achievement continuum" and "fails to acknowledge gains by students who have moved from below basic to basic or for those students who have moved from proficient to advanced." [40] All high school students are allegedly held to the same standards of progress, but the problem seems to be with the way progress is measured due to the enormous diversity in the classrooms and the range of entry levels. Essentially, AYP does not reveal anything about individual students and their progress. High schools must become proactive and create a system of evaluation that looks at the whole student and offers multiple ways of exhibiting competency. Students who need additional academic support should be able to access that support and have multiple opportunities for applying newly learned study strategies within the context of their high school coursework. It is unrealistic to believe that an academic support course or two in college will bring an under prepared student up to par. Students need rigorous courses beforehand that train them to think and reason, and this preparation takes time. Several programs with connections to both high school and college have been available to students who otherwise might not attend college. They are:

> The *TRIO Programs* are designed to "help students to overcome class, social, academic, and cultural barriers to higher education." [41] *TRIO Programs* are direct grant programs funded in rank order on the basis of competitive proposals.

According to *TRIO* statistics, "students had a 22% greater chance of entering their third year of college" than those of similar backgrounds who did not participate in *TRIO Programs*. [42] Findings from several studies indicate: "...more services bring greater success," and that "students who had the full range of *TRIO* services available at the college level (counseling, special courses, tutoring) were twice as likely to be retained." [43]

TRIO is designed to identify "promising students" *(Talent Search)*, prepare them to do college level work *(Upward Bound, Upward Bound Math/Science)*, provide information on academic and financial aid opportunities to adults, and provide tutoring and support services to students once they reach campus.

> As mandated by Congress, over two-thirds of the students must come from families with incomes under $24,000 (family of four) where neither parent graduated from college. Students enrolled in today's *TRIO Programs* mirror our nation's multi-cultural and multiethnic society. Thirty-nine percent of *TRIO* students are White, 36% are African-American, 16% are Hispanic, 5% are Native American, and 4% are Asian-American. Sixteen thousand *TRIO* students are disabled. There are more than 25,000 U.S. veterans currently enrolled in the *TRIO Programs*. *TRIO* college graduates are working in business, industry, government, medicine, law, education, communications, sales, finance, politics, transportation, publishing, law enforcement, computer science & technology, engineering, and accounting. [44]

Upward Bound is a pre-college program designed to help increase the rates at which high school freshmen, sophomores and juniors enroll and graduate from college. The goal for *Upward Bound* is to help "low family income and potential first generation college students prepare for college." [45] All *Upward Bound* projects "MUST provide instruction in math, laboratory science, composition, literature, and foreign language." [46] Participants receive instruction in literature, composition, foreign language, mathematics, and science on college campuses after school, often on Saturdays, and during the summer. There are 681 *Upward Bound* programs operating across the United States. In the early 1980's, a Research Triangle Study of *Upward Bound* found that *Upward Bound* students were "four times as likely to graduate from college as their peers who did not attend this program." [47]

The *Talent Search* program serves students in grades six through twelve and, in addition to counseling, participants receive information about college admission requirements, scholarships, and various student financial aid programs. Considered an "early intervention program" *Talent Search* helps young people "to better understand their educational opportunities and options. [48] Over 302,000 Americans are enrolled in 319 *TRIO Talent Search programs*." [49]

The *Bridge Program* offers academic preparation, intrusive, individualized academic advising and the personal attention of faculty in an intensive, yet nurturing, college environment during the summer. The *Bridge Program* is designed to strengthen academic skills, develop a peer support network and familiarize students with a campus and its resources. *Bridge Program* students are typically enrolled in an English course, a mathematics course, and a freshman seminar; academically rigorous credit bearing courses that become part of the students' official college transcript. *Bridge Program* students are generally assigned an academic advisor who will serve as their permanent advisor providing guidance on course selection, career planning, and progress towards fulfilling degree requirements. [50]

All of the above programs are designed to foster academic success through the close connections students are able to make with faculty (both high school and college) and staff throughout length of the program and are designed to strengthen academic stills and acculturate students to a college environment. [51]

The majority of these programs feature a strong mentorship component, emphasize reading, writing and math, personal counseling and may also involve the entire family as stakeholders in the process. Through these programs, students experience the demands and expectations of academic and social life on campus. This interdisciplinary approach to a course of study provides comprehensive instruction designed to enhance reading, writing, critical thinking, and time management skills. Students are able to gain confidence and experience in academia within a sheltered, supportive environment. [52]

> The most influential person for my learning was a counselor that I once had. I met her after I was an adult and I had been telling her that I was going back to school to take some courses. I was working nights, midnights as a matter of fact. She asked me why I was always talking about going back and why I had not done it…So one day I went out to the next registration for one of the junior colleges, and I signed up to take some courses. She was the person who got me started, and I kind of became what I call a drop in student for quite a number of years because I had to keep stopping my education. First it was because of money, and I couldn't get financial aid. When I ran out of money, I had to stop. A couple of my instructors had told me though that I had lots of perseverance, and I never thought of myself that way until I realized that I never gave up the things I wanted to do. [53]

How High Schools and Colleges Can Make a Difference

There is little dispute that comprehensive support systems are essential to student development and success and that the delivery and type of support systems vary widely across institutions. With many students entering higher education under prepared in multiple areas, systems are needed for emotional as well as academic support. For many there is a huge gap between high school and college coursework, and the expectations of college instructors are considerably different from those of high school faculty. The reading and writing that students must do in college is more advanced than general high school reading and writing; college students must be able to process difficult academic material and think critically.

But students entering higher education in need of academic support in more than one area are often overwhelmed and find themselves placed in more than one academic support course during their first term in college. This means they are further marginalized and without the opportunity to put what they have learned into practice in a content area. Rather than blaming high schools for not preparing their students for higher education, educators need to work across the traditional grade-level boundaries. They should talk to each other about a secondary core curriculum and the competencies that are expected for more students. In most cases, high schools have separated their "college-bound" students from others at the start by offering them a more rigorous set of courses.[54]

Unfortunately, the classification of "college-bound" is often established prior to high school, and based primarily on standardized tests. This practice leaves out the students who may not even know at that point that college could be an option for them. By the time they are ready to graduate, many of them have not acquired the basic competencies that will help them succeed in college, and they usually have not experienced a challenging curriculum. This is not due to a lack of talent; rather, it is due to a set of expectations imposed on them which assigns them to a less rigorous education. Simmons, Musoba and Chung (2004) claim the "strongest positive influences on persistence among first generation students are the opportunity to take rigorous high school curriculum and enrolling full time while in college." [55]

By collaborating, college and high school educators could work together to define curricula that would better prepare all students for college coursework. A joint determination of a set of competencies that all high school students should achieve before graduating, along with dual enrollment in high school/college, would go a long way toward setting expectations early and ensuring more meaningful access to greater numbers of students. [56]

Faculty could create teams with the high school teachers and together discuss expectations at both levels of higher education, their similarities and differences. They could work with students to help them think through their goals and begin to develop support systems in the high school that would start them on the path to higher education. An alternate model could be to work across all three systems and create paths for students that would offer choices based on their goals: high school to community college to four-year college or high school straight to the four-year college. With partnerships in place, faculty from both high schools and colleges can work together to determine standards and how to help students meet those standards.

The idea of academic support is embraced by most institutions of higher education, and providing access without developing a support system is meaningless. Access accompanied by a lowering of standards is also unacceptable; access and excellence can and must co-exist both for the sake of all students and for society. In order to ensure successful access to higher education, high schools and colleges must look for effective strategies that encompass the whole student. Because an increasingly high percentage of under prepared students are bringing a range of personal issues with them to school, if there is not some way to help them address those issues they will not succeed. Academic support cannot be solely about teaching reading, writing and math, but rather a more holistic approach that fosters self-esteem as well as the acquisition of strategies needed to succeed in a college environment. [57]

Conclusion

By establishing partnerships and working across the artificial boundaries traditionally built between high schools and colleges/universities, we can create meaningful access for increasing numbers of students. The following strategies will enhance such meaningful access:

- Creating a broader, rigorous, more relevant, curriculum starting in high school that integrates diverse teaching strategies across the curriculum and recognizes and reflects educational and cultural diversity,
- Utilizing strategies that strengthen the basic academic skills related to reading, writing and mathematics needed across the curriculum and also addressing the student's level of self-esteem, and
- Developing more effective academic support services across all levels of the educational system.

These partnerships will need to be funded, and the federal government must be involved. Its history of facilitating access to higher education acknowledges the fact that a better educated citizenry contributes to a more productive and healthy society. The government needs to work in partnership with educators and educational systems to determine how best to allocate monies across the entire spectrum of education in the United States. The following questions may provide the reader with an opportunity to reflect further on this topic.

Questions

1) What exactly is the role of government in the American system of education?

2) What data are needed to determine an equitable allocation of monies across the whole spectrum of education?

3) How can we work toward ensuring that access and quality are compatible?

4) How can we work toward a more seamless system of education where students are truly at the center and educators from K-16 work together to ensure student achievement?

Notes

1. Casazza, M.E. and L. Bauer. *Access, Opportunity and Success: Keeping thePromise of Higher Education*. Westport, CN: Praeger, 2006.
2. Banchero, Stephanie. *Chicago Tribune*, August 17, 2005.
3. Lewin, Tamar, "SAT Essay Scores Are In, But Will They Be Used?" *New York Times*, May 15, 2005.
4. Roueche, J. and S. Roueche. *National Panel Report of the Association of American Colleges and Universities,* 2002.
5. Heiser, Scott, "Soaring Costs Leave Poor Students Struggling to Make Grade,"*Financial Times,* August 22, 2005.
6. Heiser, 2005.
7. Heiser, 2005.
8. Heiser, 2005.
9. Carnevale, A. "The Coming of Labor and Skills Shortage." *T&D* 59 (January, 2005): 3
10. Carnevale, 2005.
11. Roueche, J. and S. Roueche, 2002.: 2
12. Roueche, J. and S. Roueche, 2002.: 2
13. Fry, R. *Hispanic Youth Dropping Out of U.S. Schools: Measuring the Challenge.* Washington, D.C.: Pew Hispanic Center, 2003.
14. National Center for Public Policy and Higher Education
15. Carnevale, 2005
16. Carnevale, 2005: 5
17. Chang, M. "*Racial Diversity in Higher Education: Does a Racially Mixed Student Population Affect Educational Outcomes*?" (PhD diss., University of California, Los Angeles, 1996).
18. Chang, 1996
19. Shriver, T. & R.P. Weissberg. "No Emotion Left Behind." *New York Times* Op ed. 2005. 8-16
20. Butts, R.F. and L.A. Cremin. *A History of Education in American Culture.*Troy, MO: Rinehart & Winston, 1953: 370
21. Wyatt, M. "The Past, Present, and Future Need for College Reading Courses in the U.S." *Journal of Reading.* 36(1), 1992. 10-20.
22. Casazza, M.E. and S. L. Silverman, *Learning Assistance and Developmental Education.* San Francisco: Jossey-Bass, 1996.
23. Butts, R.F. and L.A. Cremin. *A History of Education in American Culture.* Troy, MO: Rinehart & Winston, 1953.
24. Cohen, A.M. and F. B. Brawer. *The American Community College.* San Francisco: Jossey-Bass, 1982.
25. Parr, F.W., "The Extent of Remedial Reading Work in State Universities in theUnited States," *School and Society*, 31(799), 1930. 548.

26. Parr, F.W., "The Extent of Remedial Reading Work in State Universities in the United States," *School and Society*, 31(799), 1930. 548.

27. Greenburg. *Chronicle of Higher Education*. 50(40): B9, 2004.

28. Maxwell, Martha. *Improving Student Learning Skills*. San Francisco: Jossey-Bass, 1979.

29. Kantrowitz, Mark, "The Smart Student Guide to Financial Aid," *FinAid*, 2008. <www.FinAid.org>

30. "Department of Education to tighten Pell Grant eligibility," *Cable News Network LP*, 2008. <www.cnn.com/2004/EDUCATION/12/23/pell.grants/>

31. *Cable News Network LP*, 2008.

32. Heiser, 2005.

33. Heiser, 2005.

34. Heiser, 2005.

35. Duggan, M. "Factors Influencing the First to Second Year Persistence of First Generation College Students" (Paper presented at the annual meeting of the Northeast Association for Institutional Research Cambridge, MA, November, 2001); Choy, S. "Student whose parents did not go to college." Washington DC: *National Center for Education Statistics*, 2001.

36. Bills, D. *Credentials, signals and screens: Explaining the relationship between schooling and job assignment*, (Unpublished manuscript. University of Iowa, Iowa City.: 2000).

37. Shriver, T. & R.P. Weissberg. "No Emotion Left Behind." *New York Times* Op ed. 2005. 8-16

38. Loukes and Cameron, "AYP in Illinois and the Nation," 2005. <http://www.ierc.siue.edu/documents/AYP%20IERC-2005-I-1.pdf>

39. Loukes and Cameron, 2005.

40. Loukes and Cameron, 2005, 11

41. "Trio Programs," Kansas State University, April 4, 1997. <www.k-state.edu/ess/trio.htm>

42. "Trio Programs," Kansas State University, April 4, 1997. <www.k-state.edu/ess/trio.htm

43. "Trio Programs," Kansas State University, April 4, 1997. <www.k-state.edu/ess/trio.htm>

44. Upward bound, <http://www.ed.gov/programs/trioupbound/index.html>

45. Upward bound, <http://www.ed.gov/programs/trioupbound/index.html>

46. Upward bound <http://www.ed.gov/programs/trioupbound/index.html>

47. "Trio Programs," <http://www.k-state.edu/ess/trio.htm>.

48. Upward bound, <http://www.ed.gov/programs/trioupbopund/index.html>

49. Upward bound <http://www.ed.gov/programs/trioupbopund/index.html>

50. Upward bound, <http://www.ed.gov/programs/trioupbound/index.html>

51. Casazza, M.E. and L. Bauer. *Access, Opportunity and Success: Keeping thePromise of Higher Education*. Westport, CN: Praeger, 2006.

52. Casazza and Bauer, 2006.

53. Casazza and Bauer, 2006.

54. Casazza & Bauer, 2006.

55. Simmons A. B., G. D. Musoba, and G.C. Chung, "Persistence among first generation college students in Indiana: The impact of college preparation, college experience, and financial aid." *IPAS Research Report #05-01*, April 2005

56. Casazza & Bauer, 2006.

57. Casazza & Bauer, 2006.

References

Astin, A. "Diversity and Multiculturalism on the Campus: How are Students Affected?" *Change* (1993): 44-49

Bills, D. *Credentials, signals and screens: Explaining the relationship between schooling and job assignment,* (Unpublished manuscript. University of Iowa, Iowa City.: 2000).

Butts, R.F. and L.A. Cremin. *A History of Education in American Culture.* Troy, MO: Rinehart & Winston, 1953.

Carnevale, A. "The Coming of Labor and Skills Shortage." *T&D* 59 (January, 2005): 37-41.

Casazza, M.E. and L. Bauer. *Access, Opportunity and Success: Keeping the Promise of Higher Education.* Westport, CN: Praeger, 2006.

Casazza, M.E. and S. L. Silverman, *Learning Assistance and Developmental Education.* San Francisco: Jossey-Bass, 1996.

Chang, M. "*Racial Diversity in Higher Education: Does a Racially Mixed Student Population Affect Educational Outcomes*?" (PhD diss., University of California,Los Angeles, 1996).

Choy, S. "Student whose parents did not go to college." Washington DC: *National Center for Education Statistics,* 2001.

Cohen, A.M. and F. B. Brawer. *The American Community College.* San Francisco: Jossey-Bass, 1982.

"Department of Education to tighten Pell Grant eligibility," *Cable News Network LP,* 2008. www.cnn.com/2004/EDUCATION/12/23/pell.grants/

Duggan, M. "Factors Influencing the First to Second Year Persistence of First GenerationCollege Students" (Paper presented at the annual meeting of the NortheastAssociation for Institutional Research Cambridge, MA, November, 2001).

Fry, R. *Hispanic Youth Dropping Out of U.S. Schools: Measuring the Challenge.* Washington, D.C.: Pew Hispanic Center, 2003.

Greenburg. *Chronicle of Higher Education.* 50(40): B9, 2004.

Heiser, Scott, "Soaring Costs Leave Poor Students Struggling to Make Grade," *Financial Times,* August 22, 2005.

Kantrowitz, Mark, "The Smart Student Guide to Financial Aid," *FinAid,* 2008. www.FinAid.org

Lewin, Tamar, "SAT Essay Scores Are In, But Will They Be Used?" *New York Times,* May 15, 2005.

Loukes and Cameron, "AYP in Illinois and the Nation," 2005. http: //www .ierc. siue .edu /documents/AYP%20IERC-2005-I-1.pdf

Maxwell, Martha. *Improving Student Learning Skills.* San Francisco: Jossey-Bass, 1979.

Parr, F.W., "The Extent of Remedial Reading Work in State Universities in the United States," *School and Society*, 31(799), 1930. 547-54.

Roueche, J. and S. Roueche. *National Panel Report of the Association of American Colleges and Universities,* 2002.

Shriver, T. & R.P. Weissberg. "No Emotion Left Behind." *New York Times* Op ed. 2005. 8-16

Simmons A. B., G. D. Musoba, and G.C. Chung, "Persistence among first generation college students in Indiana: The impact of college preparation, college experience, and financial aid." *IPAS Research Report #05-01,* April 2005

"Trio Programs," Kansas State University, April 4, 1997. www.k-state.edu/ess/trio.htm

"Upward Bound Program," *U.S. Department of Education,* 2008. www.ed.Gov/programs/trioupbound/index.html

Wyatt, M. "The Past, Present, and Future Need for College Reading Courses in the U.S." *Journal of Reading*. 36(1), 1992. 10-20.

Chapter 8
Public Education and Privatization in the Ownership Society

Stephen Thompson

Introduction

Since President Bush came into office in 2001 more than a few commentators have noted a push towards policies that privatize public institutions like, for example, social security. Because of this perceived "privatization" agenda, enactment of the No Child Left Behind (NCLB) Act in 2002 has fueled a lot of fear and anxiety over the "real" intention of the legislation. More specifically educators believe that this is just one more attempt to increase the credibility of vouchers and charter schools or more to the point, outright funding of private schools with public funds. Most of this fear is generated by the constant push of "voucher" advocates whose voices seem to have grown louder over time and have gained a substantial audience in state capitals and Washington, D.C. These advocates come from a committed group of ideologues that at their core believe in the myth of the American as rugged individualist. Their rhetoric celebrates the individual as a master of their own domain and discourages a "robust collective life with rich networks of communal assistance."[1]

Why privatization and why now? The partial answer lies at the beginning of this country's history where the Constitution limits government's power and reserves all power not enumerated to the people. As the United States of America grew, immigration of vast numbers of people looking for a new life from the old world along with the push of people going westward, instilled a cult of "individual, pull yourself up by your bootstraps" solutions to sociological problems and an ethos of "every man for himself." Over time history has shown that this myth persists despite significant evidence to the contrary and that institutions like our public schools serve a purpose much larger than one individual or one group of ideologues.[2]

One of the accepted tenets of any modern society is that a literate and well-informed population is necessary for democracy. It is around this tenet that governmental involvement in education owes its existence; however, there are disagreements over how schools can achieve those aims that cause friction, for example, the use of public tax money to support private business. Some have been more direct by describing NCLB as a not very well-disguised effort to shift public education funding to the private sector.[3] The thrust of this chapter will therefore explore whether or not President Bush's agenda in passing NCLB is properly seen as an effort to subsidize private school tuition at the expense of the public schools.[4]

The Free Market's role in a Democracy

The free market is the sacrosanct system to distribute goods and services in the U.S. Unfortunately, unfettered free markets often lead to serious inequities, wealth imbalances and monopolies, which benefit few and harm many. Prior to the great depression of the 1930s, the U.S. government typically took a laissez-faire attitude towards any inequities created by the market and often sided with moneyed interests at the expense of the individual to uphold the status quo. This reliance on free markets has its roots in the writings of Adam Smith who believed that profit motive, free economic markets, and competition are necessary to allow for the highest efficiency and to offer the highest quality of goods and services at the lowest cost.[5] But Smith never advocated for a "hands-off" policy from government believing that government was necessary to rein in the excesses of the market.

During the Great Depression and subsequent New Deal programs a significant increase in the involvement of government created assistance to the collective public with legislation specifically designed to regulate the market. Collective bargaining and social security were two public policy initiatives that were acknowledgments that some fates that befall individuals, like poverty, are beyond the control of the individual and thus in need of governmental intervention.

For any free market to exist and function, several conditions need to be present. First, there must be numerous sellers and buyers. Parents need to and do buy education for their children, either through tuition or taxes. Lack of supply in educational providers in the inner city and rural areas will create unmet demand and hinder plans to privatize the public schools in those areas. A second essential component of a free market is the easy entry by potential sellers. Schools are expensive to start up and maintain and therefore entry into this market is difficult, but not impossible. The final component of a free market involves the prevention of monopolistic power, to say that a single provider should not be able to dictate market price but price is set by a large number of interacting buyers and sellers. If parents wish to have their children attend private schools but cannot pay the tuition then private schools cannot serve this population without some type of governmental support through help from scholarships and/or vouchers. It is through governmentally funded vouchers that financial support of private schools in certain low-income areas becomes possible. While privatization advocates complain that public education is a monopoly it is important to note that government is not operating under the same reality as private companies who might be considered a monopoly because they don't maximize price to maximize profit.

The cost to educate any one child is significant, with expenditures averaging $7,875 per pupil in 2003.[6] For low-income families there exists little choice but to send their children to the nearest public school. Further compounding the matter, there is widespread variation between funding in school districts in poor neighborhoods versus wealthy neighborhoods, often equating to thousands of dollars. Clearly some kind of public financial support is needed for children with low family incomes to attend private schools.

How and why did government become the majority provider of K-12 education in a country where the free-market is the predominant system to distribute goods and services? In the early years of this nation, K-12 education was spotty and for the most part private. Horace Mann is widely credited with developing a formal model of public education in the 19th Century. His motivation was to improve and equalize children's opportunities for education, which ironically happens to be the same goal of voucher advocates. To achieve this end he created a state board of education, surveyed the condition of the state's schools, created an institute to train teachers, increased the length of the school year and found support for increasing teacher salaries, procuring books and building schools.[7] Mann's goal was to create a common school that would act as a "great equalizer" and create an endless array of social good such as the disappearance of poverty and reduction of crime.[8] Privatization on the other hand would appear to be the antithesis of the "great equalizer" that Mann sought from a public education.

Where does this privatization push come from? Privatization of public schools is at the forefront of neo-liberal or neo-conservative ideology. Roberto Unger defines privatization as an economic program that seeks to achieve fiscal balance through: limiting federal spending instead of increasing taxes; increasing integration into the global economy with its established rules (via the World Bank and the International Monetary Fund); outsourcing services which includes the acceptance of the concept of private property inherent in capitalistic transactions; and believing in the primacy of markets.[9] What has happened under the current Bush administration is the expected reduction in taxes particularly for the wealthy but strangely we have not seen the expected reductions in spending. Instead, we have seen huge increases in spending with concomitant huge increases in the budget deficit. It is this inability to cut spending that has the Cato Institute (a conservative think tank) observing that current spending budgets surpass that of previous Democratic presidents; not viewed as a positive development by conservative scholars.[10]

The concept of public funding of private education through vouchers began with Milton Friedman who states two rationalizations for governmental participation in education.[11] One is the referred to as the "neighborhood effect" that is the education of the few children is paid for by the many adults in a given community. The second is a paternalistic concern that a community has for children and other irresponsible individuals. He saw that education was necessary to pass on a "common core of values deemed requisite for social stability," however; he didn't believe that the government needed to be the provider of that education but rather the provider of funding through vouchers that could be used in any school. Therefore, the government would no longer be responsible for providing the education, just the funding. He likened a voucher program to the GI Bill, which funded higher education through vouchers at the end of World War II for returning soldiers. Furthermore an efficiency argument could be made to support privatization as "reform of public education is impossible because of the legislative and legal mandates that government imposes and that individual schools and districts are "bogged down" by lack of clarity about mission and locus of decision-making."[12] M. Holt adds that government-run schools are an illegal restraint of trade and that "Vouchers would force the educational monopoly to reassess itself," as well as eliminating the endemic inequities in today's public school systems.[13] Holt concludes that it is only through self-determination and community building that we can accomplish the task of equalizing educational opportunity. The irony is using Mann's outcomes of improving and equalizing children's opportunities for education to support a much different system.

The process of implementing Friedman's ideas of privatization of public entities was recently highlighted in Naomi Klein's book *The Shock Doctrine: The Rise of Disaster Capitalism*.[14] Klein exposes four decades of natural and man-made disasters that were used to exploit the public's disorientation and grab control of the state's institutions to privatize them. Recent history in New Orleans after Hurricane Katrina has shown this to be t he case with public schools closed permanently on ly to be replaced by a voucher program that would send these children to a private school.[15] Milton Friedman, wrote an impassioned plea for using vouchers in New Orleans after Hurricane Katrina. "Most New Orleans schools are in ruins, as are the homes of the children who have attended them. The children are now scattered all over the country. This is a tragedy. It is also an opportunity to radically reform the educational system."[16] This disaster with its unfortunate aftermath allows free market adherents to a solution in the form of an opportunity to radically reform the educational system.

NCLB's privatization push

One obvious place to start is the ascendancy of Ronald Reagan in 1980 and the conservative backlash against the New Deal programs of Franklin Delano Roosevelt and the Great Society programs of Lyndon Baines Johnson. Grover Norquist, in particular, has been a vocal proponent of reducing the size of government through his famous quote: "I don't want to abolish government. I simply want to reduce it to the size where I can drag it into the bathroom and drown it in the bathtub."[17] This became known as "starve the beast" and the idea was to cut tax rates significantly such that the federal government (the beast) had no choice but to reduce its level of spending, particularly in the areas of social programs. Not enough spending was cut (or could be cut) to balance the budget and as a result, large budget deficits resulted.

The 1983 report "A Nation at Risk" was another major push towards privatization in that our schools were branded as "failing." Specifically, "the educational foundations of our society are presently being eroded by a rising tide of mediocrity that threatens our very future as a Nation and a people."[18] The condemnation continues:

> Each generation of Americans has outstripped its parents in education, in literacy, and in economic attainment. For the first time in the history of our country, the educational skills of one generation will not surpass, will not equal, will not even approach, those of their parents. It is important, of course, to recognize that *the average citizen* today is better educated and more knowledgeable than the average citizen of a generation ago-more literate, and exposed to more mathematics, literature, and science. The positive impact of this fact on the well-being of our country and the lives of our people cannot be overstated. Nevertheless, *the average graduate* of our schools and colleges today is not as well-educated as the average graduate of 25 or 35 years ago, when a much smaller proportion of our population completed high school and college. The negative impact of this fact likewise cannot be overstated.[19]

With this "documented" failure of public education the conservative movement increased its push for a privatized educational system similar to their current push to privatize and "fix" Social Security and Medicare.[20] The primary way used to discredit public schools was to broaden the use of shibboleths such as "Communist", "Socialist", or plain old "un-American" to mark those government programs that conservatives sought to abolish. The game plan was seen by some public school advocates as a direct mechanism to discredit public schools through the clever usage of language such as the use of misleading dichotomies like "you're either skeptical of public education or you're satisfied with mediocrity."[21] This doesn't leave much ground to argue for anything other than privatization or giving up.[22] While doing well on standardized exams mandated by NCLB might be expected to stop the push for privatization, this has not been the case. Too many students passing the exam caused the difficulty of the test to be increased until the point of failure was proven, thus reinforcing the concept that public education cannot be made better, but freedom of choice is the only way to enhance academic standards.[23] As Kohn states the object of this policy was to push the agenda that "public education is not something to be made better, it is something from which we need to be freed."[24]

One last group that stands in the way of privatization and mightily irritates the conservative faithful is the teacher unions. They are seen by the conservative establishment as the embodiment to inflexibility and resistance to change. In keeping with conservatives' clever language usage, former Secretary of Education Rod Paige in particular has labeled the National Educational Association (NEA) a "terrorist organization."[25] The idea behind the characterization is to push the concept of failing public schools in part because they are being run by an organization with values counter to that of ordinary Americans and as such need to be done away with as anti-American. This effort to weaken teacher unions together with removing money out of public education through vouchers will most certainly lead to lower membership, decreased dues and less power.[26] Also teacher unions become an attractive target because they are one of the largest supporters of the Democratic Party and this leads to the conclusion that this is much more about politics and much less about education.[27]

How would privatization benefit children?

Assuming the theme of limited government, the object of the conservative privatization movement in any arena would be to take those functions that are currently in the public sphere and hand them over to private entities that would perform more efficiently because of competition. It is the "invisible hand" of the market that will create appropriate educational alternatives for parents and their children. Instead of slow and deliberate political process through government entities, consumers would be able to opt out of one school for another for any reason at all depending on their special needs and wants. Theory predicts that each private school would cater to their students and parents in providing a relevant educational experience...otherwise their students and parents will go elsewhere with their money. This has not necessarily been the case, with the limited availability of public monies for private purposes (vouchers).

Yet the theory continues; the market will provide a variety of educational opportunities through the proliferation of schools coming into the market attracted by the influx of money. This proliferation of schools will provide flexibility and a rapid ability to cater to the students that would seek to enroll in them.

The theory rests on this: if a market-based education is to have any chance to work then vouchers must be generous, eligibility must be universal, all schools that meet specific minimum standards must be included, and there should be no mandatory measurement of performance.[28] Competition among schools will reduce costs, improve efficiency and maximize the freedom of the students and parents.

But will it? We've already seen the numerous barriers to market entry for educational providers. More problematic is the conservatives' blind faith in markets as the answer to everything that is most troubling to the educational community, particularly in areas not well served by the market in other areas of life. As Witte points out there may be a real limited understanding by conservatives of how life works in the inner city.[29] If competition is the solution for what ails the inner city have we seen any evidence that the market has improved the lives of those in these neighborhoods? From housing to grocery stores to health care and other services there is little in the way to justify faith that the market serves any meaningful role in the inner city. Thus, it just may be that market proponents might be operating out of hatred for all things governmental and bureaucratic or as a way to attack entrenched interests such as teacher unions...rather than to promote the benefits to children.

How would privatization harm children?

The downside of a market-based education is the loss of a sense of community in the schools and the loss of those items that possess no readily identified monetary cost. Since vouchers are the prevalent mechanism to provide students with the necessary funds to enroll in private schools they must be sufficient to allow for real choice. Otherwise, because every dollar that goes to a voucher leaves the public schools' budget, those students without adequate resources will be left in the same or worse situation than the public schools they go to now. Gray makes this point by concluding that the "celebration of consumer choice and private demands has undermined communities and devalued stability in personal relationships."[30] Weil further elaborates stating that government is necessary to guarantee the rights to a free and public education and that "people go to schools to learn how to live, not just learn how to make a living."[31]

While market-driven schools allow for maximizing individual freedom of school choice this freedom typically comes at the expense of the community and its values, therefore, the major tension is between individual freedom and the community's values. By electing a Board of Education in regular elections all members of the community have the opportunity to participate in the direction of the public schools. Community members have no such right in private market-based education. Only parents and students can exercise influence over a school's direction and only by threatening to leave or not come in the first place. As we shall see later universality of vouchers does not improve educational outcomes, but a more limited program can do so.

Voucher legality and the Establishment Clause ...whatever happened to the separation of Church and State?

Lemon v. Kurtzman, a twice-decided U.S. Supreme Court decision first looked at the matter of expending public monies for private schools. The use of public monies to fund private education does not violate the Establishment Clause of the Constitution if it meets a three-pronged test as follows:

> 1) The legislation must have a secular purpose;
> 2) The primary effect of the legislation must not advance nor inhibit religion; and
> 3) The legislation cannot allow for excessive governmental involvement with religion.[32]

More recently, Zelman v. Simmons-Harris states that a tuition-aid program does not violate the Constitution's Establishment clause if that aid (read vouchers) can be used at both religious and non-religious private schools.[33] Another famous case, often cited by proponents of vouchers is Brown v. Board of Education.[34] The belief is that the ideals of Brown v. Board of Education have never materialized and that government schools are unable and unwilling to change to promote equality of opportunity.[35] Clearly vouchers have achieved legal status.

What does Choice really mean?

Despite the rhetoric of what choice is and is not, there are several different types of school choice most of which involves public-to-public transfer. Cookson lists the six types of choice as intra-district, inter-district, controlled, magnet schools, charter schools and voucher plans.[36] Intra-district choice allows parents to select among public schools within their home districts. Inter-district broadens that choice out to include schools across district lines. Controlled choice allows for parents to choose a school within a specific area but may be limited to ensure balance of race, gender, etc. Magnet schools are public schools that provide specialized program or curricula. Charter schools are publicly supported schools that are free of significant restrictions under which public school districts must face. Charter schools do need to meet similar student performance standards. Lastly, voucher programs are specifically designed to use public money to fund private educational institutions.

Because privatization advocates firmly believe that public schools have not been and never will be accountable, the connection between privatization and accountability remains the cornerstone of the leap to improvement in education. Unfortunately, there is scant evidence that private schools actually improve the delivery of education and there is evidence that accountability is less in private than public schools.[37] In Milwaukee, Wisconsin where vouchers have been policy for more than 10 years it's potential consumers cannot get any private school student performance information readily.[38] Even public Charter schools do not appear to participate in open accountability, which the reader may recall is one of the necessities of a highly functioning market, that is, substantial information on school performance is key to parents making informed decisions about where to send their children. Contrary to popular conservative belief, it is the public schools that are the most accountable through the systematic measurement of student performance and the public reporting of those results.

What is the evidence on choice programs and how has choice made a difference? Cullen, Jacob and Levitt performed a couple of important studies on the matter of choice and whether or not it improved the outcomes for those students who chose to attend a different high school than their local one. In their first study they looked at the Chicago Public Schools Choice program (which is an intra-district model as defined previously), and they found little difference in outcomes between those students who opted out of their local high school and those who were left behind.[39] One significant improvement was noted in the likelihood of graduation in those students who attended a career academy. In a later study they found mixed results, in that over the short term, there were no systematic improvements in academic outcomes related to moving students to other "better" schools, but the program may be beneficial because other worthy goals are reached through open enrollment such as better fit between student and school or improved social circumstances.[40]

To look at possible outcomes of a voucher program we must look at Milwaukee who was at the forefront of this movement beginning its parental choice program in 1990. John Witte from the University of Wisconsin at Madison was asked to evaluate the voucher program after 5 years and came to the following conclusions in a series of reports summed up in an article and book.[41] Positive results of the voucher program included an attraction of "very poor, mostly minority families whose children were not doing well in public schools." The program helped to keep several private schools in the city of Milwaukee solvent and provided a real alternative to parents where none had existed before. On the negative side, the public schools lost the more highly educated and active parents, the attrition rates in the choice program and schools approached 30% each year and the achievement scores were no better in the private schools than they were in the public schools the students came from. In another study on choice, Rouse found slightly different results in that those students who attended a private school through the choice program performed better in math, but not reading.[42] She believed that one potential explanation for better student performance is lower pupil to teacher ratio in the private schools vs. the public schools as the major cause of the difference in student performance.

Yet another study found different results when the issue of choice and school productivity was examined. Hoxby asked whether student achievement increased per dollar spent in private schools vs. that in public schools.[43] She found that student achievement did rise in both voucher and charter schools. Furthermore, she found that the aphorism that private schools "cream skim" the best students from the public schools was not true and instead found that the voucher and charter schools disproportionately took those students who were performing poorly in their public schools. Contrary to Witte's findings, Hoxby found that charter school students are 4 to 5 percent more proficient in reading and 2 to 3 percent more proficient in math than their public school counterparts. In a much broader national study she found that some of the states had statistically insignificant differences and she admits that further multi-year studies based on random lotteries among charter school applicants is needed. However, a more recent study performed by Lubienski and Lubienski found that once socioeconomic status was accounted for public schools outperformed private schools in each SES quartile.[44]

Unfortunately these ambiguous results did not deter the Wisconsin legislature from expanding the program beyond the scope of offering those students and their parents who had no real choice to those who have many choices available and the money to pursue them. Witte remarked that if "choice is expanded to private and parochial schools across the state, it will not be poor, inner-city, black, and Hispanic children who will benefit, those for whom the original program was intended to serve, but rather those who had choices all along." Based on 1990 census data, 16% of Wisconsin's students attended private, mostly parochial schools. In Milwaukee, more than 84% of private school students were white, and their average family income was more than $40,000 annually. In contrast, only 33% of public school students were white, and their family income averaged approximately $25,000.[45] Expanding the program into the less needy populations will directly undermine the value of the program to those who can truly benefit, the socio-economically disadvantaged children in the inner city.

The Future of Public Schools and Privatization

The 37th Annual Phi Delta Kappan/Gallup Poll of the Public's Attitudes Toward the Public Schools tells a more positive story about public schools.[46] The number one problem identified in an open-ended questionnaire remains lack of financial support for schools with no other problem coming close and has been the number one problem for 15 straight years of the survey. As to the public's support of public education, 24% assign a high grade to public schools nationwide, however, that number increases to 57% when discussing their own community schools.[47] The number further increases when parents were asked about the school their oldest child attended. When asked to select an option between reform of the current system and some alternative system, the overwhelming preference is in favor of reform.

When specifically asked about allowing parents and student to attend private schools through the use of publicly funded vouchers only 38% of respondents favored that approach which is down from 46% in 2002.[48] The major reason given for supporting private schools via vouchers is a belief that student achievement is higher followed by increased safety and receptivity to religious practices. A little less than 50% supported the concept of charter schools, however, 80% believed they should be held to the same standards of accountability that public schools are held to.[49] Specific questions related to NCLB were asked. While more respondents are knowledgeable about NCLB than ever before it still remains a mystery to 59% of the sample.[50] Of those who know a fair amount to a great deal about NCLB, 57% view it unfavorably while 36% view it favorably.[51]

Specific objections were raised over single tests that determine whether or not schools need improvement, testing only on English and Math, the transferring out option (most parents in schools needing improvement prefer additional service be provided in the child's current school), holding special education students to the same standards as other students, disaggregating sub-group scores and using those to determine progress, and using fixed goals rather than improvement percentages. Furthermore, there is a perception that NCLB would unnecessarily lessen curricular choices to those being tested and away from those considered extracurricular and again parents favor a broader choice of curriculum beyond that being tested.

So what happens next?

Despite his misgivings about a general voucher program, W itte decries those who oppose choice as the death of public education citing a long tradition of private education in the U.S. But has the exodus from public schools toward private schools happened? In 1970 there were approximately 51.3 million students enrolled in K-12 schools. Of those 45.9 million or 83.4% attend public schools. The other 5.4 million or 16.6% attended private schools. In 2000 preliminary data shows approximately 53.4 million students were enrolled in K-12 schools. 47.2 million or 83.4% attended public schools while 6.2 million students or 16.6% attended private schools.[52] The data shows that little movement has occurred in the 30-year period highlighted above so the attraction of private education doesn't seem to have increased despite the rhetoric and support they have received in some areas in the past 25 years since the election of Ronald Reagan.

As one sifts through the evidence of school choice it is difficult because of conflicting evidence to state which policy is better for children in the long run. If the object behind privatization is to provide better educational opportunities to disadvantaged children that are languishing in bad public schools then choice through several mechanisms can and does improve their educational outcomes. If the object is obedience to an ideology of unfettered free markets and unchecked privatization then initiatives like choice will serve as nothing more than a way to shift public funds to private entities without any public oversight. Eventually once the pressure to reduce public support of education increases this could shift the burden of education from the public at-large to those who can least afford it, the parents of school aged children.

What this author really believes is at issue in the privatization push is a desire by parents who currently send their children to private schools to receive public support and funding of that choice. That is why the program was expanded in Wisconsin to include those families who can afford private school tuition. Interestingly, voucher proponents would have a much stronger argument if the program were limited to those on the lower rungs of the socioeconomic ladder because the evidence in Milwaukee has shown some limited positive net effects to student outcomes in that population. As Witte correctly points out the policy debate becomes less of "do vouchers work?" to one of how to broaden the subsidy to everyone.[53] In other words, the stated intention behind vouchers becomes less of improving educational outcomes and more a cause for redistribution of public resources to an ever widening population of less deserving people, for example, those higher on the socioeconomic scale. Once a program reaches that stage of development people stop asking questions about student outcomes and begin asking how do I get mine?

If we as a nation are moving towards a market-based model of education through vouchers what happens to those students who are defined as needing choice to escape what are clearly failing inner city schools? In the limited instances where vouchers have been tried there is evidence, previously described that show in very limited circumstances such as the inner city where schools are having significant difficulties, that choice can be beneficial to both those students who opt to attend private schools and those who are left behind in the public schools. The privatization argument falls apart as the program is broadened to include those students who attend what might be considered "good" public schools. More importantly, a "one-size fits all" program built upon rigid ideology will not fix what ails education.

While the data is far from complete, there appears to be no current evidence that privatization schemes through vouchers sufficiently improve educational outcomes across the population to make it sound educational policy. Unfortunately, privatization proponents remain a significant political lobby and at the present time they have allies in both houses of Congress as well as the Executive and Judicial branches. In short, privatization through vouchers has at its core the objective to remove education from the list of publicly consumed goods. Despite growing evidence that the wholesale privatization of education in the U.S. would fall far short of its claims, it doesn't appear that this movement will weaken or go away anytime soon. In the end policy analysts and the public must always ask *qui bono*? Who really benefits from privatizing education and does the evidence support that change in the specific circumstances being contemplated?

Questions

1) Who funds the privatization effort?
2) What are the aims of the owners of privatized services?
3) Who manages the distribution of out sourced services to public institutions like public education?
4) Who participates in the decision making when choice and voucher agendas are advocated for?
5) Who ultimately benefits from privatization? From vouchers? From Choice?

Notes

1. Morone, J.A. Hellfire Nation: The Politics of Sin in American History. NewHaven, CT, Yale University Press, 2003.
2. Morone, 2003
3. McKenzie, J., "The NCLB Wrecking Ball," *No Child Left.* November, 2003. <http://nochildleft.com/2003/nov03wrecking.html>
4. Rudalevige, A., "Forging a Congressional Compromise," in *No Child Left Behind – The Politics and Practice of School Accountability.* Peterson, P.E., and M.R. West, (eds.) Washington, D.C.: Brookings Institute Press, 2003.
5. Smith, A. An Inquiry in the Nature and Causes of the Wealth of Nations. Chicago: University of Chicago Press, 1976.
6. National Education Association (NEA), "Estimates of School Statistics Database" found in: *Statistical Abstract of the United States: 2004-2005,* Washington, D.C., U.S. Census Bureau, 2004.
7. Filler, L. *Horace Mann on the Crisis in Education.* Ohio: Antioch Press, 1965.
8. Cremin, L.A. The Republic and the School: Horace Mann on the Education of Free Men. New York: Teachers College, 1957.
9. Unger, R.M. Politics: The Central Texts, Theory against Fate. New York: Verso, 1997.
10. Moore, S. "Big Government Finds Enablers among the GOP." *The Cato-Institute.* 2003. <http://www.cato.org/pub_display.php?pub_id=3203>

11. Friedman, M. *Capitalism and Freedom*. Chicago: University of Chicago Press,1962.

12. Hill, P.T., L.C. Pierce, and J.W. Guthrie. *Reinventing Public Education*. Chicago: University of Chicago Press, 1997.

13. Holt, M. *Not Yet "Free At Last,"* Oakland, CA.: ICS Press, 2000.

14. Klein, Naomi. *The Shock Doctrine: The Rise of Disaster Capitalism*. New York: Henry Holt and Company, 2007.

15. Anderson, N., "Bush Proposes Private School Relief Plan," *Washington Post*,A12, September 17, 2005.

16. Friedman, M., "The Promise of Vouchers," *Wall Street Journal*, December 5, 2005.

17. Berlau, J. "Grover Norquist Takes on the Tyranny of Federal Taxation." *Insight Magazine*. 2005.
<http://www.insightmag.com/media/paper441/news/1998/01/26/PictureProfile/Grover.Norquist.Grover.Norquist.Takes.On.The.Tyranny.Of.Federal.Taxation-213841.shtml>

18. "A Nation at Risk." *National Commission on Excellence in Education*. 1983. <http://www.ed.gov/pubs/NatAtRisk/risk.html>

19. "A Nation at Risk." *National Commission on Excellence in Education.*

20. Berlau, J. *Insight Magazine.*

21. Kohn, A., "NCLB and the Effort to Privatize Public Education," in *Many Children Left Behind,* ed. D. Meier, A. Kohn, L. Darling-Hammond, T. R. Sizer, and G. Wood (Boston, Beacon Press, 2004a).

22. For a more engaging discussion on the use of language in policy and culturaldisputes see George Lakoff's book *Don't Think of an Elephant: Know Your Values and Frame The Debate – The Essential Guide for Progressives,* Chelsea Green Publishing, 2004.

23. Bennett, W.J., and Finn, Jr., C.I., "No Standard's Without Freedom," *WallStreet Journal Opinion-Editorial page,* December 23, 2003.

24. Kohn, 2004a

25. Johnson, D.C., and Salle, L.M. "The Goals of those Attacking Public Education, Public Education and Teachers Unions." *Commonweal Institute*. 2004.
<http://www.commonwealinstitute.org/reports/Responding_Ed_Report.pdf>

26. Miner, B. "Why the Right Hates Public Education." *The Progressive*. 2004.
<http://progressive.org/?q=node/920&PHPSESSID=7229fb843649cad--e65152ee9da22df>

27. Bast, J. and R. Wittmann. "A Marketing Plan for Education Choice." *Heartland Institute*. 1991. http://www.heartland.org/Article.cfm?artId=10211

28. Enlow, R.C. "Grading Vouchers –Ranking America's School Choice Programs." *School Choice Issues in Depth,* Vol. 2, Issue 1, 2004. Indianapolis: Milton and Rose D. Friedman Foundation.

29. Witte, J.F. The Market Approach To Education – An Analysis of America's ghghgFirst Voucher Program, Princeton, NJ, Princeton University Press: 2000.

30. Gray, J. Enlightenment's Wake: Politics and Culture at the Close of the Modern Age, London: Routledge, 1995.

31. Weil, D. *School Vouchers and Privatization*. Santa Barbara, ABC-CLIO, 2002.

32. *Kurtzman v. Lemon,* 403 US 602, (1971) and 411 US 192, (1973).

33. *Zelman v. Simmons-Harris,* 536 US 639, (2002).

34. *Brown v. Board of Education,* 347 US 483, (1954).

35. Holt, M. *Not Yet "Free At Last."* Oakland, CA.: ICS Press, 2000.

36. Cookson, P.W. School Choice: The Struggle for the Soul of American Education. New Haven, CT.: Yale University Press, 1994.

37. Elmore, R., B. Fuller, and G. Orfield. "Empirical Research on Education Choice: What Are the Implications for Policy Makers?" in *Who Chooses? Who Loses?* (New York: Teachers College Press, 1996).

38. Pryzbyla, D. "NCLB Path to Privatization of Democracy." *Education News.*2004. <http://www.educationnews.org/nclb-path-to-privatization-of.htm>

39. Cullen, J.B., B.A. Jacob, and S.D. Levitt, "The Impact of School Choice on Student Outcomes: An Analysis of the Chicago Public Schools." *National Bureau for Economic Research (NBER)*
(working paper, 7888, 2000). <http://www.nber.org/papers/w7888>

40. Cullen, J.B., B.A. Jacob, and S.D. Levitt, "The Effects of School Choice onStudent Outcomes: Evidence from Randomized Lotteries." *National Bureau for Economic Research (NBER)*
(working paper, 10113, 2003). <http://www.nber.org/papers/w10113>

41. Witte, J.F. "The Milwaukee Voucher Experiment – The Good, the Bad and the Ugly." *Phi Delta Kappan.* (September, 1999).

42. Rouse, C.E. "Schools and Student Achievement: More Evidence from the Milwaukee Choice Program." FRBNY *Economic Policy Review.* (March, 1998) <http://www.newyorkfed.org/research/epr/98v04n1/9803rous.pdf>

43. Hoxby, C.M. "School Choice and School Competition: Evidence from theUnited States." *Swedish Economic Policy Review,* 10:9-65, 2003. <http://www.ekradet.konj.se/sepr/>

44. Lubienski, S.T. and C. Lubienski, "A New Look at Public and Private Schools: Student Background and Mathematics Achievement," *Phi Delta Kappan.* (May, 2005). <http://pdkintl.org/kappan/k_v86/k0505lub.htm>

45. Witte, J.F., and Thorn, C., "Private and Public Education" in Wisconsin, Madison, Robert M. La Follette Institute of Public Affairs, University of Wisconsin Issue Paper, Table 6, 1995.

46. Rose, L.C., and A.M. Gallup. "The 37th Annual Phi Delta Kappa/Gallup Poll ofthe Public's Attitudes toward the Public Schools." *Phi Delta Kappan.* (September, 2005) <http://www.pdkintl.org/kappan/k0509pol.pdf>

47. Rose, 2005

48. Rose, 2005

49. Rose, 2005

50. Rose, 2005

51. Rose, 2005

52. U.S. National Center for Education Statistics, "Digest of Education Statistics,"found in *Statistical Abstract of the United States: 2004-2005,* Washington, D.C.: U.S. Census Bureau.

53. Witte, J.F. *The Market Approach To Education – An Analysis of America's First Voucher Program.* Princeton, NJ.: Princeton University Press, 2000.

References

"A Nation at Risk." *National Commission on Excellence in Education.* 1983. http://www.ed.gov/pubs/NatAtRisk/risk.html

Anderson, N., "Bush Proposes Private School Relief Plan," *Washington Post,* A12,September 17, 2005.

Bast, J. and R. Wittmann. "A Marketing Plan for Education Choice." *Heartland Institute.* 1991. http://www.heartland.org/Article.cfm?artId=10211

Bennett, W.J., and C.I. Finn, Jr., "No Standard's Without Freedom," *Wall Street Journal Opinion-Editorial page,* December 23, 2003.

Berlau, J. "Grover Norquist Takes on the Tyranny of Federal Taxation." *Insight Magazine.*2005. http://www.insightmag.com/media/paper441/news/1998/01/26/PictureProfile/Grover.Norquist.Grover.Norquist.Takes.On.The.Tyranny.Of.Federal.Taxation-213841.shtml

Brown v. Board of Education, 347 US 483 (1954).

Cookson, P.W. *School Choice: The Struggle for the Soul of American Education.* New Haven, CT.: Yale University Press, 1994.

Cremin, L.A. *The Republic and the School: Horace Mann on the Education of Free Men.* New York: Teachers College, 1957.

Cullen, J.B., B.A. Jacob, and S.D. Levitt, "The Impact of School Choice on Student Outcomes: An Analysis of the Chicago Public Schools." *National Bureau for Economic Research (NBER)* (working paper, 7888, 2000). http://www.nber.org/papers/w7888

Cullen, J.B., B.A. Jacob, and S.D. Levitt, "The Effects of School Choice on Student Outcomes: Evidence from Randomized Lotteries." *National Bureau for Economic Research (NBER)* (working paper, 10113, 2003). http://www.nber.org/papers/w10113

Elmore, R., B. Fuller, and G. Orfield. "Empirical Research on Educational Choice: What Are the Implications for Policy Makers?" In *Who Chooses? Who Loses?* New York: Teachers College Press, 1996.

Enlow, R.C. "Grading Vouchers –Ranking America's School Choice Programs," *School Choice Issues in Depth,* Vol. 2, Issue 1, 2004. Indianapolis: Milton and Rose D. Friedman Foundation.

Filler, L. *Horace Mann on the Crisis in Education.* Ohio: Antioch Press, 1965.

Friedman, M. *Capitalism and Freedom.* Chicago: University of Chicago Press, 1962.

Friedman, M., "The Promise of Vouchers," *Wall Street Journal,* December 5, 2005.

Goodman, A. "No Child Left Behind: A Debate on the Privatization of Education." *Democracy Now.* 2004 .http:// www .democracynow .org /article .pl ? sid = 04 /03 /12 / 1534250

Gray, J., *Enlightenment's Wake: Politics and Culture at the Close of the Modern Age.* London: Routledge, 1995.

Hill, P.T., L.C. Pierce, and J.W. Guthrie. *Reinventing Public Education.* Chicago: University of Chicago Press, 1997.

Holt, M. *Not Yet "Free At Last."* Oakland, CA.: ICS Press, 2000.

Hoxby, C.M. "School Choice and School Competition: Evidence from the UnitedStates." *Swedish Economic Policy Review,* 10:9-65, 2003. http://www.ekradet.konj.se/sepr/

Johnson, D.C., and Salle, L.M. "The Goals of those Attacking Public Education, Public Education and Teachers Unions." *Commonweal Institute.* 2004. http://www.commonwealinstitute.org/reports/Responding_Ed_Report.pdf

Klein, Naomi. *The Shock Doctrine: The Rise of Disaster Capitalism.* New York: Henry Holt and Company, 2007.

Kohn, A., "NCLB and the Effort to Privatize Public Education." In *Many Children Left Behind,* edited by D. Meier, A. Kohn, L. Darling-Hammond, T. R. Sizer, and G. Wood. Boston, Beacon Press, 2004a.

Kohn, A., "Test Today, Privatize Tomorrow," *Phi Delta Kappan,* (2004b).

Kurtzman v. Lemon, 403 US 602 (1971) and 411 US 192 (1973).

Lubienski, S.T. and C. Lubienski, "A New Look at Public and Private Schools: Student Background and Mathematics Achievement," *Phi Delta Kappan.* (May, 2005). http://pdkintl.org/kappan/k_v86/k0505lub.htm

McKenzie, J., "The NCLB Wrecking Ball," *No Child Left.* November, 2003.http://nochildleft.com/2003/nov03wrecking.html

Miner, B. "Why the Right Hates Public Education." *The Progressive.* 2004.http://progressive.org/?q=node/920&PHPSESSID=7229fb843649cad--e65152ee9da22df

Moore, S. "Big Government Finds Enablers among the GOP." *The Cato Institute.* 2003. http://www.cato.org/pub_display.php?pub_id=3203

Morone, J.A. *Hellfire Nation: The Politics of Sin in American History.* New Haven, CT, Yale University Press, 2003.

National Education Association (NEA), "Estimates of School Statistics Database" found in: *Statistical Abstract of the United States: 2004-2005,* Washington, D.C., U.S. Census Bureau, 2004.

Niskanen, W.A. "The End of Small Government?" *Cato Institute.* 2005.http://www.cato.org/pub_display.php?pub_id=4881

Pryzbyla, D. "NCLB Path to Privatization of Democracy." *Education News.* 2004. http://www.educationnews.org/nclb-path-to-privatization-of.htm

Rose, L.C., and A.M. Gallup. "The 37th Annual Phi Delta Kappa/Gallup Poll of the Public's Attitudes toward the Public Schools." *Phi Delta Kappan.* (September, 2005) http://www.pdkintl.org/kappan/k0509pol.pdf

Rouse, C.E. "Schools and Student Achievement: More Evidence from the Milwaukee Choice Program." FRBNY *Economic Policy Review.* (March, 1998) http://www.newyorkfed.org/research/epr/98v04n1/9803rous.pdf

Rudalevige, A., "Forging a Congressional Compromise," In *No Child Left Behind – The Politics and Practice of School Accountability,* edited by P.E. Peterson, and M.R. West. Washington, D.C.: Brookings Institute Press, 2003.

Smith, A. *An Inquiry in the Nature and Causes of the Wealth of Nations.* Chicago: University of Chicago Press, 1976.

Unger, R.M. *Politics: The Central Texts, Theory against Fate.* New York, Verso, 1997.

U.S. National Center for Education Statistics, "Digest of Education Statistics," found in *Statistical Abstract of the United States: 2004-2005,* Washington, D.C.: U.S. Census Bureau.

Weil, D. *School Vouchers and Privatization.* Santa Barbara: ABC-CLIO, 2002.

Witte, J.F., and Thorn, C., "Private and Public Education" in *Wisconsin, Madison, Robert M. La Follette Institute of Public Affairs, University of Wisconsin Issue Paper, Table 6,* 1995.

Witte, J.F. "The Milwaukee Voucher Experiment – The Good, the Bad and the Ugly." *Phi Delta Kappan.* (September, 1999).

Witte, J.F. *The Market Approach To Education – An Analysis of America's First Voucher Program.* Princeton, NJ: Princeton University Press, 2000.

Zelman v. Simmons-Harris, 536 US 639, (2002).

Chapter 9 Hawaii, The Fiftieth State: A Case Study of the Plantation Blues

Nancy Stone

Introduction

The Fiftieth State of the Union is in fact the Fiftieth State in Education. Is it the beautiful beaches and intoxicating rainforests that distract its students from the academic rigor that scholars of today's world need in order to compete? Or perhaps there are other factors beyond the two thousand miles of ocean that separate Hawaiian schools from the mainland?

Prior to the onset of government funded and directed public education, Hawaiians while under the authority of the missionaries were once considered the most literate people in the world.[1] S o what happened to push this state and these people into the tailspin that has sunk them to the bottom? This chapter will examine the structure, the history, the funding, the demographics, the policy practices and the politics that have driven this downward movement.

One might first look at the structure of Hawaii's education system. Unlike the rest of the country, Hawaii has a single school system. It is a state run system of education with a single Board of Education. Members spend upwards of $60,000 to buy themselves a seat on the board. This type of spending cannot be assumed by public school educators or parents of public school children, thus making these positions only attainable to the politically motivated and financially solvent. Furthermore, it is legislated that no public school teacher is allowed to serve on the board. So, the question one might ask is, "What is in it for them?" Why would a board member invest this amount of time and money to sit on a board in a non-paying position that apparently has no familial attachment?

History

A look into the history of public education in Hawaii is a blueprint of how racial discrimination can be used to control the less powerful in society. Missionaries first established education in Hawaii. Their objective was to bring Christianity to the natives. In order for the missionaries to achieve their goals they needed to erase the language barrier. They translated the Hawaiian language into written form and reduced the Hawaiian way of life both religiously and culturally.[2]

In the 1830's, an elite group of land owning Caucasians seeking to protect their property rights, established a western system of government, proclaimed a Constitution and authorized an elected House of Representatives. Centralization of the government's role in education began in 1840 with the "General School Laws."[3] By then it was established that this elite group were firmly in control of the government both economically and politically. Hawaii was established as a Caucasian controlled sugar empire. The second legislature included a limiting provision stating that no public office could be held by any man unable to read or write. Reading and writing also became a prerequisite for marriage, thus forcing western education upon the Hawaiian people.

The need for plantation workers promoted the "Master and Servants Act of 1852" and established a two-class society.[4] T his was followed by a huge influx of contracted laborers from China, the Philippines and Japan. Following the annexation of the Hawaiian Islands in 1898, the territorial governor Sanford B. Dole, placed all tax money from the counties into a centralized general treasury thereby establishing a single funding source for all schools. In 1910, Hawaii was richer than the rest of the American Union in annual per capita production of wealth, yet spending on education was a mere $2.07 per capita compared to the mainland average of $3.66. This disparity in spending on public education reinforced Hawaii as a two-class system, the elite ruling Caucasian class that represented about five percent of the population and the poor non-Caucasian class.

The non-Caucasian population was growing and resentments towards whites for stealing the land were the accepted social arrangement. Payment of teacher wages was at times trivial. Teachers were compensated with goats and soap and offered land in exchange for teaching. Preference was given to local teachers and many had only an elementary level of education.[5] T his substandard type of education served the controlling elite who educated their children in private schools and maintained the status quo.

As Japanese and Chinese immigrants received Americanized education, they also saw a chance to rise to a controlling power in this state. While Hawaiians were struggling to hold together after the fall of the monarchy, the Chinese seized an opportunity to take on the position of educating the islanders. The Japanese who aggressively sought power, however, soon replaced the Chinese dominance.

In fact, today the legislature reflects a different racial makeup compared to the population. Most of the state legislature is of Japanese ancestry. The

Department of Education's racial profile compliments the legislative profile.

The ethnic Japanese dominance in the Department of Education is apparent according to the Department of Education's EEO5 Report from December 2003 (see Figure 1. 2003 EE05 Percentage of Japanese Personnel for the State of Hawaii Department of Education).

These figures are skewed when compared to the overall Japanese population of the state which according to the 2000 Census is less than 17% of the population.

Hence, a new elite class is in control of the many.

Teachers	Principals	Board of Education Staff	Superintendent Office
35%	47%	100%	81%
Budget Branch	Classified Personnel Management	Civil Rights Compliance Office	Administrative Services
78%	65%	75%	85%

Figure 1. 2003 EEO5 Percentage of Japanese Personnel for the State of Hawaii Department of Education

Funding

Funding for Hawaii schools is still controlled by the Hawaii State Government. Whereas other districts in the country gain funding through a property tax base, the funding in Hawaii comes directly from and represents about 1/3 of the state's budget. In response to the public outcry about classrooms being under funded, the legislature passed ACT 51 in 2004, in which funds to schools would be distributed under a student weighted formula and require 70% of the funds sent directly down to the school level. However the oversight on this Act falls quite short in its implementation. In fact less than half of the 70% actually gets to the schools. Aside from all of the contracts that the D.O.E. hands out there are 278 categorical funds that get paid before the money actually gets to the schools. These funds help support various state and district level programs that many times are designed to employ friends and relatives in non-teaching positions and result in added work for teachers. Although over the last 40 years the number of public school teachers has remained constant, the middle and upper management positions have increased over 600%. This bureaucratic top heavy system of management has created a fiscal tape worm and drained the education system of desperately needed funds.

Hawaii's claim to greater equity in educational spending by eliminating the property tax, a disparity that is envisaged throughout the country, falls short in its promise. A closer examination of Hawaii schools will indeed tell the truth. Whereas, some of Hawaii's newer schools can boast of air-conditioned classrooms, computers for every student and multiple teachers to a class, most of the students in Hawaii see an entirely different reality. Aside from the year round tropical heat, most of the classrooms are lucky to get workable fans. Many classrooms, especially special education classrooms, which are usually designed as portable dwellings or converted storage spaces, don't have telephone access. In many of the schools, books are far outdated or not even available. The backlog of classrooms in need of repair has been answered with political preference by legislators who cater to special groups. As it was in 1910 it holds true today that Hawaii's student spending per capita is fiftieth in the nation. This pattern of meager spending on education in Hawaii for more than 100 years continues to divide this state and its people into a two-class system.

A closer look at a few schools might best clarify the inequity in Hawaii's schools (see Figure 2. School Demographics according to Socio-Economic Status).

The first school selected is Niu Valley Middle School located in an upper-class neighborhood on the South shore of Oahu. Niu Valley's NCLB status for school year 2004/2005 is in good standing with 65% of the students proficient in reading and 48% proficient in Math. The demographics of the school reflect that 99% are classified as Asian/Pacific Islander. Niu Valley is distinctly Japanese in staff as well as student body creating a homogeneous population and has no disabled, disadvantaged, limited English or any other racial sub-group.

The second school selected is Waipahu High School approximately 16 miles Northwest of Niu Valley on the leeward (Western) side of the island. Waipahu High School has a student population of about 2300 students of which approximately 300 are in special education. In addition to the large special education population, Waipahu High School has large sub-groups in disadvantaged students and students limited in English. Just like Niu Valley Middle School, Waipahu High School has only one racial group, which is Asian/Pacific Islander. Unlike Niu Valley, most of the students are Filipino, Hawaiian or Samoan. Waipahu was home for many years to the sugar mill and the residents of Waipahu are descendants of the pineapple and sugar plantation workers. Waipahu High School like many other schools in the poor areas of Hawaii struggle with crumbling sub standard facilities, inadequate wiring and a lack of books, resources, security and hope. Waipahu High School did not meet the AYP and its NCLB status for school year 2005/2006 is in "Constructive Action." Waipahu High School's overall proficiency in reading was 38% and the overall proficiency in math was 12%. When asked to comment on the NCLB results, a former Waipahu High School teacher, Britt Cormier said that she wasn't a bit surprised. She believes that the dominant Japanese administrators and their nepotistic practices of hiring unqualified and unprofessional staff to blindly follow their authoritarian master slave tactics towards the students perpetuate the plantation hierarchy. She stated that it is not an environment of learning, but rather training ground for students to acknowledge who is in charge. Another former Waipahu High School behavioral specialist described it as *Plantation Blues.*

Demographics

The next issue of significance to Hawaii schools is the demographics.

School Demographics	Pacific Islander	Proficient in Reading	Proficient in Math
Niu Valley Middle School	99%	56%	51%
Waipahu High School	99%	38%	12%

Figure 2. School Demographics according to Socio-Economic Status

The isolation of these islands from the rest of the country, the natural barriers that divide it, the melting pot of cultures and races as well as the prominent military presence creates a unique population in Hawaii's schools making it a minority-majority state (Figure 3. The United States Census 2000 Summary for the State of Hawaii).

In addition to the racial makeup of the state, the preliminary figures from the Federal Survey reflect that 14,700 of the almost 180,000 public school students in 2004 are military dependents. Although the military population by number is fairly consistent the actual population is frequently rotated with deployments. Although many of the military dependents are educated in schools on bases or within military housing at the elementary level, they are submerging into the culture at the middle school level.

Racial and cultural indifferences add to the fear that comes from moving to a new school. For as long as people in this state can remember, "Kill Haole Day" (Haole: Hawaiian slang for white people) has existed in the Hawaii public schools and persists still today. It is the last day of school and often white students stay home to avoid confrontations. As recent as November 21, 2007, a twelve year old white girl had her head smashed into a concrete wall after racial slurs about her being a Haole were verbally exchanged.[6]

Discrimination in not exclusive to Caucasians, but is utilized by which ever group is in power. Unfortunately in Hawaii, discrimination runs the education system and problems that result from nepotistic hiring perpetuate these unlawful practices and prevent highly qualified educators from advancing in the system if they are not part of the racially elite.

Policies, practices, and politics

The Organic Act of 1900 designed to Americanize the population in Hawaii was ill received by the people.[7] The overthrow of the Hawaiian Kingdom for the capitalistic gains of the few has left deep wounds among islanders that persist today. Along with the Asian population who desire to maintain their own

RACE	Totals	%
One race	**952,194**	**78.6**
Two or more races	**259,343**	**21.4**
By category	**1211537**	**100%**
White	294,102	24.3
Black or African American	22,003	1.8
American Indian and Alaska Native	3,535	0.3
Asian	503,868	41.6
Asian Indian	1,441	0.1
Chinese	56,600	4.7
Filipino	170,635	14.1
Japanese	201,764	16.7
Korean	23,537	1.9
Vietnamese	7,867	0.6
Other Asian	42,024	3.5
Native Hawaiian and Other Pacific Islander	113,539	9.4
Native Hawaiian	80,137	6.6
Guamanian or Chamorro	1,663	0.1
Samoan	16,166	1.3
Other Pacific Islander	15,573	1.3
Other race	15,147	1.3

Figure 3. The United States Census 2000 Summary for the State of Hawaii

culture in this country, Hawaiians are at war with themselves. To quote Q. Britt Cormier, a long time educator from Hawaii, "If we can't even live peacefully together, what makes our government think we can possibly test alike?"[8]

NCLB in Hawaii

The number of schools meeting Adequate Yearly Progress increased from 39% to 53% between 2003 and 2004. Although this appears to be positive for Hawaii schools, according to the performance outcomes from the 2004 Superintendents Reports, Hawaii schools being sanctioned under NCLB rose from 30% in 2004 to 49% in 2005.[9] Hawaii's national tests scores are consistently ranked lowest/last in the nation.

According to the Harvard Civil Rights Project, the disparities in NCLB's Adequate Yearly Progress (AYP) mechanism for identifying districts for improvement will have a disparate impact on Hawaii's public schools.[10] Hawaii's school district is considerably larger than others and certainly more diverse. Hawaii schools have repeatedly scored far below the national norms, which will require these schools to make greater gains than the higher performing districts. The report also indicates the negative impact NCLB has on low income and special education. Hawaii's schools reflect that 52% of the student population falls under the category for special needs.[11]

In Hawaii, we can certainly see a different picture regarding the subgroups. The impact of the dominant racial presence of the Japanese can be seen in the Native Hawaiian Educational Assessments from 1983 until present. In all areas and at all grade levels, the Japanese outperform all other groups including whites. Although social economics do have a big impact on the NCLB sub grouping, the racial makeup of the educators also appears to have a significant impact on the subgroups in Hawaii as well. This racial profile of educators and administrators is a variable not considered in the Harvard Civil Rights Report.

In response to the failure rates that are increasingly evident, the Board of Education in Hawaii has decided to close the gap by lowering the standards. They are currently cutting the benchmarks and rewriting the instrument used to measure proficiency in order to create the illusion of progress.

If a school is failing under NCLB in Hawaii they are either taken over by the area superintendent or choose one of three mainland curriculum initiatives to implement. The concept of the state taking over the failing state run schools is a paradox that is so typical in Hawaii. Allowing outside mainland-initiated programs to strengthen and restructure failing schools is a clash of cultures.

For example, if a school is set for restructuring they may chose a curriculum like "America's Choice" to assist in bring up the student's scores.[12] M uch needed funds are spent on purchasing these programs and teachers are brought in from the mainland to provide specific teacher training in their methods. Often these programs are underfunded and teachers sacrifice great teaching methods to follow specific guidelines. The implementation of these programs along with aligning the curriculum to the standards and mapping which standards are taught when, the test becomes a fulltime planning nightmare for teachers. Aside from the fact that the curriculum is culturally irrelevant in Hawaii, it comes with the added resistance that it is both mainland and Haole. Schools are required to test students every two weeks in constructed responses as well as provide quarterly assessments in preparation for the Hawaii State Assessment test in the spring that will determine the AYP. Focus is then placed on students who are close to being proficient in order to raise the scores.

Schools have been systematically cutting out sports and the arts to find the funding and using these teacher positions to increase help in math and reading. So, unless dramatic changes are made to Hawaii's failing education system the punitive actions under NCLB will heighten the problem of the plantation blues.

The decline in licensed teachers in Hawaii along with the increase in drop-outs is all a reflection of the brutal conditions being pushed into Hawaii's schools. The change in focus from learning to testing is a drag on professional educators who want no part of the systematic decline in superior teaching methods and replaced by programs such as direct instruction that lower the educational experience to behavioral training in the classrooms where teachers are forced to snap their fingers in students faces and socially humiliate students by sending them backwards to lower achieving groups when they fail to keep up with their classmates.

School Administration

Up until the spring of 2006, the State of Hawaii's Revised Statutes, Section 302A-605 required all principals and vice-principals to meet certification requirements of the Department of Education in the State of Hawaii. The certification requirement limited the department's ability to actively recruit qualified educational administrators from other public or private schools throughout the nation. Part of the qualifications for Hawaii's administrators is the mentoring process by which a principal will partner with a vice principal. This selection process limits teachers who may not be connected yet are highly qualified. The impact of this law is that only the handpicked few in the state will ever reach positions of authority. This same process for selecting personnel officers is again a limited pool of applicants entirely from within the school system. This system is designed to keep specific groups in power and determine the educational interest of the entire population. For this reason, the Japanese have controlled the education of Hawaii's students for over fifty years.

Hawaii has a long history of school superintendents and ministers of public instruction, each taking hold to ensure some new political agenda. Those who have tried to decentralize the control of the education system have been either removed or forced to resign.

The current acting Superintendent of Schools, Patricia Hamamoto came into office on the tailwinds of a sex scandal that resulted in the resignation of her predecessor Dr. Paul LeMahieu (Kua, Crystal).[13] Prior to Dr. LeMahieu's appointment, Hawaii Schools were placed under a court mandate called the Felix Consent Decree. The mandate was a result of the system not providing services to the students with special needs. During his term in the late 90's, Dr.

LeMahieu established standards based education in Hawaii. This is significant in the context that educational reform comes slow to the islands and is historically met with resistance and retaliation.

Patricia Hamamoto who was Dr. LeMahieu's Assistant Superintendent, recently re-contracted to her position as superintendent without question, even though Hawaii schools continue to fail. Her lack of qualifications to even meet the school code as a school administrator with her mere bachelor's degree that took her seven years to achieve was rewarded by the board and was compensated by doubling the previous superintendent's salary. Ms. Hamamoto's dedication to education was not as easily apparent after her extended schooling, since she worked for several years as a tour guide and hostess in Hawaii.[14] I f all this seems sinister, then you merely need to reflect upon the system's design to accept her placement as evidence of local control and favoritism.

Highly Qualified Teachers

Teaching positions are not advertised in the state of Hawaii. When positions become available, it is the District Superintendent's job to place unassigned teachers. Although the school code outlines priority in placement, these positions are filled at the whim of the personnel officers and principals who are not held accountable. Simply stated, if a personnel officer claims that there are no positions available for a specific teacher, neither the teacher nor the teachers union have access to the truth in this statement. This power structure, which was legislated in the State of Hawaii, has full control over who teaches in the state.

According to State of Hawaii "Teacher Employment Report 2003-2004," from 1999 to 2004 the department averaged 1,481 newly hired teachers each year.[15] O f the 1,657 newly hired teachers for the 2003-2004 school year, 1,156 were emergency hires.[16] This staggering figure of emergency hires included teachers who have not completed their praxis examination and or have not ever completed a teacher education program. These non-qualified teachers represent more than 10% of the 11,248 teachers in the state for that year. This number however does not include the number of unqualified emergency hires from the previous years that still hold these teaching positions in the state. According to the Honolulu Advertiser Jan. 25, 2008 issue, a D.O.E. contracted Oregon-based School Synergy says 22 percent or 2900 of Hawaii's public school teachers do not qualify under the No Child Left Behind law. According to the Superintendents Report for 2003-2004, only 84% of the teachers in Hawaii are licensed.[17]

The method of nepotistic hiring in Hawaii is the accepted social norm that the people have come to accept as part of being local. This sentiment is reflected in the fact that Hawaii has no licensing reciprocity with any other state. As such, teachers who come to Hawaii need to pay for retesting and take additional praxis exams that they would not have to take elsewhere.

Recruitment of new qualified teachers has been an increasing concern for the State of Hawaii since many baby boomers are retiring and the number of students entering into the education field has been diminishing. Although in recent years, recruiters have gone outside the state to satisfy a federal mandate for qualified special education teachers, preference is still given to local teachers. Many of these mainland transplants generally fulfill their contracts and head back home. The transition of moving so far, the cost of living, lack of understanding by administrators and staff regarding federal law in special education as well as the cultural barriers that exist in Hawaii are some of the reasons these mainland transplants do not renew contracts. These highly qualified educators are in fact a threat to the elite authority that gain and maintain their positions through nepotistic hiring. The Japanese who now control the government and education system perpetuate these feelings and often utilize their positions to discriminate. Mainlanders who are confronted with this racial atmosphere are often confused by the rejection of the local population and return to their mainland homes.

A current strategy for teacher recruitment is to tap into the military resource of personnel since Hawaii is home to the United States Pacific Command (CINCPAC). This however is a temporary fix since these new teachers are residing in Hawaii at the whim of the military. In addition, their temporary status provides no threat to the ruling elite.

In addition to recruitment problems, Hawaii is now facing problems of losing long time teachers who are buckling under the new pressures. Administrators are now required to make weekly walkthroughs in the classrooms where they evaluate everything from standards being posted on the board to questioning students about what standard they are working on. Requirements such as current student work on display and student participation at the time of the observations become part of the teacher's evaluation. Academic rigor is the only focus and there is no time for teaching moments or even smiling.

Recently, the Department of Education placed random drug testing on the ballot for teacher raises, thus holding their well deserved increases hostage to trading in their right to privacy. As a result of all the new mandated requirements teachers are simply throwing in the chalk.

Conclusion

The establishment of legislated education in Hawaii has had devastating effects on the people in this state. Teachers are limited and voiceless, parents have little choice except for private schools and home-schooling, and the students have historically been left behind. There is no vehicle for change since the legislature controls the school system and they are protected under states rights, which are supported by our federal government.

Like other districts, Hawaii's bureaucrats can juggle the numbers, regroup the students, lower the standards and even extend out the school year, but eventually they will fail. The idea that an even larger bureaucracy, the federal government will ultimately control the education system is an even greater threat. When the education of our children is decided and mandated by the powerful few our freedoms of what we learn and how we learn will be lost. This frightening scenario is a reality in Hawaii and if we don't learn from their mistakes, all the teachers, parents and students dependent on public education will be left behind.

Recently when I informed my students that they were getting another test, two girls approached me and said, "We want to be left behind!" Children still want to be children, and not lab rats and teachers want to teach without their hands tied. According to a longtime Hawaii educator Charles Manning, "Basically NCLB looks like and feels like a case of the emperor's new clothes. "The narrow-mindedness which the act reflects is truly an example of regression of our educational system. The effects are the loss of quality learning, learning reduced to teaching the test, diminished course offerings, and over testing the students."

Administrators who were asked to provide their input on the topic have declined to comment out of anger, fear and exhaustion. We are a warring country and the federal government has declared war on education, which is the last guard to protect our democracy. Children will be stripped of the opportunity to learn higher level thinking skills by the forced programs through rote methods and memorization in efforts to pass a test. Higher level thinking skills will be available only to the well off who can afford private schools. Their catchy slogan "No Child Left Behind" was indeed the same idea within the Organic Act of 1900. The islanders weren't left behind; they were simply sent to the back of the canoe.

According to Plato, the moral training of citizens is insurance to a democratic society.[18] An immoral system of education will undoubtedly become its downfall. Teachers (those who diffuse knowledge) have historically been held to a higher standard of morality for the insurance of a moral society. Politicians however have no prerequisites other than their age, residence and citizenship. They are not tested for competency to hold their positions and they assume no responsibility for the moral training of citizens.

The informal education we are receiving in this country is that teachers are responsible for an unjust society. If our country's leaders show disrespect to teachers, the public will be socialized to agree. If a parent disrespects teachers their children will see no need to respect them either, thereby, rendering educators impotent in their function. Teachers today are better trained and qualified than in any other time in our history, how unfortunate our leaders are not.

The world needs to remember how the Nazi Party used the education system to teach people to hate a particular group. Political mind control is a threat to a moral society. If "Knowledge is Power" then controlling knowledge is true power. Albert Einstein said, "Imagination was more important than knowledge." So try to imagine: what would life on Hawaii be like if the early elites had been more accepting of differences in others? When the missionaries first came to Hawaii, they found a peaceful people living harmoniously side by side. If they had taken the time to learn from the Hawaiians about their values such as Aloha (love), Kupono (honesty), Ho'ihi (respect) and Lokomaikai (generosity) . . . then perhaps paradise might still exist on earth.

Chapter Question

In 2004, Hawaii Governor Linda Lingle proposed to the legislature to break apart the existing Department of Education into separate districts. Her efforts were defeated in congress. Governor Lingle then attempted to change the system through a referendum. The public who was educated by the legislature also defeated this. This absolute control of public education by the legislature in Hawaii can only be changed through the legislative process. Public educators in this country are protected under the "Academic Freedom" clause to maintain a democratic society. With the deadline of 2014 for all schools to maintain 100% proficiency under NCLB, the chance that any public school will prevail is virtually unachievable. When the destruction of public schools is achieved what protections will ensure a democratic society in the future?

Notes

1. See Gavan Daws, *Shoal of Time: A History of the Hawaiian Islands*. (New York: The MacMillan Company, 1968).

2. Daws, 1968.

3. Daws, 1968.

4. Daws, 1968.

5. See Cecil K. Dotts and Mildred Sikkema, *Challenging the Status Quo: Public Education in Hawaii, 1840-1980*. (Honolulu: Hawaii Educ. Assoc., 1994).

6. See *Hawaii Tribune Herald*, "School Violence Sparks Alarm," 11/21/07.

7. Dotts, 1994.

8. See Britt Cormier, interview by author, Aiea Hawaii, October, 2005.

9. See "Superintendent's Report" 2003-04, Hawaii State Department of Education.

10. See Christopher A. Tracey, Gail L. Sunderman, Gary Orfield, "Changing NCLB District Accountability Standards: Implications for Racial Inequity," *Harvard Civil Rights Project, Harvard University*, June 2005.

11. See Tracey, Sunderman, & Orfield, June 2005.

12. See *America's Choice Ramp Up to Literacy I Teacher Edition*, (NCEE, America's Choice 2005, Washington, D.C. 2005).

13. See Crystal Kua, "LeMahieu quits: The Board of Education accepts the resignation effective immediately," (*Honolulu Star Bulletin*, October 19, 2001).

14. "Superintendent Pat Hamamoto's Resume," Hawaii State Department of Education, 2003. <www.doe.k12.hi.us>

15. "Teacher Employment Report 2003-2004," Hawaii State Department of Education, <www.doe.k12.hi.us>

16. "Teacher Employment Report 2003-2004," Hawaii State Department of Education, <www.doe.k12.hi.us>

17. "Superintendent's Report" 2003-04, Hawaii State Department of Education.

18. *Vintage Classics*, "The Republic by Plato," (New York: Random House, 1991).

References

Cormier, Britt, interview by author, Aiea Hawaii, October, 2005.

Daws, Gavan. *Shoal of Time: A History of the Hawaiian Islands.* New York: The MacMillan Company, 1968.

Dotts, Cecil K. and Sikkema, Mildred. *Challenging the Status Quo: Public Education in Hawaii, 1840-1980.* Honolulu: Hawaii Educ. Assoc., 1994.

EEO5 Report, Hawaii State Department of Education, Honolulu, HI: 2002, <www.doe.k12.hi.us>

Hawaii Public Schools List School Year 2003-04 Adequate Yearly Progress (AYP) Results and Corresponding School Year 2004-05 Accountability Status. Hawaii State Department of Education, Honolulu, HI: November 2, 2004, <www.doe.k12.hi.us>

Hawaii State Teacher's Association, Honolulu, Hawaii: *2004, <www.hsta.org>*

Hawaii Tribune Herald, "School Violence Sparks Alarm," 11/21/07.

Hurley, Timothy and Trina Shapiro, "BOE may lower bar to pass No Child tests," *Honolulu Advertiser,* August 5, 2005.

Kanaiaupuni, Shawn Malia Ph.D. and Koren Ishibashi, M.P.P., "Left Behind? The status of Hawaiian Students in Hawaii Public Schools," *PASE Report 02-03:13,* Kamehameha Schools, June 2003.

Kua, Crystal, "LeMahieu quits: The Board of Education accepts the resignation effective immediately," *Honolulu Star Bulletin,* October 19, 2001.

Manning, Charles, interview by author, January 2008, Pahoa, Hawaii.

NCEE. *America's Choice Ramp Up to Literacy I teacher edition.* Washington, .C.: America's Choice 2005.

Niu Valley Middle School, *NCLB School Report SY 2004-05 Native Hawaiian Educational Assessments,* Kamehameha Schools Publishing, 2005.

"No Child Left Behind" State Education Report, School Year 2003-04, Hawaii State Department of Education, Honolulu, HI: 2004, <www.doe.k12.hi.us>

School Year 2003-04 Preliminary AYP Results and Corresponding School Year 2004-05 Accountability Status by Complex, Hawaii State Department of Education. Honolulu, HI: August 16, 2005. <www.doe.k12.hi.us>

Superintendent Pat Hamamoto's Resume, Hawaii State Department of Education. Honolulu, HI: 2003. <www.doe.k12.hi.us>

Superintendent's Report 2003-04, Hawaii State Department of Education. <www.doe.k12.hi.us>

Tibbetts, Katherine, "Losing Ground: Longitudinal Trends in Hawaii DOE Test Scores for Major Ethnic Groups," *Policy Analysis & System Evaluation Report No. 2001-02:* 16. Kamehameha Schools Publishing, 2002.

Tracey, Christopher A., Gail L. Sunderman, Gary Orfield, "Changing NCLB District Accountability Standards: Implications for Racial Inequity," *Harvard Civil Rights Project, Harvard University,* June 2005.

United States Census, US Census Bureau, 2000, <www.census.gov>

Vintage Classics, "The Republic by Plato," New York: Random House, 1991

Waipahu High School, *NCLB School Report SY 2004-05 Native Hawaiian Educational Assessments,* Kamehameha Schools Publishing, 2005.

Chapter 10
The Modification of School Improvement and Staff Development Efforts in Response to the Failure to Make Adequate Yearly Progress

John W. Hunt

Background

Since the implementation of the federal No Child Left Behind Act (NCLB) in 2002, the impact upon America's schools has been significant in many areas. In a positive sense, NCLB has caused schools and school districts to examine the performance and academic achievement of subgroups, often for the first time. This examination has certainly highlighted the fact that the academic performance of many of our subgroups is below that of students, as a whole. Historically, when teachers and administrators examined standardized achievement scores they were often satisfied if their students were achieving at, or above, the national average. The review of cumulative test data often masked the poor performance of students in various subgroups. The implementation of NCLB has certainly changed that situation.

Based upon the overall requirements of NCLB, one hundred percent of the nation's public school students are to be meeting or exceeding academic standards by the year 2014. While states have been given some flexibility in the pace at which their students will meet these standards, the process is similar, nationally. Increasing percentages of students must meet these standards on a graduated basis. Successfully achieving these standards is referred to as making Adequate Yearly Progress (AYP). The schools and districts not meeting these standards are being subjected to a series of sanctions, which become more severe with each year's subsequent failure.

The NCLB Act has been in existence long enough that some schools and districts across the nation are beginning to face sanctions. The first level of this penalty process occurs when students in a particular subgroup fail to make adequate yearly progress for two consecutive years. As increasing numbers of schools and districts have reached the initial two-consecutive year failure stage, termed Academic Early Warning (AEW), reports of declining teacher and administrator morale have begun to abound. According to the principal of one school, "When you work in a school and there is a dragon on your backyard, you had better prepare for the dragon. The dragon, of course, is the accountability system…"[1]

Students, teachers, and administrators alike suffer morale problems in lower-performing schools. One failure leads to another, and soon, those in the school are caught in a downward spiral of emotions. Nichols (2005) addressed the phenomenon by stating: "So, once a school has been labeled failing, the children of that school belong to a failure. Leaving that school may not be a real option for many of the children, so they are stuck in an inferior school. Further, each such labeling depresses the job quality of the teachers and administrators in those schools."[2]

Beyond the morale issues, there seems to be a growing body of evidence that high-stakes tests are having unintended consequences on our nation's schools. A number of studies have shown that such tests can narrow the curriculum and seem to move instruction toward the teaching of lower level cognitive skills.[3]

The study outlined in this chapter is an outgrowth of the "narrowing" concept mentioned above. Specifically, what impact is the failure to make AYP having on selected school districts in terms of both school improvement and staff development efforts?

Research Design and Methodology

This survey was conducted during the months of February and March of 2006. The superintendents of 240 Illinois public school superintendents were asked to respond to a thirty item anonymous online survey regarding the impact of NCLB on their districts. The 240 targeted districts were those that had failed to make AYP for two or more consecutive years, as of the end of the 2004-2005 school years. These districts were identified from a list readily available on the website of the Illinois State Board of Education (www.isbe.net). Only Title I eligible districts were surveyed. The superintendents submitted their responses to a secure server and once their responses were received, their email addresses were deleted. The superintendents of 63 Illinois school districts completed the online survey, which constituted a response rate of just over 26%. Surveys were received from a wide range of districts in terms of size of student enrollment, student ethnicity, and socioeconomic level.

Superintendents were surveyed regarding a range of topics and areas of information. First, the respondents were asked to address the demographic and socioeconomic nature of their districts. They were also requested to identify the student enrollment of their districts, and whether they considered their districts to be rural, small to medium sized communities, suburban, or urban in nature. They were instructed to designate the specific areas of AYP failure, as well as to identify the particular subgroup or subgroups that had failed in those areas. They were also asked to divulge whether these failures had been at the individual building level, the district level, or both. Additionally, they were asked about the organizational type of their districts. Illinois is somewhat unique because state law allows for elementary districts, high school districts, and K-12 unit districts. Superintendents were also requested to comment upon the degree of funding that their respective districts received from the state in relation to local taxpayer funding.

Once the nature of the participating school districts was established, the respondents were asked to answer a series of questions regarding the types of changes, if any, that had been instituted in their districts in the areas of school improvement planning and staff development efforts. Specifically, they were asked to reveal whether their school improvement planning and staff development efforts were becoming more focused and more content oriented as a result of the failure to make AYP for two or more consecutive years. Additionally, they were requested to respond to questions regarding any changes in spending on staff development, any sources of outside assistance in their efforts to again meet AYP, and were they were in terms of the entire sanctions process? Were they being required to offer school choice and/or tutoring? Were all of their teachers highly qualified according to NCLB standards? What had been the reaction of their communities to their respective districts' failures to make AYP? Finally, they were asked to comment upon the impact of the failure to make AYP on their own lives and jobs.

Results of the Survey

There was a range of district types and service areas represented among the responding districts. Nearly 37% of the responding superintendents categorized their districts as rural in nature. Almost 27% said that their districts were comprised of small and medium sized communities. Just over 30% reported that they were suburban, and slightly over 6% called themselves urban.

Harkening back to the unique structure of Illinois public school districts, 45.3% of all Illinois school districts are elementary districts, 11.5% are high school districts, and 43.2% are K-12 unit districts. Among the districts responding to the survey, nearly 24% of the districts were elementary districts, 17% were high school districts, and almost 59% were K-12 unit districts. It is clear from viewing the nature of the districts responding to the survey, the K-12 and high school districts are overrepresented and the elementary districts are underrepresented in the pool of respondents. These numbers would seem to confirm the folklore on the street that high schools and middle schools have often been the first to run into AYP difficulties.

The average free and reduced lunch count of the 63 responding districts was 34.5%, compared with an overall Illinois state average of 40%. The two largest minority groups represented in Illinois public schools are African-American students, at 20.3% of the total state student enrollment and Hispanic students, weighing in at 18.3 % of the total. The percentage enrollment of these two subgroups among the responding districts showed an average African-American enrollment of 15% and a Hispanic enrollment of 15%.

Table 1, below, shows the student enrollments of the responding districts:

Table 1.	**Student Enrollments of Responding Districts**
Under 500 students =	3.2%
501-1000 students =	12.7%
1001-3000 students =	55.5%
3001-5000 students =	15.9%
Over 5000 students =	12.7%

Upon examining the areas in which the surveyed districts failed to meet AYP, forty of the districts failed to meet the standards in mathematics and thirty-five failed to meet the goals in language arts. There is some overlap in the sense that some districts failed in both mathematics and language arts, accounting for a total larger than 63.

An examination of the specific subgroup failures proved to be quite illuminating. Whether in mathematics or language arts, students with disabilities constituted, far and away, the largest failing subgroup. This group was cited as failing to make AYP in 69.8% of the responding districts. Ethnic or racial subgroups failing to make AYP were reported in 27% of the districts, and low income students were identified as failing in 25.4% of the surveyed districts. Eleven percent of the districts cited failure among their Limited English Proficient (LEP) students and 1% of the districts stated that either their male or female subgroups failed.

Moving into the heart of the survey, nearly 62% of the superintendents reported that the failure to make AYP had impacted their school improvement planning either significantly or very significantly. An additional 28.5% reported that their school improvement planning had been impacted somewhat by their failure. In a related, but separate topic, 54% of the respondents said that AYP failure had made either a significant or very significant impact upon their staff development efforts. Another 36.5% stated that this failure had caused somewhat of an impact in the area of staff development.

Specifically, the respondents' comments regarding the nature of the impact on school improvement planning are outlined in Table 2, below.

Table 2.	**Impact of Failure on School Improvement Planning**
More Narrow Focus =	55.5%
More Content Oriented =	52.3%
More Teacher Involvement =	43%

In an overwhelming fashion, the superintendents reported that both the focus and content of school improvement planning were increasingly being targeted towards mathematics and language arts.

In a related series of questions, superintendents were polled regarding the impact of the failure of their schools or districts to meet AYP upon staff development efforts. Their specific comments pertaining to this area are shown in Table 3.

Table 3. Impact of Failure on Staff Development Efforts

More Narrow Focus =	57%
More Content Oriented =	59%
More Teacher Involvement =	41%.

Again, the superintendents reported that both the focus and content of staff development efforts were being increasingly directed towards mathematics and language arts. However, a third topic was commonly mentioned regarding evolving staff development efforts. Many districts reported an increase in training teachers to assist students with test-taking skills.

Fifty-seven percent of the respondents reported that their spending on staff development had increased, or increased significantly, as a result of their failure to make AYP. Over 77% of the surveyed districts had sought outside assistance to help with their AYP issues. About two-thirds of the districts had called upon their area Regional Office of Education and/or their Educational Service Center for help. These are intermediate levels of assistance available in Illinois under the auspices of the Illinois State Board of Education. Another 35% of the districts employed private consultants in their improvement efforts and approximately 14% utilized the services of university personnel. Some districts used multiple sources of external assistance.

Some of the districts surveyed were already involved in sanctions as a result of their AYP failures. A third of the responding districts had been required to offer school choice to their students. While most of this had been offered internally, within the district, over 12% reported that their students had been offered external choice. In both cases, students of chronically failing schools were given the opportunity to transfer to another school. A great majority of the districts that offered choice reported that fewer than 5% of the eligible students had taken advantage of this option. However, one school district indicated that up to 15% of the eligible students had exercised the choice option.

Nearly 21% of the surveyed districts have been required to offer tutoring services to their students due to their repeated failure to make AYP. Typically, these services have been offered by a variety of private firms. In most of the districts, less than 5% of the eligible students have taken advantage of the tutoring. However, in two districts, up to 15% of the students have availed themselves of this opportunity and two districts reported that up to half of the eligible students have been involved in tutoring. One district stated that over 50% of its students have participated in outside tutoring.

A major area of concern uncovered by the survey pertained to the issue of highly qualified teachers. By July 1, 2006, all public school teachers were required to be highly qualified according to NCLB guidelines. In general, being highly qualified means that a teacher holds the proper certifications for the areas in which he or she is teaching. However, each state must have its definition of highly qualified approved by the United States Department of Education. This was an area of significant confusion among the superintendents surveyed. When this survey was administered, just a few months before the federal deadline, 63% of the districts claimed that their teachers were highly qualified. However, over 25% of the districts stated that they had some teachers not meeting the highly qualified requirements and over 11% admitted that they were confused regarding this issue and could not give a definitive answer. Of those districts admitting that they had unqualified teachers, the reported deficits were in the following areas: special education; bilingual education; middle level teaching; recently employed full-time substitute teachers; and vocational education teachers. The special education and bilingual deficits were most frequently cited, with middle school certification running a close third.

Two final areas were addressed by the survey. The question of community reaction to a district's failure to make AYP, or to its admission that it is employing teachers that are less than highly qualified, was one topic queried. Interestingly, over 77% of the respondents reported that they had noticed little community reaction to this failure and only 22% reported a moderate community reaction. None of the responding districts reported a significant community reaction.

The final major area examined was that of the impact of the failure to make AYP upon the jobs of the superintendents of the failing districts. Seventy percent of the superintendents surveyed reported that this issue had brought about either a moderate or significant impact upon their daily professional lives. In this section of the survey, respondents were given the opportunity to provide unstructured comments in via a drop-down box. The angst and frustration were evident in several repeated themes. Among these was the narrowing of focus of school improvement planning and staff development to mathematics and language arts, often to the exclusion of other subject areas, such as the arts. Respondents also frequently mentioned the feeling of loss of control on the part of teachers, which led to morale issues and increased anxiety levels.

Some superintendents also expressed concern over the increasing amount of dollars that their districts were spending on AYP issues.

Conclusions

One of the first findings of the study was that failure to make AYP is an equal opportunity employer in Illinois. In other words, districts of all sizes, ethnicities, and financial backgrounds are beginning to fail to meet the AYP hurdles in Illinois public school districts. The results highlight the fact that this struggle with academic achievement is not primarily an urban, or even rural, phenomenon. Indeed, the bulk of the districts failing to make AYP described their service areas as either small to medium size communities, or suburban. A similar pattern emerged in terms of student enrollments. While some very small and some urban districts did report AYP failures, over 84% of the failing districts had student enrollments between 501 and 5000 students. Among these, districts in the enrollment range of 1001-3000 students led the pack, with 55.5% admitting AYP failures.

A number of authors have decried the impact of socioeconomic conditions on the ability of some districts to produce high levels of academic achievement and there seems to be the underlying assumption that most of the AYP failures are occurring in the poorer districts. For example, authors claimed the following in one article: "One of these problems begins with the acknowledgement that high income districts receive many more applications for each position than do low-income districts. Another is that in districts with schools that serve families at both ends of the socioeconomic scale, teachers tend to seek transfers from schools with large numbers of children from low-income families to those with a higher percentage of children from wealthier families."[4]

Another author is convinced that our educational problems are social in nature, and the solution must expand beyond the individual school building, or even beyond a school district, and addresses this by saying: "As any inner-city teacher can tell us (and many rural and suburban teachers as well), to pretend that schools can single-handedly overcome a lifetime of deprivation through a "whole-school action plan" or through rigorous and intensive adherence to a particular reading program is more an exercise in ritualistic magic than a realistic solution to social, economic, and personal problems."[5]

This author subsequently reinforced this theme by stating, "Six hours of instruction a day for 180 days a year cannot overcome the effects of a deprived and impoverished home environment for 18 hours a day, 365 days a year."[6]

While it may be difficult to dispute that socioeconomic factors have an impact upon student achievement, this study showed that all types of Illinois public school districts were failing to make AYP. As previously stated, the average percentage of students entitled to free and reduced price lunches from the responding districts was over 5% below the Illinois state average. It is also instructive to examine the funding mechanism for Illinois public schools when examining this particular issue. Illinois, like several other states, uses a foundation level approach in its funding of schools. Illinois schools are funded through a combination of local property taxes, flow through funding, state funding, and federal dollars. However, all districts do not receive the same proportion of general state aid funding. In actual fact, the percent of state funding varies greatly, depending upon the local property tax contribution. In general, as the proportion of a district's income derived from local property taxes increases, the corresponding proportion of the district's revenues received from the state decreases. Typically, those districts relying more heavily upon local property taxes are able to spend more money educating each child in Illinois. With this in mind, it is interesting to note that 50.8% of the districts involved in this study, i.e., those failing to make AYP, reported that a majority of their funding came from local sources. Another 36.5% received a majority of their funding from the state, and the remaining 12.7% reported that their levels of local and state funding were fairly balanced.

An important finding of this study was that those Illinois public school districts that have failed to make AYP for two or more years have begun to make changes in both their school improvement planning and their staff development efforts as a result of their failures. Clearly, both school improvement efforts at the building and district level, as well as staff development efforts at the same levels, are now much more focused and targeted. More efforts are being directed toward improving teacher practice, and subsequent student achievement, in mathematics and the language arts. In this respect, it could be said that NCLB may be beginning to have the impact desired by its framers in these districts. As with many issues, there are both positives and negatives associated with this approach. In 2004, researchers working under the auspices of the Civil Rights Project at Harvard University surveyed the teachers of Fresno, California, and Richmond, Virginia, regarding their perceptions regarding NCLB. The response rate was 77.4% and included teachers from schools making AYP and from those needing to improve. The authors commented:

> In Richmond, we asked teachers "what overall effect do you think NCLB is having on your school?" Teachers in Richmond were divided about the overall effect of the law, perhaps reflecting the complexity of the law. Close to half the teachers believed that the overall effect of NCLB was negative, with 45.7% of the teachers in improvement schools and 47.3% in adequate schools responding negatively. But substantial numbers of teachers also thought the overall effect was positive, with 36.4% of teachers in improvement schools and 39.4% of teachers in adequate progress schools responding positively. Few believed that NCLB was having no effect.[7]

This study adds to the previously mentioned concept that there seems to be a growing body of evidence that high-stakes tests are having unintended consequences on our nation's schools. In a more recent study of four public schools in Chicago, the researchers found that higher and lower performing schools responded differently to assessment results, when they stated: "In probation schools, responses focus narrowly on complying with policy demands, focusing on improving the performance of certain students, within benchmark grades, and in certain subject areas. In contrast, higher performing schools emphasize enhancing the performance of all students regardless of grade level and across all subject areas."[8]

In a study that was released at the same time that the results of this survey were being tabulated, the Center on Education Policy found a clear narrowing of the curriculum in response to NCLB. The study, which included 299 school districts with representatives from all 50 states concluded:

> Seventy-one percent of the school districts we surveyed reported that they have reduced elementary school instructional time in at least one other subject to make more time for reading and mathematics – the subjects tested for NCLB. In some case study districts, struggling students receive double periods of reading or math or both – sometimes missing certain subjects altogether. Some officials in case study districts view this extra time for reading and math as necessary to help low-achieving students catch up. Others feel that this practice has shortchanged students from learning important subjects, squelched creativity in

> teaching and learning, or diminished activities that might keep children interested in school.[9]

Some scholars believe that NCLB has taken us away from our historical roots in American schools – the education of the whole child. According to Nell Noddings :

> Some people argue that schools are best organized to accomplish academic goals and that we should charge other institutions with the task of pursuing the physical, moral, social, emotional, spiritual, and aesthetic aims that we associate with the whole child. The schools would do a better job, these people maintain, if they were freed to focus on the job for which they were established. Those who make this argument have not considered the history of education. Public schools in the United States – as well as schools across other different societies and historical eras – were established as much for moral and social reasons as for academic instruction. In his 1818 *Report of the Commissioners for the University of Virginia*, for example, Thomas Jefferson included in the "objects of primary education" such qualities as morals, understanding duties to neighbors and country, knowledge of rights and intelligence and faithfulness in social relations.[10]

Many of the survey respondents echoed the sentiments of Noddings, and Jefferson, in their comments. They expressed concern over the narrowing of the school improvement and staff development foci in their districts. A common theme was that "the only thing we do is mathematics and language arts." Several expressed concern over the lack of attention being paid to other subject areas – particularly the arts. At the same time, some of the superintendents saw a silver lining in the NCLB cloud and were determined to make the best of the situation.

Finally, the morale issue cited by responding superintendents seems to be of growing importance. Students, staff, and administration alike suffer moral problems in lower-performing schools. Superintendents frequently expressed concern for the feelings of their staff in the era of NCLB. Their fear is that, soon, their schools will be caught in a downward spiral of emotions previously mentioned.[11]

While most of the administrators polled certainly would not label their schools as "inferior," they are struggling with what must often seem like an uphill battle. Increasing numbers of districts are consistently failing to make AYP for multiple years. According to federal guidelines, after districts offer school choice and tutoring, they must next move into the uncharted area of school restructuring. While some responding administrators are optimistic that they can meet the challenge, many of the superintendents surveyed would echo the sentiments of James Popham when he said:

> Although I've never been a death-row inmate awaiting execution, I can imagine how such prisoners must feel, as they watch their attorneys exhaust, one by one, all eligible appeals. Even though public school educators in the United States may not realize it, they are now facing a similar end-of-the-line scenario

with respect to adequate yearly progress (AYP), the accountability cornerstone of the No Child Left Behind Act (NCLB).[12]

Notes

1. C. Craig, "The dragon in school backyards: The influence of mandated testing on school contexts and educators' narrative knowing." *Teachers College Record* 106 (2004): 1129-1257.

2. D. Nichols, "Brown v. Board of Education and the No Child Left Behind Act: Competing ideologies." *B.Y.U. Education and Law Journal* (2005): 151-181.

3. S. Klein, L. Hamilton, D. McCaffrey, and B. Stretcher, *What do Test Scores in Texas Tell Us?* (Santa Monica, CA:RAND, 2000). D. Koretz and S. Barron, *The Validity of Gains on the Kentucky Instructional Results Information System (KIRIS).* (Santa Monica, CA:RAND, 1998). D. Koretz, R. Linn, S. Dunbar, and L. Shepard, "The effects of high-stakes testing: Preliminary evidence about generalizations across tests." (paper presented at the annual meetings of the American Educational Research Association and the National Council on Measurement in Education, Chicago, Illinois, 1991). R. Linn, "Assessments and accountability." *Educational Researcher,* 29 no. 2 (2000): 4-16. R. Linn, M. Graue, and N. Sanders, "Comparing State and District Test Results to National Norms: The Validity of Claims that "Everyone is above Average." *Educational Measurement: Issues and Practice,* 9 (1990): 5-14. B. Stretcher, S. Barron, T. Kaganoff, and J. Goodwin, *The effects of standards-based assessment on classroom practices: Results of the 1996-1997 RAND Survey of Kentucky Teachers of Mathematics and Writing (CSE Technical Report 482)* (Los Angeles: Center for Research on Evaluation, Standards, and Student Testing, 1998).

4. H. Burbach and A. Butler, "Turnaround Principals." *School Administrator* 62 (2005): 24-31.

5. W. Mathis, "Bridging the Achievement Gap: A Bridge too Far?" *Phi Delta Kappan,.* (2005): 590-593.

6. See note 5 above.

7. G. Sunderman, C. Tracey, J. Kim, and G. Orfield, *Listening to teachers: Classroom realities and the No Child Left Behind Act* (Cambridge:MA: The Civil Rights Project at Harvard University, 2004) 1-47.

8. J. Diamond and J. Spillane, "High-Stakes Accountability in Urban Elementary Schools: Challenging or Reproducing Inequality?" *Teachers College Record* 106 (2004): 1145-1176.

9. Center on Education Policy, "From the Capital to the Classroom: Year 4 of the No Child Left Behind Act. Summary and Recommendations" (2006): 1-10.

10. N. Noddings, "What Does it Mean to Educate the Whole Child?" *Educational Leadership* 63 (2005): 8-13.

11. See note 2 above.

12. J. Popham, "AYP Wriggle Room Running Out." *Educational Leadership* 63 (2005): 85-87.

References

Burbach, H. and A. Butler, "Turnaround Principals." *School Administrator* 62 (2005): 24-31.

Center on Education Policy, "From the Capital to the Classroom: Year 4 of the No Child Left Behind Act. Summary and Recommendations" (2006): 1-10.

Craig, C. "The dragon in school backyards: The influence of mandated testing on school contexts and educators' narrative knowing." *Teachers College Record* 106 (2004): 1129-1257.

Diamond, J. and J. Spillane, "High-Stakes Accountability in Urban Elementary Schools: Challenging or Reproducing Inequality?" *Teachers College Record* 106 (2004): 1145-1176.

Klein, S. and L. Hamilton, D. McCaffrey, and B. Stretcher, *What do Test Scores in Texas Tell Us?* (Santa Monica, CA:RAND, 2000).

Koretz, D. and S. Barron, *The Validity of Gains on the Kentucky Instructional Results Information System (KIRIS).* (Santa Monica, CA:RAND, 1998).

Koretz, D. and R. Linn, S. Dunbar, and L. Shepard, "The effects of high-stakes testing: Preliminary evidence about generalizations across tests." (Paper presented at the annual meetings of the American Educational Research Association and the National Council on Measurement in Education, Chicago, Illinois, 1991).

Linn, R. "Assessments and accountability." *Educational Researcher,* 29 no. 2 (2000): 4-16.

Linn, R. and M. Graue, and N. Sanders, "Comparing State and District Test Results to National Norms: The Validity of Claims that "Everyone is above Average." *Educational Measurement: Issues and Practice,* 9 (1990): 5-14.

Mathis, W. "Bridging the Achievement Gap: A Bridge too Far?" *Phi Delta Kappan*,. (2005): 590-593.

Nichols, D. "Brown v. Board of Education and the No Child Left Behind Act: Competing ideologies." *B.Y.U. Education and Law Journal* (2005): 151-181.

N. Noddings, "What Does it Mean to Educate the Whole Child?" *Educational Leadership* 63 (2005): 8-13.

Stretcher, B. and S. Barron, T. Kaganoff, and J. Goodwin, *The effects of standards-based assessment on classroom practices: Results of the 1996-1997 RAND Survey of Kentucky Teachers of Mathematics and Writing (CSE Technical Report 482)* (Los Angeles: Center for Research on Evaluation, Standards, and Student Testing, 1998).

Sunderman, G. and C. Tracey, J. Kim, and G. Orfield, *Listening to teachers: Classroom realities and the No Child Left Behind Act* (Cambridge: MA: The Civil Rights Project at Harvard University, 2004) 1-47.

Chapter 11
Unintended Consequences: The Teacher's Story

Anne Grall Reichel

INVITATION:
As you read my chapter, I encourage you to construct your own meaning of the term "highly qualified" and to reflect on the stories our veteran teachers have to tell about how their life world and that of the children they serve has changed under the demands of NCLB.

To be considered "highly qualified", by our federal government's definition, one must hold a bachelor's degree, pass state licensure or certification requirements and prove that they know each subject they teach. Yet, I am left wondering, does this definition of "highly qualified" truly get at the essence of teaching?

I encourage you to consider this question as you read on.

Setting the Stage: Vision versus Reality

As an educator, it would be impossible to ignore the spate of literature focused on the need to humanize school change. Evans (1996) aptly titled his book on leadership *The Human Side of School Change.* The literature strongly endorses the notion of collaboration and collegiality. Relationships are viewed as "more fundamental than things."[1] Leaders are encouraged to build reform efforts upon trust and consensus. Relational trust is viewed as the "antidote to vulnerability."[2] Educational leaders are forewarned that their efforts to build communities of learners without relational trust will quickly erode. Sergiovanni (2005) describes the "hopeful leader" as one who recognizes the gifts and the potential that each person brings to the table.[3] Teachers are to be viewed as equal partners contributing in extraordinary ways to continuous growth and improvement. "The members of the organization feel a unity of organizational purpose that transcends individual circumstances and emphasizes the interest of the whole."[4]

But how far is this vision from the reality that exists in our schools under the demands of NCLB? How often do teachers have a voice in their own professional development? What support do they receive to implement the "simultaneous multiple improvements"[5] that are cast in their direction with little explanation? Our teachers are suffering from a deluge of teach to the test strategies, that often stand in contrast to that which they know to be effective in nurturing the development of critical thinkers and problem-solvers.

Emerging from the literature base is the need to further study the potential of professional collaboration and the meanings teachers ascribe to it. Several researches have identified the need for further research on the nature of professional collaboration and the dynamics of the relational trust that rests at the very soul of the collaborative process. Of interest, to researchers, is the teacher's perception of professional collaboration. What do teachers have to say about their relationships in schools? What voice do they have in the collaborative process? Do teachers feel a sense of trust or a sense of betrayal?

Sergiovanni (2005) identifies relational trust as a hallmark of a community of practice.[6] Bryk and Schneider (2002) discuss the significance of the role of social capital in effective functioning of social institutions and clearly communicate that this aspect of schooling has been overlooked.[7] Their research identifies a common theme:

> The quality of social relations in diverse institutional contexts makes a difference in how they function. This scholarship, together with field observations, directed our attention to a critical but often overlooked aspect of school reform. Schools are networks of sustained relationships. The social exchanges that occur and how participants infuse them with meaning are central to a school's functioning. Moreover, the character of these social exchanges is especially salient in times of broad scale change.[8]

It would be impossible to ignore the fact that our schools are in the midst of sweeping reform efforts, particularly in the arena of professional development. Change is the charge of the day. Emerging from the studies on change is a growing interest in the importance of trust within organizations. Hargreaves (2002) conducted an interview- based study with 50 Canadian teachers. He elicited responses from teachers on their emotional relationships to their work, their professional development and change in education. He discovered that amongst the strongest sources of negative emotion amongst colleagues was the opposite of trust - betrayal.[9] Furthermore, Leonard and Leonard (2004) conducted an extensive quantitative study analyzing the responses of 565 Canadian teachers on dimensions of organizational culture. They concluded their study with a call for further research into the phenomenon of collaborative cultures.

> "Although the use of quantitative investigation methods and statistical analysis may have provided some additional information and insights into this complex

phenomenon, only deeper, richer qualitative investigations are likely to move us substantially further toward fuller comprehension"[10]

Inspired by the call for deeper qualitative studies I set out, almost two years ago, to tell the teacher's story. I wanted to find out how far the vision for education was from the reality of the life world of our teachers attempting to carry out the mandates set forth by NCLB. I discovered that our teachers are living in discordant harmony. Our veteran teachers are dangerously off center. The vision of collegial learning communities where all voices are celebrated is distant from the reality of our teachers. They know that, under the demands of NCLB, the assessment pendulum has swung to an impossibly distant place, perhaps further disconnected from the reality of the child's world than during the period of social efficiency. Teachers report that they have little to no voice in that which they are asked to implement. We have failed to monitor the "unintended consequences"[11] of NCLB by silencing the teacher's voice.

Unintended Consequences

"Unintended consequences," I've borrowed the words quite freely from Lortie's timeless sociological study of teachers. The words seem to resound more purposefully than ever as I consider the catastrophic impact of No Child Left Behind on our veteran teachers. My premise is really quite simple; we have failed to examine the unintended consequences of our intervention (NCLB), because we have failed to listen to the people doing the work. My purpose, in writing this chapter, is not to villainize the authors and legislators of NCLB, or the administrators who must enforce it. My purpose is to bring the teacher's voice to the discussion to better inform our future actions.

I want to make it perfectly clear that I've attempted to bring this voice to the forefront for over a year now. I started out, encouraged by my dissertation committee, to get my research published. After many futile attempts I found myself drowning in a sea of rejection letters. Next, my wise dissertation chair Dr. Tafel suggested that I think of my dissertation as a political document. She suggested that I send it off to several senators. That was interesting at best. Senator Clinton's office sent my dissertation back in an envelope with no response. Senators Durbin & Kennedy have not responded. Senator Obama sent a very nice letter and expressed interest in reading my work.

I had previously talked with Senator Obama's Education Fellow on the perils of the Illinois Science Standards and had documented the fact that they were not aligned with the recommendations of the American Association for the Advancement of Science. Senator Obama's Fellow, a former high school science teacher, was highly receptive on the science issue.

Cognizant of my own failure to bring the teachers' voices forward, I was filled with the desperate sense that I had failed the veteran teachers who so generously gave of their time and stories. Attempting to heal, I returned to my own university teaching and abandoned my efforts to publish. I also began to separate myself from my staff development work throughout Northern Illinois.

At one time, I had experienced the joy of concentrating on integrated unit design, scientific inquiry, critical thinking, conceptual mapping in science and social science, problem-solving and differentiated instruction. I found myself immersed in "Teach to the Test" gigs that made it almost unbearable to get up in the morning. I noticed that the faces of the teachers, I had grown to respect and admire, had changed. Our "charge" changed, the teachers and I. We no longer discussed the joy of scientific inquiry or integrated unit design, instead we discussed Illinois Standard Achievement Test preparation. I no longer sensed joy in them and I certainly did not feel it myself. I chose to leave a lucrative consulting business behind to work with alternative certification candidates committed to urban education. That helped, but the need to bring the teacher's voice forward continued to gnaw away at my inner soul. After almost a year of abandoning my quest to tell the teacher's story, Dr. Todd Price asked if I would explicate the teacher's voice for a book he and several colleagues were writing. And so.... I find myself struggling to represent the teacher's voice one more time.

Einstein stated; "The deeper we search, the more we find out there is to know and as long as human life exists I believe that it will always be so." Sometimes, I wish that I had not been inspired by Einstein's words. Sometimes I wish I had not explored deeply into the life world of teachers because the stories that emerged, under the demands of NCLB, were so dark. But, the optimist in me, is reminded of the wisdom that Campbell (1988) put forth in *The Power of Myth*. Campbell believed that it was necessary to embrace the darkness in order to experience a soulful transformation.[12] I fully believe that unless we embrace the darkness, unless we think deeply about the stories that our veteran teachers have to tell we cannot move forward with the conviction to undo that which has been done in the name of NCLB.

For some period of time, before I started my study, I wondered why teachers were not more proactive when it came to NCLB. I wondered why they did not speak out when they were being forced to teach in ways that were counterintuitive to everything that they had learned about effectiveness and best practice. As I interviewed them, I came to understand that they are not in a position to speak on their own behalf. The fear of retribution runs deep within them compromising their health and well being like a deep thrombosis threatening the life-giving circulation that keeps the human body going. The teachers' fear became completely transparent when I attempted to triangulate my dissertation data through member checks. As a nascent researcher, I naively sent my first transcription of an interview via e-mail. That evening I received a call from the teacher whom I had interviewed. She stated: "Anne please do not send any more transcriptions via e-mail, we all fear the consequences." I learned to conduct interviews in restaurants and coffee shops. I met teachers in towns that were distant from the ones they worked in. I navigated via snail mail and home phones to protect their anonymity. Each teacher, who voluntarily came forward, shared that the experience was cathartic. Just last week, as I was riding the train into Chicago, I happened to sit down next to a teacher from a northern district. She said; "Anne you will be disappointed in me, I'm taking early retirement." I asked why? She shared; "I just can't teach to the test anymore." I told her about my study and assured her that she was not alone. When we got off the train we shared an emotional moment and she encouraged me to keep trying on behalf of the teachers. I knew at that moment that the story of the heroines, I had had the privilege to interview, must be told. If only, for the sake of helping other teachers know that their intuitions were synchronous to other teachers forced to teach to the demands of NCLB.

The women who participated in my study were all veteran elementary teachers. Through my work as a staff developer throughout Northern Illinois, I had the privilege of working with most of them for a minimum of 10 to 12 years. I purposefully selected and interviewed the teachers Parker Palmer would have identified as the teachers who celebrated their work as their calling. They were the teachers who came early and stayed late, some were nationally board certified. All had continued to grow professionally and had served as mentors to young teachers. They had served on endless committees and spent their summers engaged in professional growth. Some had even come to my home during the summer to work on science units. As I conducted interviews, it did not take long to reach the realization, that under the demands of NCLB, these extraordinary teachers were being forced to dance to cacophonous tones.

> "Like hermit crabs who skitter about in the tide pools wearing the shells of dead snails, we don our belief systems that do not always fit too well, and go about our business. Most of us are not so much believers as possessors of beliefs."[13]

My observations and conversations with teachers have led me to believe that they, like the hermit crab, skitter about as technocrats fulfilling the demands of reform. They carry the unthinkable burden of implementing reform initiatives fixed in an antiquated paradigm of social efficiency. The teachers' shells do not perfectly fit that which they intuitively know about children and learning, yet they like scavengers, under the demands of NCLB, scurry about looking for the next best technical strategy to raise the scores. They are not believers in what they are doing and they are silenced under the shadows of their leaders, parents and legislators pushing for the best scores. No longer can they create the kind of innovative lessons that gave life to their teaching at one time. They feel betrayed, forced to wear shells that can only lead to the death and stagnation of thinking processes. The teachers I interviewed feel betrayed by the system. It is only logical to ask: Why do our veteran teachers feel betrayed?

My study revealed that teachers feel betrayed on several accounts. Teachers believe that we have lost our focus on the whole child. They believe that their voices have been silenced. Despite all the literature focused on the importance of relationships and communal effort in improving schools our teachers find themselves in situations where their voices are not heard. They find themselves struggling to keep up with the frenetic pace that comes with the spate of continuous reforms mandated by their central office.

> "The result of simultaneous multiple improvements is almost invariably dispiriting: no single project receives adequate attention, resources, planning or dissemination: staff time and effort are fragmented; frustrations abound."[14]

The teachers find that their efforts to joyfully collaborate have turned into technical sessions on score improvement. Veteran teachers find themselves protecting younger colleagues and "sneaking" to provide recess, and meaningful learning experiences that move children beyond test preparation. "Sneaking" has become a means of survival.

It is the teachers' stories about the whole child, the loss of voice, the frenetic pace, and the strength and resiliency to trust intuition in order to survive that I will share throughout the remainder of this chapter. The words of these remarkable teachers are not for the faint of heart. The voices of the teachers you are about to hear from are struggling to stay afloat in a tumultuous sea of standardization and bureaucracy. Their voices cannot be heard over the continuous waves of reform, and the children they once had time to embrace, have become numbers. Occasionally the teachers and their students duck under a wave long enough to engage in scientific inquiry or simulations of democracy only to emerge to the next wave of test taking strategies and test preparation booklets. Noddings (1992) astutely notes that if tests were central to growth and development, then parents would find a way to give them regularly at home.[15]

Throughout the remainder of the chapter I will be quoting veteran teachers. In an effort to protect their anonymity they will remain nameless. It will suffice to say that they are from school districts in Northern Illinois. As I talk to teachers in different parts of the country I believe that the voices represented on these pages are representative of teachers everywhere. I have over 140 pages of single spaced teacher transcriptions collected to date. I gathered my data through semi-structured interviews and hermeneutic circles. I have the deepest admiration and respect for the highly professional teachers who took the time to participate in my study. They are a gift to the children.

The Whole Child

Teachers reported that under the demands of NCLB our children are being reduced to numbers. Unfortunately numbers do not always represent the gifts and talents that our children have to offer. One teacher shared that in the last seven to eight years of her thirty-three year career that teaching had changed drastically. Under the "gun" of control she felt the pressure to quantify, that which was not quantifiable. She felt as though she had been forced to defy her own wisdom on the best way of seeing the children. "We are under the gun to quantify every skill of learning possible and unfortunately when you try to quantify something you lose the quality. There are some things you cannot possibly quantify when it comes to looking at student work."

Another shared that the remarkable talents of some children can easily be lost when the score is held as the pinnacle of success.

> I have a little boy in my room who is the very brightest in my class, but he cannot write worth a darn. You talk to him and he is at a whole different level. He is going to score high on some of the things, but there are some he is going to bomb out on. He doesn't have the motor coordination to do it and he can express himself beautifully in words, but that is not shown on the test. And I think those kids answer questions on a totally different level that is not tested with those kinds of tests.

Many of the veteran teachers I interviewed questioned the reliability of the scores. They described some of the human variables that make it virtually impossible to measure a child's ability in a moment in time. They cited an array of variables that impact scores including illness, a poor night's sleep, and family situations. Underlying one teacher's description of some of the human frailties that stand in the way of accurate test scores was the ominous message that our children are experiencing tremendous anxiety associated with high-stakes testing.

> I had one student who was such a perfectionist and if every circle was not filled in exactly perfectly she had massive anxiety. As a result, this very bright little girl, probably one of the brightest enrichment students wasn't able to finish the test and scored way below grade level. Well I knew why, I knew even before looking at the details of the test that the reason behind her score was that she had only finished six or seven items in a twenty-minute test.

Pressing further into the notion of the "whole child" I discussed differentiated instruction with the teachers. These wise teachers lamented the fact that with an emphasis on preparing for the test there was less time for differentiating instruction and more time on test preparation. They felt that instead of their curriculum being student driven and based upon the individual needs of the students that the curriculum had become "test driven.

> So basically our curriculum revolves around what is going to make those students score higher, and do they really understand the concepts? We don't know? Can they pick the correct answer? Instead of curriculum being student driven and on an individual need it is test driven.

One teacher suggested that if we were to truly honor children we would test them in ways that took their disabilities into account. Her compassion for all children was evident. Her words moved to unthinkable territory as she suggested that teachers begin to think of children as liabilities because they can bring class averages down.

> Those remedial students have so much information to share, but often they can't write it because they have a writing disability, but they can tell me and express it in other ways and I think we just think of them as being disabled. We start to look at them as bringing down the scores and heaven forbid if a child moves into your district who has learning problems and he moves in right before the test and you haven't had time to prep him. He is lost. Maybe he came from a district that didn't spend as much time as you did preparing for the

> test and he is going to bring your whole class average down and you are going to look like a horrible teacher. It will show up in the newspaper.

After listening to the above account I found myself hoping that this was an isolated incident. Surely teachers were not beginning to view children in their classrooms as liabilities? Unfortunately the story was corroborated upon over and over again. Another teacher shared the comments of a colleague who was commiserating over a student who brought her class average down. "I heard a comment when our scores came back from a teacher who said one child in her class brought her class percentage down and if only he had been sick or absent she would have had an incredible class average. But, as it is now, she is below the district percentage for that grade level because of that one child. Well, that one child deserves to be educated and it is just too bad for that child."

The teachers reported that in some cases administrators had gone to great lengths to find "creative ways" to eliminate the scores of the children classified as liabilities. Underlying these words was a sense that the children with low scores had become "the other", "the they", as if not part of "us" of "our school community". "Well they are in our district, and I constantly hear the administrators saying things about how we can get their numbers not to count. I think that it is terrible. To say you are in the 98th percentile and not counting in the scores of all the kids is not an accurate look at the building at all."

I asked the teacher for further clarification. "So you mean instead of focusing on ways of helping that child, they were more focused on not counting the score?" The teacher sadly replied; "Yes, and there was a child who came in from a private school in Chicago and was taking our tests and the principal was down right upset that her scores would count. She didn't want her score in. I said I didn't think it was a liability, but they found a way to remove her."

As I listened to the stories I was reminded of Nieto's (2002) description of children as "walking sets of deficiencies."[16] I had always quietly hoped that it was not true; I had hoped Nieto was wrong.

One teacher shared that we sent the message to children that there was something "grossly wrong" with them if they could not earn a high score. Another shared that she was concerned about the children who were denied a spot in a special reading program based upon their scores. She shared that teachers were forced to resort to dishonesty to get children the help and support they needed. "We are told they have to have a score of 34 or below to be in the reading program. I had some kids who were 35, so they never got help last year."

I asked if the children had received help the following year. She responded in a justifiably indignant tone: "Yeah they are, but why did we wait a year? Because of one little number? You know, where is that early intervention? Research shows how important early intervention is, there are teachers who have lied, they've made up the scores, they've lied because they knew the kid wasn't going to get any help. "

Many teachers expressed anger and frustration regarding cutoff scores. One expressed concern over the children who missed the cutoffs on both ends of the scale. "If the ones just below the gifted cutoff got a little extra help they would be able to achieve. But, they are all put into a room with one teacher because of legislation. Consequently, there are kids at both ends who are just falling off and I see it and the frustration level is very high."

One teacher recalled a technological design project she gave to her class several years ago. She remembered that the children who were most successful at challenging problem-solving were not the top test takers. She shared how the children had persisted in continuing the project on their own during the summer, fueled by perhaps one of their first chances in school to be successful.

> That was the interesting thing; they were not the top kids in the class. I think that was what was so impressive about it. These were the kids who you could see the light turn on and this was a chance, maybe the first time that they were able to be successful at something at school that was academic. They knew they had a chance because they knew if they were taking a standardized test and had to read and write to choose A, B, or C or write an extended response answer on something about design they wouldn't have been able to do it. Here was a situation where they were able to excel. They actually continued their work in the summer and consulted each other.

I asked the teacher if she had continued the project. She remorsefully shared that she been forced to abandon this lengthy project in order to do more test preparation. We live in a time where problem-solving and critical thinking will be essential to survival and yet we seem to have less and less time to engage children in higher order thinking. It is quite frankly alarming to think about what we are sacrificing in the name of testing.

Our children are starving. They have been placed on a steady diet of test preparation curriculum devoid of opportunities to problem-solve and create. They hunger for an opportunity to think. Their teachers hunger to engage them in meaningful work.

> Education has become an act of depositing, in which students are the depositories and the teacher is the depositor. Instead of communicating, the teacher issues communiqués and makes deposits which the students patiently receive, memorize and repeat. This is the banking concept of education, in which the scope of action allowed to the students extends only as far as receiving, filing, and storing the deposits. They do, it is true, have the opportunity to become collectors or cataloguers of the things they store. But in the last analysis, it is people themselves who are filed away through the lack of creativity, transformation, and knowledge in this misguided system.[17]

Our children have been filed away, they are starving, living inside a neat little box of test taking strategies and scores. They hunger for creativity, transformation and the genuine experience of knowing.

We have created a web of bureaucracy and standardization that may lead to our own demise. Our misguided focus on testing and standardization fails to see the unique talents of many children in our schools. Ironically, in our attempts to leave no child behind, we appear to be leaving more behind. Our teachers have been forced to teach in a wasteland, delivering stagnated curriculum designed to improve test scores. They long for the chance to invite problem-solving, critical thinking and opportunities to give children the freedom to create. Our children scrambling to be the best test takers they can be are "at the end of living and the beginning of survival."[18]

Despite the fact that "teachers have an intimate unique knowledge of students"[19] they are being forced to assess in unauthentic ways. Worse, they must use the results of tests for student placement even when they stand in contrast to their professional judgment. " Objectivism has led us into actions so inharmonious with reality that catastrophe seems inevitable if we stay the course."[20] I can't help but wonder what kind of angry adults we will nurture if we continue to view our children as scores and liabilities.

Loss of Voice

As I approached the subject of voice during my semi-structured interviews I realized that the vision for schools as collegial places where teachers contributed in extraordinary ways was far from the reality of the teachers I interviewed. They appeared to relish the chance to discuss the loss of voice that they had experienced since the onset of NCLB. One teacher highlighted the lessons learned by big business when they failed to listen to the voices of the workers.

> I would very much like for our educational system to be a collaborative effort, a true collaborative effort between the federal, state, and local level. Teachers need to be given a voice because we are the ones in the trenches. Everything I've read about GM and other big businesses, when they failed to listen to the people who were doing the work that is required, it did not go well and this is not going well. We are producing anxiety ridden children who see school as an extremely stressful place to be. I do remember as a child loving to go every single day. I remember thinking, "what are we going to do today". And even most of my fourth graders come in with that expectation and I feel horrible when I have to push them and this is just so wrong. It is so inhumane.

Many of the teachers I interviewed, believed that committee decisions were made long before the first committee meeting. The teachers shared that the decisions that were made by the administration before the meeting often revolved around the selection of materials that their administrators perceived would be the best purchases to raise test scores. The teachers often saw these materials as lacking the depth of understanding that they knew was critical to student engagement and conceptual understanding. I asked the teachers how they felt when they were asked to serve on these committees.

> Oh horrible! And it has been brought up many times by teachers who have gone to the administration and said, "We really resent the fact that we know that you made a decision before we started, don't insult us by having us on a committee and try to make us believe we have input." And we have been told, "Oh your opinion did count!" But, when you look at the results of the voting for whatever the curriculum change is and when you tally what people's

> opinions were, you know that isn't the case, or that you've been swayed in a given direction. So, you really don't feel like you are empowered.

Similar to Hargreave's findings, I came to understand that the teachers viewed scenarios, like the one above, as acts of betrayal. The bonds of trust that they once shared with their administrators were quickly eroded when their voices were not heard, particularly when they had spent a great deal of time serving on a committee. The teachers felt violated, they felt as though they had taken the time to behave professionally, offering a voice of contribution and were silenced.

> We will go to meetings and make recommendations and talk about things and then what comes out isn't anything at all that we have talked about. Why bother? If they are going to tell me what to teach and not listen to me, don't waste my time. Then just adopt a program and tell me what to do and I'll accept it, but don't pretend that we have a part in it. Just don't waste my time.

As I listened to the teachers I clearly sensed that they were off center. Underlying their comments were important issues of anger, frustration, betrayal and protection of self through retreat. I'm left wondering what will become of the profession if those with invaluable insights become so angry and frustrated that they withdraw from contribution? The intricate web of relationships within schools appears to be damaged .It seemed that no matter what topic I discussed with teachers the conversation always came back to the layers of bureaucracy, control and the test scores. Even on the subject of voice this was evident. The test score appeared to be overriding the teacher's voice and good sense. One teacher shared her frustration in trying to initiate early intervention in reading for first graders. Due to the layers of documentation of data that were required the intervention process was slowed down significantly.

> The administration asks us to show them the test scores, well a test score for a first grader isn't always as valid as it might be for some of the older kids. So I just get so aggravated and then we have to file it, and then you have to analyze the data and you know as a teacher, you look at those kids and you know which ones needs additional reading help. You truly do, but we have to assess them on the ISOL and then we have to give them the Gates and then we have to meet with the parents and explain why we think the child is weak and then because of all the documentation we have to wait six weeks before we can start any of the early intervention. We are just doing so much more than we really need to do and it is all because we have to have paperwork and paperwork and I just get so aggravated with it. I feel like, (hesitates) I just feel so frustrated, no one is listening to us about this.

I found the statement above to be particularly alarming. . Not only had this teacher lost her voice, but it appeared that her professional judgment was not valued, it had been lost, sucked into the black hole of paperwork, test scores, bureaucracy and control. In my next hermeneutic circle I couldn't help but ask the next obvious question. "Do you feel valued?"

A highly respected teacher, who lived her life in self-discovery constantly taking courses and improving her own practice lowered her head. All eyes were cast on this unassuming, professional teacher. As she raised her head she quietly whispered the unspeakable. "We are not valued at all." Another highly respected teacher quickly joined the conversation as we continued to discuss teachers as equal partners who served as valued contributors.

> Couldn't be further from the truth, not that we shouldn't be, but we are not equals. No! Not that! I've always expected that I have superiors and if a decision is made I have to follow through with that and I've always respected that, but in the past year I feel further and further down and that our voices are not being heard and I'm not to this point yet, but I know people who are already so bitter that they are going to sit quietly, shake their head and not do what they are told. People are going to leave and people are getting burnt out, and we are just going to carry out a curricular plan that we know isn't good, it isn't the way it should be and we know it is not in the best interest of kids.

The teachers' stories of diminished voice are characteristic of high fear organizations. High-fear organizations are "still locked in a style of operation characterized by fear, mistrust and control."[21] Clearly, there was little receptivity to the openness that is an essential ingredient in a high trust organization. Reina and Reina (1999)[22] highlight the importance of people coming to their work from a place of contribution.

The teachers did not feel that their voices were heard. They were silenced. They were no longer contributors in systems that once valued their input. This led to anger, frustration and retreat. They were incapable of making a contribution because they were not heard. In the very act of not hearing the teachers' voices the administrators were severing the potential for establishing managerial trustworthiness. A high capacity to trust others is associated with a fluid work style that allows for sharing of information and dependency on others. Without voice it is impossible to openly communicate information rendering the potential for dependency on others null and void.

The administrators, focused on raising the test scores and implementing the demands of NCLB had failed to listen to the voices of the people doing the work. As I mentioned earlier, I do not wish to villainize the administrators. They are living with an unspeakable burden as they try and orchestrate the mandates of NCLB. I am certain that, unintentionally, they have, in some instances, lost sight of the teachers as everyone works at a frenetic pace to raise the scores. Interestingly, one compassionate teacher provided an explanation for the shift in the administrators approach under NCLB.

> And I'm sure they feel they are listening to our voices. And part of it is, I think, the fact that they have not taught themselves in years. And they never have had to do it under these circumstances from the state and they are telling us we have to do this and this!

The Frenetic Pace

The teachers from Northern Illinois reported that there were more and more demands eating away at their time. Some reported having common assessments in every discipline and highly structured curriculum guides that have essentially made them automatons in their own classrooms. They reported having more and more to do and that the quality of their work was suffering as a result of it. A National Board certified teacher with a stellar reputation as a calm, reasonable, woman was one of the first to bring the frenetic pace to my attention.

> We have a lot of assessments. Even in the science alone there is this assessment, that assessment, the next assessment and then there is a lot of vocabulary and we are trying to get all the vocabulary in because of the ISAT test. You are very aware of all that ecosystems vocabulary that we have to make sure the kids know, so all of that. I think the kids are getting a lot out of it, but I mean I feel like I'm frazzled because I feel like I am cramming all of this stuff down their throats. I don't know, it is just the stress level, I feel like I am more intense. In fact, I even shared this with our principal, I feel like sometimes regarding not just assessments, but regarding meetings and having to be here and having to be there and not having time to converse with your colleagues and to plan, and you know just to be more relaxed about your teaching and it just feels like you have to do this and you have to do that and it is all so structured and regimented and you know I've got some special needs kids in here who cannot handle that pace. They breakdown and I've got several in my classroom who will come up to me and they talk much slower and they need more explanation and I find myself looking at my clock and I'm thinking, "What am I doing?" You know I need to slow down and help these kids learn and not just now we are doing this and now we are doing that (voice speeds up with a frenetic tone) and it is the frantic pace.

There was not a single teacher that I interviewed who was not feeling the intensity of the demands. You see, the common assessment model they had fallen victim to, was designed for a high school. No one had carefully studied the impact of attempting to take a high school model and foisting it upon teachers and children in an elementary setting where teachers teach all subjects. The assessment model was put into place rather quickly in most of these elementary districts and the curriculum guides that came with the assessments were highly prescriptive, leaving little time for authentic inquiry and problem-solving. Another teacher came forward, she had found the courage to listen to her inner voice.

> Well, it is virtually impossible to teach everything we have to teach for the test and differentiate for everyone, we try our best to differentiate and to do everything, but we feel like we are on a treadmill, falling off the back, getting nowhere, falling right off the back of the treadmill. And then there are moments where you just close the door and say to yourself, "I'm doing the best I can." Keeping in mind that I'm there to do more than pour knowledge into their heads, because they are whole people.

As I collected story after story from veteran teachers, I couldn't help but wonder if their younger colleagues were feeling the same pressure. I asked the veteran teachers what they had observed?

> Everybody is frantic. You talk to any teacher and they can't get everything done in one day, they can't keep the pace up, and it is teachers of all ages. For awhile we thought it was just the more experienced teachers but the younger teachers are feeling that way too.
> I am always running to catch up! And you are reading all of this (teacher shows me a huge curriculum guide, one of four she is required to use) and you are trying to figure out what you can implement and you are figuring out how you can cut corners so you can get done, rather than kind of digging deeper into things of certain interest for kids.

I asked the teachers if the quality of their teaching was being sacrificed in the name of quantity. A teacher reminisced on methods that she had sacrificed to meet the parameters at hand.

> Every one of us is experiencing an awful lot of stress over this. I have always believed, and I believe most professionals believe, less is more. You should teach fewer things and you should teach them in more depth. Now more! They want more and more and more and we are getting less and less and less and we are producing less and paying a very high price for it.

> I don't think there is much time for deep conversation. We haven't had enough time to barely teach the foundation, they can't understand the foundation much less engage in higher order thinking.

I asked the teachers about subjects like science and social studies that help children understand their relationship with the earth and with their fellow human beings in different parts of the world. The teachers reported having little time for these important subjects and also had to sacrifice teaching research based programs in the way they were designed because of time constraints.

> So lots of time we will alternate science and social studies rather than doing them both because the time just isn't there. Our math program started and was very successful. It was supposed to take an hour and fifteen minutes a day. Well, I think people are down to about an hour a day now and they are leaving out some of the things which they felt weren't quite as vital. If you are going to teach the math program as it was meant to be, you have to have all the time to do it.

I asked one teacher if she felt the test-taking curriculum she was required to teach prepared the children for the world. "No, I think they frustrate them. I think a child will remember a lot longer by doing rather than lecturing. But time is restricted on all of those things too.

After listening to many harrowing tales of that which had been lost in the frenetic pace of test-taking preparation, I asked the teachers if this pace had impacted their relationships with children. A teacher softly responded, "Oh I am sure it does because we are stressed. Definitely! Come on we have to get through this, got to get through that, we have to get this unit done and this and this and this. Of course it does, of course it does."

A first grade teacher shared that she had to give up a much needed recess break that was once a standard part of the first grade morning.

> We don't give them recess in the morning, they get it just before lunch, and now the kids who need remediation are kept in one day a week and the administration says it is a fun activity. It isn't a fun activity for the children. The kids ask, "Do I have to?" It is not fun for these kids to miss recess, but, "Oh the test scores!"

Clearly our teachers find themselves working at a frenetic pace to fulfill the demands of NCLB. They have lost all semblance of coming full circle in their work with children. Instead of predictable patterns they find that life in the classroom just clips along at an alarming pace. Campbell (1988) observed that we inherited the concept of the circle from Sumerian mythology, the four cardinal points and the three hundred and sixty degrees. "The temporal aspect of the circle is that you leave, go somewhere, and always come back. Now we are losing this sense of the circle in relation to time, because we have digital time, where you have time just buzzing by."[23]

Time is just ticking away for our teachers. They clearly have more to do than the hours, minutes and seconds will allow. When they listen to their own intuition they know that they are off balance. They know that the demands are impossible for themselves and for the children. The freneticism of raising the scores has spiraled out of control sucking our teachers and children into a perilous black hole devoid of light. "There's a center of quietness within you, if you lose that center, you are in tension and you begin to fall apart."[24] We can't afford to have our teachers fall apart. We are forcing them to live in a world of fragmentation that can only lead to their demise. I wonder who will be left to teach if we continue on this absurd frenetic pace.

Survival: Trusting Intuition

As I continued my interview process it became increasingly apparent that veteran teachers had learned to survive by finding ways to trust their intuition in order to do what they felt was best for the children. As they described experiences in which they had followed their intuition or bliss they also used words like "sneaking", "guilty", and "cheating". One primary teacher shared that it had become increasingly difficult to find the time to take the children out for recess. She knew that the first graders desperately needed the reprieve, but she shared that she had experienced a sense of guilt when she listened to her intuition and took the children outside. "You feel guilty when you take the children outside, which I did Friday because I knew it would be one of the last nice days. There are so many things we can do outside related to our science units. But, then you feel guilty."

I continued to question the primary teacher: "Am I hearing you say that there is not a lot of time to trust your intuition?" The teacher affirmed that I was hearing her correctly. I was surprised when a fourth grade teacher described diverting from the curriculum to buffer the tension her students were feeling as cheating.

> I cheat, a little bit here and there. Shame on me! I have noticed that the children are a lot more anxious and a lot less willing to tune in when we are hitting one skill after another, rushing through things. They are tuning out and coming to school unable to sleep and unable to pay attention and they are very upset with the testing that gets done. To the point of crying, to the point of not sleeping, some to the point of just backing away from it all together. I think that is a huge, huge problem. It also does not allow us to be a community of learners where it is just fun, relaxing, and interesting.

One teacher shared that at times she makes the decision to "close the door" and teach in ways that help the children to see the connections. It appeared that the closing of the door was another indicator of this need "to sneak" so that children could have rich connected learning experiences.

> And now we have kids coming to us with blank looks on their faces because they aren't from this country and now we can't teach about other parts of the world, our curriculum is all US History. So there is so much we teach that these children cannot tie to their experience. Then the local assessment we give focuses on dates. I tell them I'm more interested in them understanding what went on in this time period. Sometimes, I close my door and do what I think is best for kids.

It seems quite amazing that our veteran teachers describe the times that they followed their intuition as cheating and sneaking. I asked the veterans if this was different for younger teachers? An experienced teacher described the way she was teaching writing and compared herself to what a younger teacher would have to do.

> I am focusing on good writing. I have twelve laptops in my room right now. You know what, I made a decision the other afternoon. I thought, "If it takes me a half day to finish it, we are just going to do it." You know, it was such a calm afternoon, and the kids were so engaged and excited about it. I will teach the children what makes a good extended response. Am I going to do it every week? No! But, I know a new teacher. She has to!

Another teacher described the canned lessons she had been given in the new ISAT preparation curriculum guides, "I am standing my ground. I am not using this. But, a new teacher. Could they stand their ground? Absolutely not!"

It appears that veteran teachers find ways to teach in depth following their intuitions constructed through years of successful teaching. It is in these moments that they appear to be following their bliss despite feelings of guilt. They know their younger colleagues do not have this luxury.

It seems that we fallen upon the darkest of times in education. Our schools, for the most part, have become lifeless, dreary places where the focus rests on standardization, testing and control. I worry that there is not much to sustain the young women in the profession if they incapable of ever following their bliss. I worry that following intuition, for veteran teachers, is associated with feelings of guilt.

If you are following your bliss, you are enjoying the life that is within you[25].

As I reflected on the fact that our teachers are incapable of truly following their bliss I realized that they are in dire need of an advocate. Unless we clearly and intelligently communicate the perilous situation at hand in our schools, I'm fairly certain that the younger teachers, who cannot feel the joy of teaching from their inner self will leave. The children will be left drowning in a sea of tests and standards and the authors and administrators of NCLB will be left wondering what happened to the educators who were fulfilling their commands? Surely, we cannot allow this to happen. We will have successfully created a society of test takers with no one left to teach them. When a problem of great magnitude occurs the adults, schooled under the demands of NCLB, will be left searching for the answers that lie hidden within. They won't know how to sort through the information, they won't know how to be critical consumers of the facts and we will suffer the unintended consequences of NCLB. Recalling the words of Chief Seattle.

Man does not weave the web of life, he is merely a strand in it.
Whatever he does to the web, he does to himself.[26]

I'm left wondering if we can build trusting relationships in schools under the pressure of NCLB? I'm left wondering what stands in the way of building collaborative cultures where all contribute in extraordinary ways? For the teachers, I interviewed, it was clearly betrayal. Betrayal, like some cancers, may rapidly mutate destroying the healthy relationships within a community, at other times the cancer insidiously grows beneath the surface undetected by the community as a whole. As I interviewed these exceptional teachers, I became more and more interested in trying to understand the depth of their betrayals. Reina and Reina (1999)[27] proposed that those who care most deeply about an organization, are the ones who often feel most betrayed by the organization. The teachers I interviewed cared deeply about their profession. Their profession was their calling. They had been forced to teach in a wasteland that was counterintuitive to everything that they had come to understand about best practice. They were forced to dance to cacophonous tones. They were indeed in discordant harmony.

I fully believe that our teachers are in need of the support and compassion of gentle healers. They need people who are willing to compassionately listen to their needs and reassemble the fragmentation we are experiencing in schools as a result of NCLB. I'm certain our teachers and administrators cannot survive the demands unless we find ways to honor them with compassion.

My research has left me thinking a great deal about the notion of isolation that Lortie (1975/2002)[28] discusses in his timeless work *Schoolteacher*. If retreat allows for healing and if creation of new ideas comes from intuition and quiet moments, then perhaps the isolation of the classroom is not the evil we may consider it to be. I have believed for some period of time that we need the balance. Palmer (1998)[29] refers to this as the inner ground and the community of fellow teachers. Without this balance I'm afraid we will remain off center. I think the thing that is most disturbing to me is that in the world of standardization we have stripped away the inner ground. We have denied teachers of the place for creation, growth and new ideas. This notion is what wakes me from my sleep most often, tearing away at my silence and my harmony. I think it is the seed of my compassion for our teachers. Who amongst us wants to be reduced to an automaton? We need to restore the inner ground if we are ever to create the new stories for our time.

Campbell (1988) believed that we are lost, that we have not created the stories for our times.[30] He saw the need to create new myths for our times. Darwin believed that it was not the strongest of the species, or the most intelligent that survived. For Darwin, it was the members of the species that were most responsive to change. We are in dire need of new stories. We are in dire need of responsiveness to change. The trouble is that we keep creating recipes and "how to" books. We keep creating the next best strategy to prepare for the test. It is rather simple, the recipes don't work everywhere because they are not responsive to the needs of the individuals in unique times and places.

I encourage my readers to move beyond the old paradigm of assessment that, in Stiggins (2007) words, sorts children into winners and losers.[31] Under the punitive rules of NCLB we unfortunately create winners and losers. We perpetuate a sense of hopelessness and defeat amongst the learners most in need of our unconditional support and guidance. Assessment can be used to inform the instructional process. As I see it, assessment can be humane when it is used to provide feedback to learners on how they can improve. In the new paradigm for assessment we have the potential to focus on the growth of all learners rather than their failures. Imagine if our new myths celebrated the stories of "losers" who became "winners" because assessment was used to chart a path for success.

I challenge each of my readers to embrace the dilemma created by NCLB. I encourage you to create new stories that blend the best of traditions within your unique time and place. I encourage you to revisit the teachers' words. If you are a teacher, please read these stories and use them as a means of understanding that you are not alone. If you are an administrator, please use them to reflect upon the community within your building. Use them to think about the impact that NCLB is having on both you and your staff. If you are a legislator please reconsider the impact of No Child Left Behind. We are my friends in desperate need of a new order. My new chant is a timeless one: *Novus Ordo Seclorum.* (A new order)

In a dark time, the eye begins to see,

I meet my shadow in the deepening shade...
A fallen woman, I climb out of my fear.[32]

I have climbed out of my fear, I have embraced the dark side of NCLB. I encourage you to do the same. Our children deserve to be more than numbers. They deserve a varied curriculum that celebrates thinking and novel approaches. They deserve to be judged on their individual growth rather than on their test score. They deserve to experience a world of education that is full of possibilities instead of tests.

Notes

1. P. Senge, Scharmer, C.O., Jaworski, J., & Flowers, B.S. *Presence: Human purpose and the field of the future.* (Cambridge: The Society for Organization Learning, Inc. 2004) p. 199.
2. Sergiovanni, 2005, p.70
3. Sergiovanni, 2005.
4. K.A. Knutson, A.O. Miranda, & C. Washell, "The connection between school culture and leadership social interest in learning organizations." (*The Journal of Individual Psychology, 61(2),* 2005). p.27
5. R. Evans, *The human side of school change.* (San Francisco: Jossey-Bass. 1996.) p.127
6. Sergiovanni, 2005.
7. S. Bryk, & B. Schneider, *Trust in schools.* (New York: Russell Sage Foundation, 2002). p. *xiv*
8. S. Bryk, & B. Schneider, 2002. p. *xiv*
9. A. Hargreaves, Teaching and betrayal. (*Teachers and Teaching: Theory and practice, 8* (3/4), 2002). 392-407.
10. P. Leonard, & L. Leonard, "The collaboration prescription: Remedy or reverie." (*International Journal of Leadership in Education 4,* 383-399, 2004). p.21
11. D.C. Lortie, *Schoolteacher.* (Chicago: University of Chicago Press, 1975/2002). p. 214
12. J. Campbell, *The power of myth.* (New York: Anchor Books, 1988).
13. W.T. Anderson, *Reality isn't what it used to be: Theatrical politics, ready to wear religions, global myths, primitive chic, and other wonders of the postmodern world.* (San Francisco: Harper & Row, 1990). p. 9.
14. Evans,1996, p.77
15. N. Noddings, *The challenge to care in schools: An alternative approach to education.* (NY: Teachers College, 1992).
16. Sonia Nieto, *Language, Culture, and Teaching: Critical Perspectives for a New Century.* Lawrence Erlbaum Associates, 2002.
17. P. Freire, *Pedagogy of the oppressed.* (New York: Herder & Herder, 1970). p.72)
18. Campbell, 1988, p.43
19. Lortie, 1975/2002, p.*x*
20. Palmer, 1998, p.56
21. Ryan & Oestreich, 1998, p.5
22. D.S. Reina, & M.L. Reina, *Trust in the workplace: Building effective relationships in your organization.* (San Francisco: Berrett-Koehler, 1999).
23. Campbell, 1988, p.269

24. Campbell, 1988, p.203
25. Campbell, 1988, p.113
26. Chief Seattle.
27. Reina and Reina, 1999
28. Lortie, 1975/2002
29. Palmer, 1998
30. Campbell, 1988
31. R. Stiggins, "Assessment through the student's eyes." *Educational Leadership.* 64(8), 2007.
32. Roethke

References

Anderson, W.T. *Reality isn't what it used to be: Theatrical politics, ready to wear religions, global myths, primitive chic, and other wonders of the postmodern world.* San Francisco: Harper & Row, 1990.

Bryk, S., & Schneider, B. *Trust in schools.* New York: Russell Sage Foundation, 2002.

Campbell, J. *The power of myth.* New York: Anchor Books, 1988.

Evans, R. *The human side of school change.* San Francisco: Jossey-Bass, 1996.

Freire, P. *Pedagogy of the oppressed.* New York: Herder & Herder, 1970.

Hargreaves, A. Teaching and betrayal. *Teachers and Teaching: Theory and practice, 8* (3/4), 392-407, 2002.

Knutson, K.A., A.O. Miranda, & C. Washell, "The connection between school cultureand leadership social interest in learning organizations." *The Journal of Individual Psychology, 61(2),* 25-36. 2005.

Leonard, P. & Leonard, L. The collaboration prescription: Remedy or reverie. *International Journal of Leadership in Education 4,* 383-399, 2004.

Lortie, D.C. *Schoolteacher.* Chicago: University of Chicago Press, 1975/2002.

Nieto, Sonia. *Language, Culture, and Teaching: Critical Perspectives for a New Century.* Lawrence Erlbaum Associates, 2002.

Noddings, N. *The challenge to care in schools: An alternative approach to education.* NY: Teachers College, 1992.

Palmer, P. *The courage to teach: Exploring the inner landscape of a teacher's life.* San Francisco: Jossey-Bass, 1998.

Palmer, P. *A hidden wholeness: The journey towards an undivided life.* San Francisco: Jossey-Bass, 2004.

Reina, D.S. & Reina, M.L. *Trust in the workplace: Building effective relationships in your organization.* San Francisco: Berrett-Koehler, 1999.

Ryan, K.D. & Oestreich, D.K. *Driving fear out of the workplace: Creating the high-trust, high-performance organization.* San Francisco: Jossey-Bass, 1998.

Senge, P., C.O. Scharmer, J. Jaworski, & B.S. Flowers, *Presence: Human purpose and the field of the future.* Cambridge: SoL (The Society for Organization Learning, Inc.) 2004.

Sergiovanni, T. *Strengthening the heartbeat: Leading and learning in schools.* San Francisco: Jossey-Bass, 2005.

Stiggins, R. "Assessment through the student's eyes." *Educational Leadership.* 64(8), 2007.

Chapter 12
A Ray of Hope: Service-Learning Insures Success for All

Virginia Jagla

> Education is a social process. Education is growth. Education is not a preparation for life; education is life itself. – John Dewey

Who can argue with the premise of the No Child Left Behind law? Of course we want success for all students. Most teachers and administrators realized the one-size-fits-all approach originally adopted within the law would prove to be too challenging to fulfill. Now that the essential component of flexibility is being added to this federally mandated law, there may be a ray of hope. Rather than ponder the myriad facets of this complex piece of legislation, this chapter considers one school's approach to addressing and meeting academic standards through the use of service-learning.

In her influential book, Cathryn Berger-Kaye[1] tells us that:

> Service-learning can be defined in part by what it does for your students. When service-learning is used in a structured way that connects classroom content, literature, and skills to community needs, students will:
>
> - apply academic, social and personal skills to improve the community.
> - make decisions that have real, not hypothetical, results.
> - grow as individuals, gain respect for peers, and increase civic participation.
> - experience success no matter what their ability level.
> - gain a deeper understanding of themselves, their community.
> - develop as leaders who take initiative, solve problems, work as a team, and demonstrate their abilities while and through helping others.

The National Service-Learning Partnership[2] defines service-learning as "a teaching method that engages young people in solving problems within their schools and communities as part of their academic studies or other type of intentional learning activity. Service-learning helps students master important curriculum content by supporting their making meaningful connections between what they are studying and its many applications."

The intention of service-learning is to experience democracy in action by planning and carrying through worthwhile activities to benefit others in society. Service-learning can be a meaningful variable affecting student learning. Contemporary service-learning programs address learning standards, respect students' individual learning styles, and link educational and service goals with the responsibilities of citizenship in a democratic society. Students learn through the experiences themselves as well as reflection on the process. Service-learning is a powerful pedagogy which engages the use of academic skills to address and solve real-life problems in the community. It is a true "ray of hope" for educators looking to engage all students in order to meet and exceed standards in all schools.

National Middle School Association dedicated their March, 2005 issue of *Middle School Journal* to the "Behind the scenes of No Child Left Behind." In this issue the editor, Tom Er[3] points out the immense concern with the standards and the tests focuses us on what happens before and after instruction. He cautions educators to place more emphasis on what occurs amid standards and tests. Strong, engaging instruction is what will advance true learning. In his article, "Accountability for Academics and Social Responsibility through Service-Learning," David Smith [4] gives us a look at a strong program in a middle school in Connecticut. The service-learning component provided the high quality "authentic" assessment required by the standards. Service-learning is being utilized in many schools as a natural bridge with academic standards.

The number and depth of high-quality service-learning programs is increasing in schools. Service-learning has been a part of Field Middle School for about twelve years. It began with just a few programs. "You have to start out small," said Mary Beth Hulting, the Service-learning Coordinator at Field Middle School in Northbrook, IL. Northbrook is a northern suburb of Chicago. Field Middle School is a nationally recognized "Leader School" for its incorporation of service-learning.

Dr. Robert Machak has been the principal of Field Middle School for six years. Service-learning at the school predates him. It was not integrated into the curriculum at that time. Through researching "the paper trail," he believes that service-learning has been part of Field Middle School for approximately twelve years. "I think service-learning is a more integral component if you look at overall curriculum today than it was ten or twelve years ago when the program started." Service-learning at Field Middle School initially was implemented sporadically, usually one day or less spent on a given project. Such projects were few and far between. None of them were connected with curriculum. "We are aligned with state learning standards now... It is not an add-on or extra. It really is part of who we are and what we do." The passion of conviction comes through loud and clear as Machak reiterates many essential elements of the embedded nature of service-learning at Field Middle School.

Research abounds regarding the use of service-learning in K-12 schools. Much of the research addresses academic learning. Various studies have been done to gain more insight into the pedagogy. One such study found that students in quality service-learning schools showed moderate to strong positive gains on student achievement tests in language arts and/or reading, engagement in school, sense of educational accomplishment and homework completion.[5] Other studies have found that students who participated in service-learning have achieved higher scores on the state test of basic skills.[6] Further research indicates that elementary and middle school students who participated in service-learning had improved problem-solving skills and increased interest in academics.[7] In their comprehensive book, *Serve and Learn: Implementing and Evaluating Service-Learning in Middle and High Schools*, Pritchard and Whitehead[8] show how service-learning can improve intellectual development because of its constructivist nature. They further illustrate how service-learning increases academic achievement and can be instrumental in accelerating school reform.

Hulting teaches humanities and science at Field Middle School. The rest of her time is spent in coordinating the various service-learning projects which permeate the academic curriculum as well as nonacademic subjects like physical education, art, and home economics. She has learned much regarding service-learning pedagogy during her five years at the school. When she first started at Field Middle School, she understood the community service aspect. She has grown to understand that this "needed to truly be connected with the curriculum... it needs to connect somewhere within the curriculum to state standards to what you are doing and make it a real life experience for the kids."

It takes time and patience to understand how to connect service-learning to state standards. As Hulting says "It is not something you can force on any teacher." Some teachers have a natural proclivity for service-learning, yet others are easily persuaded to attempt this method once they have seen it in action and have grasped the understanding. By perusing the standards which are expected to be addressed in the appropriate grade level, teachers can decided which ones lend themselves to service-learning projects. The academic learning standards should be made transparent to the students at the middle and high school level. Often the students come up with ideas or a different twist to an established idea.

Regarding service-learning's interdisciplinary nature, Hulting indicates "Sometimes you get two subjects connected doing one project. There is really no magic formula... you get one, two, or three connected doing one project." Many middle schools are organized into interdisciplinary teams. Formulating a service-learning unit with such a team can provide students with increased understanding at a deeper level than if one teacher planned the project. The team approach enhances the likelihood of success as there are more individuals to accomplish the necessary tasks. It is essential to involve the students in the planning. Their ideas are usually helpful and the cornerstone to a constructivist model of teaching.

Service-learning is slightly chaotic as it evolves. It is not as orderly as a teach-and-test method of teaching. Any teacher who employs the pedagogy of service-learning necessarily must place a lot of value in this approach. If the teacher is reluctant it is not going to work. When an enthusiastic community partner pairs with amenable teachers, as Hulting says "you'll have a program that is unbelievable." The key is working with the faculty who are open to the pedagogy. Starting small with those who are enthusiastic, while demonstrating the power of the pedagogy, can spark others who were not opposed but, for whatever reason, were slightly apathetic to the approach at first. At Field Middle School, service-learning has become so much a part of the culture that now when a new idea is proposed the buy in is almost automatic.

Hulting credits service-learning with helping students in a variety of academic endeavors. Evidence relating higher achievement at Field Middle School with the embedded nature of service-learning is anecdotal. There are, however many studies which delineate this correlation. Research studies have found that students involved in service-learning have earned higher grades.[9] In another study 83% of schools with service-learning programs reported that grade point averages of participating service-learning students improved 76% of the time.[10] Middle and high school students who participated in service-learning tutoring programs increased their grade point averages and test scores in reading/language arts and math and were less likely to drop out of school.[11]

Machak feels that when people talk about curriculum revision, they are often referring to additions in what he refers to as "the mile wide and an inch deep" method. Many educators feel pressured by the No Child Left Behind mandate to "cover" vast amounts of curriculum in their lessons. "We are trying just the opposite." By spending more time with the service-learning projects, he feels the students gain deeper understanding rather than surface knowledge. The trick here is to "uncover" the comprehensive understandings inherent in any subject.

Machak refers to less integrated service-learning endeavors as "good P.R stuff." When he became principal, there were a few one day service projects which were "not tied to any curriculum goals," and involved students taking a trip into Chicago. He felt there was more that could be done within their own community which would match the curriculum goals and standards of the school. He worked to develop more intergenerational service-learning activities with the seventh grade classes. "That is when we stared… the computer partners. We developed an intergenerational garden and the whole idea for Veterans Day and adopting a grandparent for each advisory."

He credits Mary Beth Hulting as being instrumental in steering the direction of service-learning toward compatibility with state standards and district goals. He is proud of the faculty's ability and willingness to revise, edit or stop some well meaning activities if they do not "fit philosophically what we are trying to do."

Hulting advises looking at the curriculum first. Faculty members can ask "What are we already doing that lends itself to an element of service-learning?" It is important not to think of service-learning as an "add on" or extra activity not integrated with the curriculum. James Bean[12] delineates how curriculum integration naturally occurs as social issues are addressed in middle schools. In their significant book, *Social Issues and Service at the Middle Level*, Samuel Totten and Jon Pedersen proclaim that "a study of social issues and involvement in service are ideal ways to begin to interweave a meaningful exploratory component throughout the curriculum."[13] Totten & Pedersen's book highlights a wide array of middle level service-learning projects which are both interdisciplinary and exploratory.

An important factor in exemplary teaching is student ownership of their learning. Involving students in planning their curriculum is a necessity of good middle level philosophy. At Field Middle School there is an established hierarchy of service-learning involvement. In sixth grade students are mainly involved with service to the school. In seventh grade the focus is on community. The eighth graders are more globally involved. Hulting says "We do guide the sixth and seventh graders. We tell them where we are headed, what ideas we might have or might be able to work with." Field Middle School has an advisory period every day. Two or three advisory periods a week are dedicated to service-learning. "It is during that time the kids can brainstorm with the teacher... what can we do for this... how are we going to contact community members? They really come up with the ideas."

The eighth graders come up with service ideas with their advisor as their guide. There are a few established concepts regarding the books they read. *The Seven Habits of Highly Successful Teens*[14] is one such book. They also read books about homelessness. The eighth graders attend "a big leadership conference. From that leadership conference they come up with ideas and do things from there. Sometimes we might plant an idea and they will run with it."

As I inquired about the high school the Field Middle School students will attend, Hulting indicated that "many of our kids end up being the class presidents and end up running big service projects... We tracked some of the kids. With Field being so small, and considering there are four different districts in Northbrook, there are almost always two of the four top offices -- president, vice president, secretary or treasurer from Field." She proudly tells stories of how engaged the students are at Field Middle School. This obviously translates to future involvement in high school and beyond. Research has shown that middle and elementary school students who participated in service-learning were better able to trust and be trusted by others, be reliable and accept responsibility. [15]

Further studies have shown that students who participated in high quality service-learning programs displayed an increase in measures of school engagement and achievement in mathematics than their peers in control groups.[16] Another study found that students who participated in service-learning endeavors came to class on time more often, completed more classroom tasks and took the initiative to ask questions more often. [17] In a variety of research studies schools that sustain service-learning programs convey that student engagement has resulted in increased attendance each year during a three-year period of time.[18] In studies with students involved in service-learning, research has shown they had higher attendance rates when compared with their contemporaries in control groups.[19] The replication of studies depicting increased attendance rates is significant. When students are engaged and choose to come to school more regularly, they can acquire more consistent understanding in all subject areas. Lack of motivation is an underlying cause for students being "left behind" in schools. Service-learning pedagogy affords more impetus to learn and sparks enthusiasm as well as meaningful understanding.

Hulting has organized a multitude of binders which detail many of the aspects of established service-learning projects at Field Middle School. The ideas are aligned with the State of Illinois learning standards. Curricular goals are delineated and aligned with the outcomes of the projects. Community partners are highlighted with ongoing assessment to be sure their needs are being met. These service-learning units provide a base for total school participation. They are constantly being updated and revised with input from students and faculty.

I inquired as to how they go about researching the community partners and working with them to make sure that the projects are actually helping. Some of their established community partners actually sought them out. Such partners, like the senior center and the local hospital "find out through the paper that we do service-learning." In the spring the student council hosts "a breakfast where we invite community leaders from churches, synagogues, hospitals, shelters... the kids sit down with those community leaders and they determine some issues... or what types of problems they are having and how might we help."

Since educators at Field Middle School are looking to start new service-learning projects, this information will be particularly useful at this time. They will look at the information gleaned from the potential partners and determine, based on the needs of the community partners, "where the kids might help out and then look at our curriculum and see what we can do." Often the students, especially those in eighth grade, will come up with ideas in line with news reports of what is happening in the world. Hulting indicated that some of these global issues are presented by the local community leaders.

Hulting feels that one of the major accomplishments at Field Middle School has been to get everyone in the school involved in service-learning. "Not only core classes but you also have the art classes doing it as well. As you know, often change can be hard and a lot of times schools starting with service-learning really have trouble with some teachers buying in and there is some resistance to new programs." Many teachers feel that service-learning is going to be so much extra work and they really do not feel they can extend themselves in that manner. In some schools service-learning coordinators are quite pleased when the majority of teachers participate. At Field Middle School, as Hulting says, "There has been one hundred percent student participation and one hundred percent staff, faculty and administrative participation also."

Many of the service-learning projects piloted at Field Middle School have been so successful that they have been continued as a regular part of the curriculum. There are at least ten such programs in existence which have found their niche in particular grade levels. One example is their STARS (Students Tutoring And Responding to Students) program in which eighth graders take on mentoring roles for many of the sixth graders in need. This program also involves peer mediation when necessary. "We just had mediation yesterday with kids after training and they did wonderfully. I am happy that a lot of the programs that were initiated and piloted really took off."

Another such program is the Computer Partners. A senior is coupled with a seventh grader. The seventh grader teaches basic computer skills to the senior in a comfortable one-on-one situation in the middle school's computer lab. The class includes a juice and cookies break when seniors and young adolescents can engage in relaxed conversation. These classes continue with the same pairs once a week for three weeks. There are three such cycles in the school year, allowing for three groups of computer partners. Jim Zabel, the former State of Illinois service-learning coordinator, said he thought it was the first such program in the country. It is impressive to observe the self esteem boost it gives to the young adolescents as they impart their knowledge and technology skills. Many of the seniors are thrilled to get the knowledge to be able to email their grandchildren and do other basic word processing endeavors as well as use the internet.

Since Hulting is a teacher of humanities and science, I inquired as to the integration of those subjects. The two major service-learning programs for the sixth grade are an environmental unit with recycling and a unit based on wellness. As a science teacher, "we teach a lot about environmental studies with recycling components. We teach that all through the science program in an academic way. We do recycle with the kids during advisory. During the week they do some clean ups. There is also a unit in which they investigate and research certain topics dealing with the environment and present it to younger kids... and talk about the importance of recycling... It is not just doing recycling here but spreading the word."

The wellness unit is an integration of humanities and physical education. Much of the academic portion of this unit is "done through gym, where the kids spend about three to four weeks talking about wellness and diet." Drug and alcohol awareness is included in this unit. The sixth graders plan and implement a 5K walk for K-5 students and the community. As a part of this event, the middle level students disseminate the information they have learned. "They write papers on it in PE, and then we hold our own 5K where we invite community members, moms and dads and talk about wellness. We print out their papers and pamphlets... There is also a raffle portion that goes with the 5K. The sixth graders do a lot of the research and investigating through their humanities class. They write letters to community members to solicit donations for raffle prizes... Much of the money that we earn from that raffle goes to the charity that they have selected through their research in class." Math skills are increased through the money raising efforts. Math classes also chart the course for the 5K run/walk.

The middle level students gain much through the service-learning experiences besides the academic knowledge. Leadership qualities are strongly enhanced. Hulting insists that "Throughout the three grades the students come to understand that what they are learning is applicable to real life situations." This relevancy to life is paramount for young adolescents who often seems to be in a place of practicing for their lives to be.

How affirming it is to be able to do significant work for their community. One of the eighth graders told me "You get a sense of pride and satisfaction out of doing certain things and it really makes you feel good." This type of learning experience reaches far beyond the academic realm. The students at Field Middle School are comfortable with doing for others and not just looking out for themselves. Research has shown that students who participated in service-learning enjoyed helping others with projects, became more dependable for others and felt more comfortable communicating with ethnically diverse groups.[20]

At Field Middle School service-learning involvement has planted the seed. The students are becoming engaged citizens and hopefully that continues, even beyond high school. Students feel comfortable with their ability to work with diverse populations. They are comfortable with organizing and running events. These are experiences they can draw on in the future. Another eighth grader told me "Although it's meant to serve the community, I think I've learned more how to interact with people of different ages and who have different challenges in life... I think that the biggest thing I've learned is how to be patient..." These feelings are not unique to the students at Field Middle School. Research has shown that many other students who engaged in quality service-learning programs have reported increased acceptance of cultural diversity.[21] Additional studies demonstrate that students who engaged in service-learning showed progression over time in their awareness of cultural differences and attitudes toward helping others.[22]

When curriculum is enriched by service-learning pedagogy, much more than academics is enhanced for the students involved. One research study found that high school students who participated in high quality service-learning programs were more likely to develop bonds with more adults, agreed that they could learn from and work with the elderly and disabled and felt that they trusted others besides parents and teachers to whom they could turn for help.[23] Another study demonstrated that students who engaged in service-learning showed greater empathy and cognitive complexity than comparison groups.[24]

Middle school is a great time in students' lives to be involved in such significant ventures as service-learning. One eighth grader at Field Middle School summed up his point of view. "You get a good feeling because you're helping someone when they need your help... you can give something to them... I just hope more kids do service-learning. I think it's really good experience."

Thoughtful service-learning pedagogy engages the whole learner in meaningful, constructive scholarship. Thoroughly engaged students are constructing their own knowledge, which stretches far beyond the typical facts and information imparted in many daily lessons. The goal for our students should be to surpass standards, not just meet them. Service-learning can help reach this goal. The teach-test model furthers automatism in students. True mastery or concept attainment requires more in depth, constructive learning. Students are not being left behind at Field Middle School. Students, teachers and administrators agree that service-learning contributes greatly to their academic success.

Notes

1. Cathryn Berger-Kaye. *The Complete Guide to Service-learning: Proven, Practical Ways to Engage Students in Civic Responsibility, Academic Curriculum, and Social Action*, 2004) p. 7

2. National Service-Learning Partnership. (2005). <http://www.service-learningpartnership.org/site/PageServer>

3. T. Erb, "Transforming abstract standards into solid performances." (*Middle School Journal*, 36(4) (2005): 2.

4. D.B. Smith, "Accountability for academics and social responsibility through service-learning." (*Middle School Journal*, 36, 4, 2005): 20-25

5. D. Weiler, A. LaGoy, E. Crane and A. Rovner, *An evaluation of K-12 service-learning in California: Phase II final report.* (Emeryville: RPP International with the Search Institute, 1998).

6. V. Anderson, C. Kinsley, P. Negroni, P. and C. Price, "Community service-learning and school improvement in Springfield, Massachusetts." (*Phi Delta Kappan*, 72, June 1991): 761-764.

7. L. Stephens, *The complete guide to learning through community service, grades K-9.* (Boston: Allyn and Bacon, 1995).

8. F.F. Pritchard and G.I. Whitehead III, *Serve and learn: Implementing and evaluating service-learning in middle and high schools.* (Mahwah: Lawrence Erlbaum Associates, Publishers, 2004).

9. R. Shumer, "Community-based learning: Humanizing education." (*Journal of Adolescence*, 17, 4, 1994) 357-367; B. Shaffer. *Service-learning: An academic methodology.* Stanford, CA: Stanford University Department of Education, (1993). Cited in R. Bhaerman, K. Cordell, & B. Gomez, *The role of service-learning in educational reform.* (Raleigh, NC: National Society for Experiential Education and Needham, MA: Simon and Shuster, Inc. 1998); L. Dean and S. Murdock, "The effect of voluntary service on adolescent attitudes toward learning." (*Journal of Volunteer Administration*, Summer 1992): 5-10.; O'Bannon, F., "Service-learning benefits our schools." (*State Education Leader*, 17, 3, 1999).

10. J. Follman, *Florida Learn and Serve: 1996-97 outcomes and correlations with 1994-95 and 1995-96.* Tallahassee, FL: (Florida State University, Center for Civic Education and Service, August, 1998); O'Bannon, F., "Service-learning benefits our schools." (*State Education Leader*, 17, 3, 1999).

11. J. Supik, *Valued youth partnerships: Programs in caring.* (San Antonio: Intercultural Research and Development Association, 1996); C. Rolzinski, *The adventure of adolescence: Middle school students and community service.* (Washington, DC: Youth Service America, 1990).

12. J.A. Bean, *A middle school curriculum: From rhetoric to reality.* (Columbus: National Middle School Association, 1991).

13. S. Totten and J.E. Pedersen, eds, *Social issues and service at the middle level.* (Needham Heights: Allyn & Bacon, 1997).

14. S. Covey, *The seven habits of highly effective teens.* (New York: Fireside, 1998).

15. L. Stephens, *The complete guide to learning through community service, grades K-9.* (Boston: Allyn and Bacon, 1995).

16. A. Melchior, *Summary Report: National evaluation of Learn and Serve America.* (Waltham: Center for Human Resources, Brandeis University, 1999).

17. D. Loesch-Griffin, L.A. Petrides, & C. Pratt, *A comprehensive study of Project YES- Rethinking classrooms and community: Service-learning as educational reform.* (San Francisco: East Bay Conservation Corps, 1995).

18. Follman, J, *Florida Learn and Serve: 1996-97 outcomes and correlations with 1994-95 and 1995-96.* (Tallahassee, FL: Florida State University, Center for Civic Education and Service, August, 1998); O'Bannon, F., "Service-learning benefits our schools." (*State Education Leader*, 17, 3, 1999).

19. See Shaffer, 1993; Supik, 1996; Shumer, 1994.

20. Loesch-Griffin, D., L.A. Petrides, & C. Pratt, *A comprehensive study of Project YES- Rethinking classrooms and community: Service-learning as educational reform.* (San Francisco: East Bay Conservation Corps, 1995).

21. A. Melchior, *Summary Report: National evaluation of Learn and Serve America.* Waltham: Center for Human Resources, Brandeis University, 1999.; T. Berkas, *Strategic review of the W. K. Kellogg Foundation's service-learning projects,1990-1996.* (Battle Creek: W. K. Kellogg Foundation, February, 1997).

22. Shaffer, 1993; Stephens, 1995.

23. W. Morgan and M. Streb, *How quality service-learning develops civic values.* (Bloomington: Indiana University, 1999).

24. J. Courneya, An evaluation of the Native American school's water quality testing program. Cited in M. Neal, R. Shumer & K. Gorak (Eds.), *Evaluation: The key to improving service-learning programs.* (Minneapolis, MN: Minnesota Department of Education and the University of Minnesota, 1994).

References

Anderson, V., C. Kinsley, P. Negroni, P. and C. Price, "Community service-learning and school improvement in Springfield, Massachusetts." *Phi Delta Kappan*, 72 (June1991): 761-764.

Bean, J.A., *A middle school curriculum: From rhetoric to reality.* Columbus: National Middle School Association, 1991.

Berger-Kaye, Cathryn. *The Complete Guide to Service-learning: Proven, Practical Ways to Engage Students in Civic Responsibility, Academic Curriculum, and Social Action*, (2004, p. 7)

Berkas,T. *Strategic review of the W. K. Kellogg Foundation's service-learning projects,1990-1996.* Battle Creek: W. K. Kellogg Foundation, February, 1997.

Courneya, J. An evaluation of the Native American school's water quality testing program. In M. Neal, R. Shumer & K. Gorak (Eds.), *Evaluation: The key to improving service-learning programs.* Minneapolis, MN: Minnesota Department of Education and the University of Minnesota, 1994.

Covey, S. *The seven habits of highly effective teens.* New York: Fireside, 1998.

Dean, L. and S. Murdock, "The effect of voluntary service on adolescent attitudes toward learning." *Journal of Volunteer Administration*, Summer (1992): 5-10.

Erb, T., "Transforming abstract standards into solid performances." *Middle School Journal*, 36(4) (2005): 2.

Follman, J. *Florida Learn and Serve: 1996-97 outcomes and correlations with 1994-95 and 1995-96.* Tallahassee, FL: Florida State University, Center for Civic Education and Service, August, 1998.

Kaye, C.B., *The complete guide to service-learning: Proven, practical ways to engage students in civic responsibility, academic curriculum, and social action.* Minneapolis: Free Spirit Publishing, Inc, 2004.

Loesch-Griffin, D., L.A. Petrides, & C. Pratt, *A comprehensive study of Project YES-Rethinking classrooms and community: Service-learning as educational reform.* San Francisco: East Bay Conservation Corps, 1995.

Melchior, A., *Summary Report: National evaluation of Learn and Serve America.* Waltham: Center for Human Resources, Brandeis University, 1999.

Morgan, W. and M. Streb, *How quality service-learning develops civic values.* Bloomington: Indiana University, 1999.

National Service-Learning Partnership, 2005. <http://www.service -learningpartnership .org/site/PageServer>

O'Bannon, F., "Service-learning benefits our schools." *State Education Leader*, 17, 3 (1999).

Pritchard, F.F. and G.I. Whitehead III, *Serve and learn: Implementing and evaluating service-learning in middle and high schools.* Mahwah: Lawrence Erlbaum Associates, Publishers, 2004.

Rolzinski, C., *The adventure of adolescence: Middle school students and community service.* Washington, DC: Youth Service America, 1990.

Shaffer, B. *Service-learning: An academic methodology.* Stanford, CA: Stanford University Department of Education, 1993. Cited in R. Bhaerman, K. Cordell, & B. Gomez, *The role of service-learning in educational reform.* Raleigh, NC: National Society for Experiential Education and Needham, MA: Simon and Shuster, Inc., 1998.

Shumer, R., "Community-based learning: Humanizing education." *Journal of Adolescence*, 17, 4 (1994) 357-367.

Smith, D.B.,. "Accountability for academics and social responsibility through service-learning." *Middle School Journal*, 36, 4 (2005) 20-25.

Stephens, L., *The complete guide to learning through community service, grades K-9.* Boston: Allyn and Bacon, 1995.

Supik, J., *Valued youth partnerships: Programs in caring.* San Antonio: Intercultural Research and Development Association, 1996.

Totten, S. and J.E. Pedersen, eds, *Social issues and service at the middle level.* Needham Heights: Allyn & Bacon, 1997.

Weiler, D., A. LaGoy, E. Crane and A. Rovner. *An evaluation of K-12 service-learning in California: Phase II final report.* Emeryville: RPP International with the Search Institute, 1998